Built upon Love

Built upon Love

Architectural Longing after Ethics and Aesthetics

Alberto Pérez-Gómez

The MIT Press
Cambridge, Massachusetts
London, England

MIT Press books may be purchased at special quantity discounts for business or sales promotional use. For information, please email special_sales@mitpress.mit.edu or write to Special Sales Department, The MIT Press, 55 Hayward Street, Cambridge, MA 02142.

This book was set in Sabon by Graphic Composition, Inc., and was printed and bound in the United States of America.

Library of Congress Cataloging-in-Publication Data

Pérez-Gómez, Alberto, 1949–
Built upon love : architectural longing after ethics and aesthetics / Alberto Pérez-Gómez.
    p. cm.
Includes index.
ISBN 0-262-16238-5 (hc : alk. paper)
1. Architecture—Aesthetics. 2. Architecture—Moral and ethical aspects. 3. Love. I. Title.

NA2500.P455   2006
720.1—dc22

2005056164

10 9 8 7 6 5 4 3 2 1

Contents

Acknowledgments

This book brings together voices from multiple disciplines and times. It is a multilayered story that has been constructed over many years. I am therefore deeply grateful to my colleagues and students, both locally and internationally, for the many conversations that I have often translated into my own concerns. I am fortunate to work in the academic context of the graduate program in History and Theory of Architecture at McGill University in Montreal, where seminars with students and guests constantly bring "erotic" knowledge alive in often marvelous and unexpected ways.

Along the way, the book acknowledges its many (and profound) debts to architectural writers and philosophers. While less obvious, the voices and works of three dear colleagues were particularly important. Dalibor Vesely and Karsten Harries on the poetics and ethics of architecture were pivotal points of departure. Juhani Pallasmaa's "generative" theory addressing specific architectural topics was a constant source of inspiration.

Assisting on research, Marc Neveu and Carolinne Dionne read sections of this work and provided criticism. Lian Chang and Christina Contandriopoulos contributed bibliographical work under the auspices of the Institut de Recherche en Histoire de l'Architecture. My colleague Stephen Parcell from Dalhousie University read the manuscript with great care, raised important questions, and edited the language. His suggestions on content and style were invaluable. I am deeply grateful for his unconditional help.

My wife and colleague Louise Pelletier also read the manuscript and made insightful comments, providing much-needed dialogue throughout the long process of writing.

The resources of both the Rare Books and Special Collections Library at McGill University and the library of the Canadian Centre for Architecture were important for this project. I would like to thank the staff of both institutions for their support.

Last but not least, I wish to express my deeply felt gratitude to the staff of the MIT Press. Over the years their care and dedication have contributed immeasurably to the realization of my projects. I am particularly grateful to Alice Falk for her loving and rigorous editing, and to Roger Conover for helping me dream about an architectural book without images, and for his pointed suggestions about the title. With two words he helped define the true nature of this project.

Built upon Love

Opening conversation

Eros is lord of the world: he pushes, directs, controls and appeases everyone. . . . Semen is of many kinds, Venus is of many kinds, love is of many kinds, bonds are of many kinds. . . . All bonds are either reduced to the bond of love, depend on the bond of love or are based on the bond of love . . . for he who loves nothing has no reason to fear, to hope, to praise, to be proud, to dare, to condemn, to accuse, to excuse, to be humble, to be competitive, to be angered or to be affected in other ways of this sort. . . . This examination should not be considered to be far removed from public affairs just because it is more important and more wonderful than the field of public affairs.

Giordano Bruno, "A General Account of Bonding" (trans. Robert de Lucca and Richard J. Blackwell)

Do not be bewildered by the surfaces; in the depths all becomes law. And those who live the secret [of sexual love] wrong and badly, lose it only for themselves and still hand it on, like a sealed letter, without knowing it.

Rainer Maria Rilke, *On Love* (trans. John J. L. Mood)

The act of love starts on its heathenish way to end up blessed by a transfixing spasm from the world beyond.

Malcolm de Chazal, *Sens-Plastique* (trans. Irving Weiss)

However uncertain we are about whether the absence of beauty from our own lives is a benefit or a deficit, once we see the subject from a distant perspective, it instantly becomes clear that the absence of beauty is a profound form of deprivation.

Elaine Scarry, *On Beauty and Being Just*

We speak about love all the time, we often experience it, but we fail to understand it.

Love does not derive from the ego, but precedes it and makes it a gift to itself.

Jean-Luc Marion, *Le phénomène érotique*

Introduction: Architecture and Human Desire

It is perhaps obvious that human desire has shaped the built environment, sometimes in ways that today we may judge as unsuitable for the common good. Impressive buildings were constructed to fulfill spiritual needs that seem almost absurd from a late-modern perspective—totally "impractical" edifices such as magnificent funerary monuments to commemorate the dead, and temples to celebrate strange divinities. Buildings have also been objects possessed by the wealthy and powerful, symbols of decadent consumption and means for an elite to exert control over the masses. Representing ideologies and institutions in the manner of false idols, they have often contributed to repressive environments.

Modernity has rightly judged this sort of building practice faulty and dangerous. As a pragmatic alternative it has proposed that buildings should fulfill the wishes of individuals in a democratic society: a desire for shelter and protection from the elements, for a home and a place to work where humans may live their lives in as pleasurable a way as possible. In the wake of God's demise, arguably nothing else may be necessary. More recently, under the rubric "sustainable development," these aims have been interwoven with a sense of responsibility for the environment and the well-being of humanity at large. A meaningful architecture would efficiently fulfill humanity's material needs, while at the same time remaining mindful of the world's resources for the perpetuation of human civilization.

This book argues that the materialistic and technological alternatives for architecture—however sophisticated and justifiable they may be, in view of our historical failures—do not answer satisfactorily to the complex desire that defines humanity. As humans, our greatest gift is love, and we are invariably called to respond to it. Despite our suspicions, architecture has been and must continue to be built upon love. I will endeavor to show how this foundation possesses its own rationality, one that the built environment will not follow if it is based on premises drawn from normative disciplines or abstract logical systems. While recognizing the dangers of traditional religions, moral dogmas, and ideologies, true architecture is concerned with far more than fashionable form, affordable homes, and sustainable development; it responds to a desire for an eloquent place to dwell, one that lovingly provides a sense of order resonant with our dreams, a gift contributing to our self-understanding as humans inhabiting a mortal world.

The overriding aim of this book is to interpret the relationship between love and architecture in order to find points of contact between poetics and ethics: between the architect's wish to design a beautiful world and architecture's imperative to provide a better place for society. Thus I will seek the origins of architectural meaning beyond the traditional, often polarized understanding of aesthetics as an eighteenth-century science of beauty and ethics as a collection of normative rules, clarifying architecture's quest for beauty and the common good. Ethics and aesthetics reduced to rules are useless: ethical action is always singular and circumstantial. It always seems miraculous and unique, a transformative experience that is, significantly, analogous to our encounter with beauty in works of art.

Recent "postcritical" discourses (particularly in North America) have expressed a deep dissatisfaction with formalist and "hard" computer-generated architectures as being unable to respond to the expectations of cultures in the early third millennium. For more than two centuries, architects, critics, and theoreticians have been arguing functionalist and formalist positions, opposing art to social interests and ethics to poetic expression. Architectural writing ranging from popular professional journals to sophisticated theoretical books perpetuate this polarization that diminishes architecture's capacity to embody beauty and to promote social development. In stepping away from these prevalent oppositions, my aim is to uncover the deep connections between ethical and poetic values in the primary tradition of our discipline.

Modern Western civilization takes for granted a quest to pursue individual happiness and freedom. It is driven by what it perceives as a "natural" right to seek pleasure and avoid pain, a fundamental accomplishment of democracy brought about by the political revolutions at the end of the eighteenth century. For a hedonistic culture, architecture's vocation is to ensure the greatest pleasure and least pain for each individual. Our technological building practices, even when mindful of ecological responsibility or claiming high artistic aspirations, still pursue a functionalist utopia in which all desires are fulfilled through material means,

eliminating all irritants and always aiming at greater economy and comfort: maximum efficiency, economy, commodity, and entertainment value.
Consumption and possession prevail as the bastard aims of desire. Their
overwhelming presence in contemporary life enhances our propensity to
forget that we *are* our mortal bodies whose very flesh is also that of the
world, a common *element* that grants the light of reason and immortal
thoughts, while pulling us down into the darkness of the earth. We forget
that love and death, pleasure and pain are inextricably linked through our
embodied consciousness. We go even further and tend to deny the very
existence of love (as technology may wish to deny the existence of death).
Fragmented into multiple emotions in our materialistic culture, the cynic
and intellectual alike have trouble acknowledging love in view of our modern difficulty to grasp it as a gift, often contradictory since it is *beyond*
the rules of economic transactions. My wager, with José Ortega y Gasset
and Jean-Luc Marion, is that love not only exists but is crucial to our humanity; that despite its contradictions it is of a piece, and can indeed be
spoken about.

Built upon love, architecture engages the inhabitant as true *participant,* unlike the remote spectator of the modernist work of art or the consumer of fashionable buildings-*cum*-images. If this engagement is not
obvious, it is partly because architectural meaning has been "explained"
through a deceptively simple assumption that confuses our human quest
for happiness with hedonism. Love, in its multiple incarnations as desire,
is as open-ended as life itself and remains the ground of meaning even in
times of obsessive materialism. According to Plato, this erotic principle is
operative not just among human souls but everywhere in the universe.[1] Yet
love and our transcultural quest for beauty will never be reduced to a mere
pursuit of pleasure. A poor understanding of this issue is evident in recent
writings foregrounding the interest in algorithms to generate novel architectural forms; in critical practices that stress the social history of architecture, emphasizing political correctness and a critique of "authorship";
and even in architecture driven by well-meaning ecological concerns. A partial or total ignorance of the deep relationship between love and architectural meanings has dire consequences, perpetuating the modern epidemic
of empty formalism and banal functionalism, condemning architecture
to passing fashion or consumable commodity, and destining the cultures
it frames to their present dangerous pathologies. This book will attempt to
show how the appropriate engagement of desire by articulating ethical and
political positions in the form of seductive projects is the fundamental responsibility of architecture.

Eloquent myths, poems, stories, and philosophical accounts from multiple traditions have described the nature of human space as the space of desire. Regardless of culture, age, wealth, and social status, humans suffer a *lack,* which is also a gift. Unlike other animals in our planet, we have an essentially linguistic being that keeps us "apart" from the world. Throughout our lives we constantly look for "something," something that is missing and that might complete us—be it the physical presence of another, the acquisition of knowledge, or the experience of art and architecture. This lack is always present. It does not disappear with the fulfillment of practical needs or with the possession of goods. Despite its paradoxical nature it is perhaps the most obvious manifestation of our spiritual specificity. Christians have identified this lack with a longing for God, its satisfaction the state of grace reserved for the just in the afterlife. Buddhist teachers, on the other hand, identify the illusory nature of this lack as the source of unhappiness and insist on the dangers of those desires to which we are unduly attached, leading us to forget the ephemeral nature of all things human and creating perpetual frustration by denying us the possibility of living fully in the present. While a simple answer for the spiritually aware might be asceticism, Prince Siddhartha himself soon discovered that this was not the solution. His enlightenment led him to realize that we must accept desire (and suffering) as fundamental to the human condition and *engage* it as a vehicle for knowledge, always remembering its deceitful power of attachment.

Desire is associated with our inherent lack in the face of nature. Unlike other animals, humans have a very limited capacity to adapt to the environment and instead developed poetic and magical techniques. Animals possess a remarkable ability to communicate and construct, often far more sophisticated than humans' natural capacities. Termites, for example, can communicate across a 2-inch steel plate and still build a perfectly symmetrical nest. The structure they construct, however, is always the same nest.[2] Humans faced with the analogous problem of building across a divided habitat would either build completely different structures on each side of the plate, running the risk of failure and extinction if they lacked some particular expertise, or else develop a technique to perforate the plate in order to communicate and build a polity, one that depends on linguistic translation and will every time be a *different* city. This activity was named *poiēsis* by the Greeks, signifying the sort of technical making proper to humans: a poetic making in the sense that it always aimed at *more* than preserving life.

Even for the most sophisticated apes, desire is externally motivated and can be understood as a closed structure, a kind of complex mechanism: hunger is physiological while sexual behavior is seasonal. For humans, in contrast, desire is experienced as an open horizon. The erotic "phenomenon" is, according to Marion, primary in all things human. It is possessed of a rationality that flies in the face of logic and encompasses experiences as diverse as charity and lust.[3] While the behavior of apes around dead fellow creatures indicates indifference, the burial of corpses in primitive humanoid societies seems to have a relationship with the awareness of sexual desire and an obscure coincidence with an awareness of death as the limit of life. The many artifacts and mythical narratives of various cultures that express the need to propitiate or change external reality convey a sense of transgression: shame or guilt. Adam and Eve are punished with eventual death for their knowledge of love, Prometheus is punished for stealing the fire of the gods, and Cain is condemned to toil the earth and build cities. In mythical cultures, sacrifice usually accompanied technical works and deeds in the hope of renewing a sense of reconciliation with the more-than-human world.

Historical origins of *erōs* and *philia*

The complex constellation of transformations that took place during the archaic and classical periods of Greek culture created the conditions for an understanding of love and the space of desire that would resonate through Western culture up to our own time. This is a crucial reference point for my investigation. Ritual was transformed into art; drama and classical tragedy became a model for architectural representation and had their origins in rituals dedicated to Dionysos.[4] In the genealogy of architectural "objects," the primitive *xoana*, sacrificial objects usually burned as offerings upon altars, which were modeled after the deceptive "wooden bride" manufactured by Zeus himself on the advice of the clever Cithaeron to obtain Hera's favors, are related by Pausanias and others to *daidala*. These are a class of objects named in early Greek literature (Homer, Hesiod), such as those eventually attributed to Daedalus, the first architect in the Western tradition whose story has been preserved. *Daidala* are constructions made of *well-adjusted pieces,* capable of inducing wonder and providing existential safety for a community.[5] In later periods of Greco-Roman culture, the same wonder or *thaumata* remained the salient quality of artifacts that today we recognize more readily as "architecture," such as theaters, temples, and the space and political institutions of the agora and the forum. They provided for modes of cultural participation that were eventually celebrated by Vitruvius as "order." Architecture's harmony, its most important quality, is identified with *venustas,* "beauty." This is a seductive quality that binds the spectator through a distance. The products of architecture, Vitruvius tells us, are also the product of cunning (*sollertia* in Latin), whose primary technical device is "optical adjustment."

Both Eros, the name of the divinity who accompanies Aphrodite (Venus for the Romans), and *philia,* the love of friendship that entails mutual responsibility among equals, were born during the cultural transformation that culminated in classical Greece. The early lyric poets invented Eros, an invisible force that remains at the root of our capacity for creation and comprehension of the poetic image. The first part of this book examines the nature of architectural form in the light of *erōs,* seduction, and the tradition of the poetic image in Western architecture. Successive chapters examine relationships between *erōs* and creation, *erōs* and the Western understanding of space, *chōra* and limits, and love and the primary modes of recognition and representation in architecture.

Philia, perhaps drawn from geometry by philosophers and politicians, is the emotional link that enables the participation of equal citizens in the new democratic polity and its institutions, both sacred and profane. After a brief interlude arguing for the common ground among seemingly diverse forms of love, the following chapters discuss the connections between *philia* and architectural program, tracing its history through ritual and exploring the position of architecture at the limits of language. A chapter is dedicated to the examination of linguistic analogies that underscore the inception of modernist theories, followed by a comparative study of the late-eighteenth- and early-nineteenth-century theories of the Viel brothers, who articulated complementary positions regarding the communicative capacity of architecture as a political act. The book concludes by drawing points of contact between ethics and poetics that can be gleaned for a contemporary practice of architecture under the sign of love, incorporating both *erōs* and *philia* and drawing especially on the notion of the project as a promise driven by a quest to further humanity's spiritual evolution.

I *Erōs*, Seduction, and the Poetic Image in Architecture: Form

It is banal to devote oneself to an end when that end is clearly only a means. The quest for wealth—sometimes the wealth of egoistic individuals, sometimes wealth held in common—is obviously only a means. Work is only a means.

The response to erotic desire—and to the perhaps more human (least physical) desire of poetry, and of ecstasy (but is it so decisively easy to grasp the difference between eroticism and poetry, and between eroticism and ecstasy?)—the response to erotic desire is, on the contrary, an end.

Georges Bataille, *The Tears of Eros* (trans. Peter Connor)

1 Eros and Creation

Opening conversation

Love is the master and governor of the arts. . . . [N]o one can ever discover or learn any art unless the pleasure of learning and the desire of discovering move him. . . . [A]rtists in all of the arts seek and care for nothing else but love.

Marsilio Ficino, *Commentary on Plato's Symposium On Love* (trans. Sears Jayne)

Poetry is not born from rules, except in some negligible cases; rather it is the rules that derive from poetry. This is why there are as many kinds and genres of true rules as there are kinds and genres of true poets.

Giordano Bruno, *De gl'heroici furori*

Therefore, he who knows how to bind needs to have an understanding of all things, or at least of the nature, inclination, habits, uses and purposes of the particular things that he is to bind.

Giordano Bruno, "A General Account of Bonding" (trans. Robert de Lucca and Richard J. Blackwell)

But whoever has no touch of the Muses' madness in his soul approaches the gates of poetry and thinks that he will get into the temple by the help of art (*technē*)— he, I say, is not admitted, and the poetry of the sane man is utterly eclipsed by that of the inspired madman.

Plato, *Phaedrus* 245a (trans. Benjamin Jowett)

In the beginning, the god Eros was beautiful, but not necessarily winged. There is an important distinction between two different forms of Eros in Greek mythology and cosmogony. Eros is best known to us as Amor or Cupid, the mischievous attendant of Aphrodite who is responsible for sexual desire, seduction, and procreation; but in Hesiod's *Theogony* there is also a primordial Eros with markedly different characteristics. While Aphrodite's Eros will be crucial for our understanding of architecture as the space of desire in chapter 2, primordial Eros provides important clues about the relationship between love and creativity.[1]

This first chapter sketches the story of primordial Eros in Western philosophy and art, tracing the relationship between love and creativity: love as both compassion (for the other) and obsession (for the pursuit of beauty). The role of the architect has changed historically, and today it is complicated by extremely diverse demands and complex technologies. The architect's relationship with a work that eventually occupies the public realm is unlike the painter's or sculptor's insofar as it is almost invariably mediated, dependent on manifold circumstances. While acknowledging this complexity, I want to illuminate connections at a deeper, more personal level that involve the architect's thoughts and deeds and define his or her grasp of reality. These issues, fundamental in defining a *praxis* (or practical philosophy), also affect the proper transmission and teaching of the discipline. Drawing on relevant sources from antiquity to modernity may help us reconsider our current role as "creators" and may advance our practice in ways that avoid dead-end debates over formal or functional questions.

Primordial Eros

"First there came into being Khaos," wrote Hesiod, "and afterwards Gaia [deep-breasted Earth] and Eros [the love that softens hearts], the most beautiful of the immortal gods."[2] Khaos, the humid "primordial space/ substance" that Plato would later associate with *chōra*, is a neuter name; it cannot produce children. Instead, it causes other divinities to "come into being." Gaia, on the other hand, is feminine and does bear children, but her offspring are her two future male partners, Ouranos (Sky, crowned with stars) and Pontos (Sea). Both are "brought forth," not sexually conceived. Unlike the later exploits attributed to Aphrodite, her action is not one of feminine amorous tenderness, but it has a definite cause. This is where primordial Eros comes in. In the absence of a male sex, primordial Eros "softens" the first creative entities and causes them to bring to light what was hidden within them.

After drawing the night sky out of herself in a moment prior to human time, Gaia copulates permanently with Ouranos. Ouranos covers Gaia and discharges into her without stopping. Before the cycles of day and night that mark human temporality, before the birth of Olympian light, the earth and the sky were compulsively united—but not from prior sexual attraction, since the two divinities had never been separated. Paradoxically, this continuous copulation, according to Hesiod, blocked the multiplication of divinities and subsequent human genealogies.

Hiding in Gaia's bosom, Kronos (Time) grabs the genitals of Ouranos and castrates him with a sickle. The blood of Ouranos falls onto the earth and his genitals fall into the sea. This violent act separates the earth from the sky, the feminine from the masculine and thus marks the beginning of human space-time. In daylight the division between earth and sky is now visible to all: the human world under the light of speech (*logos*). At night, however, when the horizon disappears and the sky again unites with the earth, their earlier primordial state seems to return, reminding humanity of a potential wholeness pregnant with creative force. After this primordial phase of Eros comes to an end, he is reincarnated in his more familiar guise as Cupid, a character who operates between the two sexes. He accompanies Aphrodite, the goddess who was born from sea foam mixed with the sperm of Ouranos, and now presides over tricks of seduction.

For Hesiod, primordial Eros as origin (*archē*) was chaotic excess, with a power of beauty that could inspire divinities to create a *fair* cosmos. Later, Neoplatonism would identify primordial Eros with the *One*, that supreme unity qualitatively unlike any other number into which the dispersion and multiplicity of particular existences may be reconciled—a sign of completed plenitude sought by humanity, to which reason, mystical practices, theurgic magic, and also art could contribute. In each case, primordial Eros is quite unlike Cupid, the attendant of Aphrodite/Venus, who is responsible for the relationship between two (or three) individuals based on desire. The original Eros expresses the overabundance of being— plenitude rather than lack. It is the completed *one*, as well as the movement by which this complete entity gives birth out of him/herself. This is the Eros described in the Orphic fragments as androgynous, simultaneously male and female, a monster with two pairs of eyes and two sets of genitals over the buttocks. Orphic Eros is *artistic power,* a power of "separation" rather than deliberate, rational composition, and this notion would be echoed many centuries later by Marsilio Ficino, Giordano Bruno, and Paracelsus in the Renaissance; by Romantic writers and philosophers in the early nineteenth century; by the surrealists in the twentieth century; and more recently (fully accounting for a postmodern understanding of subjectivity), by phenomenological theories of creation. Eventually it would represent the power of beauty as inspiration, its capacity to replicate itself, and in this particular sense it still holds important lessons for the contemporary architect.

Eros as creative power in classical philosophy

Not surprisingly, the attributes of the two mythical embodiments of *erōs* became blurred when the presence of desire was articulated in philosophical discourse only a few centuries after Hesiod's writings. Ultimately, these are all human stories, so it is difficult to keep Eros's attributes apart. This creative confusion influences our understanding of architecture in the Western tradition, as will be apparent in these pages. Plato speaks of *erōs* mainly as it affects humanity, through sexual desire. In *Phaedrus,* however, Plato also describes erotic delirium as a form of divine madness: possession by a supernatural power, mystic initiation with successive stages, and a final epiphany of beauty. This, he believed, was the same delirium that took hold of the poet and enabled him to craft better works than a sane man. One who has been correctly initiated in the ways of love will have this transformational experience of beauty, as will one who has been seduced by a luminous work of art that shines like the eyes of the beloved. For Plato, this experience was comparable to a religious epiphany.

The question of beginnings is crucial. For Socrates, love begins as an external force. It comes out of nowhere "as if on wings," taking control of one's psyche and dominating one's body; it even affects the lover's vital organs. The beginning is the one moment you can't control: it brings good and evil, it is bitter and sweet, and it comes gratuitously and unpredictably, a gift of the gods. Falling in love, according to Socrates, is both madness and a revelation of the world *as it really is.* The Greeks associated love with Dionysos, god of madness, the feast, and transgression. The divine essence of madness is the origin of Greek tragedy and the Western work of art. For Socrates, the initial mania is the most important moment to grasp. According to Anne Carson, Socrates proposes to assimilate the *now* of love so that it can be prolonged throughout one's whole life and beyond.[3] Unlike the earlier poets, who were distressed by the force of Eros, Socrates vindicates mania because one can keep one's mind only at the cost of shutting out the gods. The incursions of Eros instruct and enrich our lives: prophets, healers, and poets conduct their art "by losing their mind."[4] Erotic mania is the instrument of this intelligence: it puts wings on the soul of the *demiourgos.* The architect/creator (always a craftsman of materials, never a creator ex nihilo) may share this experience by making works that have a similar effect on society.

Socrates went even further. He believed that the disruptive, transformative effect of love enables humanity to glimpse true wisdom. Consequently, Clement of Alexandria (ca. 200 C.E.) mentions Socrates among other *iatromantes* (shamans) of classical and ancient Greece.[5] The term *iatromantes* is composed from *iatros* (healer) and *mantis* (prophet), this second word being etymologically related to mania or madness. While Dionysos was the divinity who inherited the powers of the goddesses from the matriarchal civilizations of archaic Europe and the ancient Near East, the *iatromantes* were said to be possessed by Apollo of Hyperborea, the sun. Pythagoras and Socrates were among this group, as were other healers (*iatroi*), seers (*mantes*), purifiers (*kathartai*), interpreters of oracles (*chrēsmologoi*), travelers of the air (*aithrobatai*), and wonder-workers (*thaumatourgoi*).[6] The ancient architect Daedalus was obviously an *iatromantis* who worked by the light of Apollo, creating wondrous artifacts, including a *choros* or dance platform for the rituals of Dionysos. Not surprisingly, Socrates claimed Daedalus as one of his ancestors. The architect as *iatromantis* harnesses the power of the poetic image to engage others in a communion with other worlds *within* our world. Through light, materials, and words, he or she helps us confront the darkness that affects our lives to the point of distress. Like shamans in many cultures around the world, the architect enables us to fly and eventually become healed.

Diotima, the expert on questions of love, adds another fascinating story about Eros. In Plato's *Symposium* she explains that Eros is neither a mortal nor an immortal god, but actually "a mean between the two."[7] Recasting Eros as a "great spirit" or *daimōn,* she adds that his role is to communicate between gods and men. Diotima's story includes a genealogy of Eros that helps us understand his place in artistic creation (*Symposium* 203b). On the day of Aphrodite's birth there was a great feast of the gods. One of the guests was the god Poros (Efficacy), the son of Metis (Intelligence). While sleeping off his intoxication, Poros was seduced by Penia, a poor mortal woman who had come to the feast to beg, and thus they conceived Eros, the future attendant of beautiful Aphrodite. Eros inherited the qualities of his parents: cunning intelligence from Metis and Poros, and poverty and want from Penia. He is always in need: never settled and forever in transit, always scheming to obtain what is beautiful and good. He is rough and squalid, bold and enterprising, "a lifelong philosopher, awesome as an enchanter, sorcerer, sophist" (203d–e). He avoids the curse of both destitution and wealth, of pathological lack and fulfillment, and valorizes love as a primordial gift, for "that which is always flowing in is always flowing out" (203e). Despite his status as demigod, it is obvious that Eros stands here for a superior form of humanity, the paradigm of the architect/philosopher. A god cannot love wisdom, for he or she is already wise. Lovers of wisdom are neither the wise nor the foolish but those in between. "Love is also a philosopher," for wisdom is beautiful and love is of the beautiful (204b–c).

A few centuries later, Vitruvius would explicitly link architectural theory to philosophy. Although architecture has its own set of techniques, it embodies the values of philosophical contemplation and shares its theory with other disciplines. Vitruvius characterizes an architect's main quality as *sollertia,* Latin for *mētis* (cunning intelligence). This characterization is repeated many times in his *Ten Books on Architecture,* and echoes the much older Greek account of Metis as the mother of Daedalus. *Sollertia* is far more important than an architect's other talents or technical knowledge. Vitruvius also states that the architect must seek *venustas,* the erotic beauty that is embodied in Venus/Aphrodite. Eros as philosopher, enchanter, sorcerer, and sophist is therefore a figure for the architect who seeks wisdom in words and wonder in deeds. As Diotima clarifies later in the *Symposium,* those who are pregnant in the body beget children, while "those who are pregnant in their souls" conceive wisdom and virtue. Such creators are poets and artists who deserve to be called inventors (209).

While the earlier poets deplored the sense of loss induced by Eros/ Cupid, Socrates contemplated how humanity could profit and grow from the disorienting and revealing experience of falling in love. In a somewhat veiled manner, Socrates' Eros recalls aspects of its original Orphic incarnation. Eros's inability to be satisfied by worldly things points to the beyond: this lack is a vehicle for self-understanding and higher ethical aims. Lovers want something beyond an amorous embrace; while they often seek copulation with their "other half," they don't want to be united forever. According to Hephaistos, even if we were to attain our original mythical status as spherical beings, we would probably roll back to Olympus in search of something else (192d–e). The transformation from incompleteness into supracompleteness is the epic of Orphic Eros in a tradition that would be recovered by Renaissance Neoplatonism, and reinvigorated by Romanticism in modernity.

Renaissance incorporations

"Love should be put into action!"
  screamed the old hermit.
Across the pond an echo
  tried and tried to confirm it.
Elizabeth Bishop, "Chemin de Fer"

In contrast with Socrates' optimism, during the Christian Middle Ages the infatuation that we associate with falling in love was assumed to be a sickness of the soul.[8] Doctor Bernard de Gordon (ca. 1258–1318), professor of medicine at Montpellier, described "lovesickness" as *heroes,* the "melancholy anguish caused by love for a woman. The cause of this affliction lies in the corruption of the faculty to evaluate, due to a figure and face that have made a very strong impression."[9] Symptoms include sleeplessness, loss of appetite, and a general weakness of the body. This condition may be benign, but it can also become very serious, leading to mania and even death. Treatment of the ailment may start with gentle persuasion; but if there is no visible improvement, stronger methods should be used, such as travel, erotic pleasures with several women, and even whipping.

In this context, it is not surprising to find that the only visions and dreams deemed worthy of attention were those that concerned God's glory. Indeed, the poetic images manifested in the great cathedrals and medieval artifacts were always thought to have originated not in human consciousness but in divine will. The abbot who dreamed of the images was simply the medium, and the master mason then functioned as his hands. The true architect was God, and the vehicle was his love, *agapē*.[10]

While the changes brought about by medieval Christianity would have far-reaching consequences for European consciousness, Dante's *Divine Comedy* (ca. 1313) recovered the creative power of *erōs* for the Renaissance. Dante's understanding of the divine came through his own imagination, with the erotic guidance of Beatrice. Although the imagination for Dante was a light that comes from a Christian God, his engagement with Platonic *erōs* was a sign of a changing world. During the Renaissance, love became a magical power and the architect became a magician capable of marvelous seduction.

Marsilio Ficino inaugurated the equivalence between *erōs* and magic in the Renaissance. He noted that the lover and the magician use the same techniques to manipulate "images"[11]—techniques that also happen to be analogous to those of the architect. The architect is emerging as a magus who can produce seductive *and* ethical artifacts that enable others to dwell in accordance with the heavens, in physical and spiritual health.

Like many of Ficino's works, *Liber de vita* (*The Book of Life*) began as a commentary on a classical text—in this case, Plotinus's *Enneads.* Ficino called it *De vita coelitus comparanda* (*On Making Your Life Agree with the Heavens*) and completed it in 1489. Ficino declares that man is a magus who pursues psychosomatic health and possesses a certain power over a nature that is permeated by astrological sympathies and whose every part is linked by hidden ciphers and signs. At least five chapters in his book are devoted to talismans, images, and formal concerns. Depending on one's innate temperament or state of being, appropriate colors, smells, forms, images, and even music contribute to individual physical and spiritual well-being. This interaction has an impact on all formal aspects of life, ranging from our dress to the form and quality of our personal dwellings, including the paintings we place on our walls. Ficino's belief aligns with the Renaissance desire for perfect proportions and exquisite form. Yet the issue is not some abstract pleasure attained through a detached aesthetic interest. Beautiful buildings were believed to contribute significantly to health and justice, both personal and collective.

The question of creation, moreover, is never a simple formal manipulation. Ficino elaborates in a key passage:

It is probable that if images have some force they do not acquire it suddenly through the figure so much as they naturally possess it through the affected material. If this force were acquired while the figure was being sculpted, it would not so much be obtained through the figure as through the warming up that comes from chiseling it. . . . This chiseling and warming up, when done in harmony, like the heavenly harmony which once powered into the material, arouses that power and strengthens it the way wind does a fire, and makes manifest what was hidden before, as fire will bring out letters written in onion-juice that were previously invisible[;] . . . so perhaps the chiseling and the warming alone produce the power lying in some material. . . . If one wanted to prepare metals and stones, it would be best to strike them and warm them up, rather than shape them. For anything beyond this is, I think, but an empty image, and we ought to admit that this is close to idolatry.[12]

In a later passage, Ficino goes even further: "The intention of the imagination has its force not so much in images or medicines as in the act of applying them and using them."[13] The architect/magus/physician must *lovingly* transform the *prima materia* of the world to reveal a hidden order with restorative powers. Doing so requires a harmonic, rhythmic action that becomes embodied in a building, a sculpture, a sonnet, or an herbal medicine. Much of the image's power comes from the subject's own faith. Ficino reminds us that Hippocrates and Galen already knew that the love and faith of a sick man make the work of a doctor much more effective. It is "the power of love to transform. . . . Love itself, and faith in the heavenly gift, is often the cause of the heavenly gift, and love and faith obtain this perhaps sometimes because the kindness of heaven favor this in us."[14] The architect/magus/physician is endowed with a heavenly gift of love and a keen capacity to identify beauty, a capacity that is indeed a kind of madness. To produce wonders, he must both love his work and care profoundly for the Other to whom it is addressed.

The sixteenth-century physician and alchemist Paracelsus understood the creative function of Eros even more literally. For him, the whole world was one reality, *prima material,* and creation was an act of *separation* induced by the imagination.[15] First, the "vital fluid" is converted into active semen by the male's imagination, which is responsible for discovering "flammable" beauty, just as heat from the sun can ignite wood. Procreation would not occur unless the "loadstone [womb/matter] attracts the semen."[16] This understanding could be applied at various levels: the macrocosm, the microcosm, and human experience. Thus, in medicine, sympathy is a key to healing. Paracelsus invented the concept of homeopathic medicine, in which a sickness is cured by its like. Small doses of poison are administered to the patient, and disharmony caused by lovesickness is cured by additional love. Healing also requires the doctor to be compassionate toward the patient, with unconditional love that closely resembles the Christian *agapē:* God's unconditional love for all his creatures, regardless of the creature's inherent values.[17]

Giordano Bruno's essays on magic provide the clearest exposition of the early-modern magus.[18] He describes how a magician can directly influence objects, individuals, and human society in the same way that a lover can use his or her talents to gain control of the beloved. By understanding the nature of "chains," the magician can use them to "bind" things for his purposes, relying on analogies between individual *pneuma* (soul, breath, or mind) and universal *pneuma.*[19] Recalling the astonishing "modernity" of Machiavelli,[20] Bruno declared that knowledge of the appropriate "chains" could lead to a dream of "universal mastery," adding with apprehension that such a dream would be unethical and unrealizable.

According to Bruno there are a few, very special professions that require disciplined imagination: poetry, art, and architecture. Since the imagination is the main gateway for all magical processes, these professions are associated with magic. Most mortals are subject to uncontrolled fantasies, but members of these professions must learn to exert total control over their imagination to avoid being seduced by the very objects they create. This is an ethical imperative. For a magical process to succeed, both the performer and his subjects must have faith in its efficacy.[21] Faith is the prior condition for magic, and the magus indeed must believe in his own work. Furthermore, Bruno observes that while the magus/architect has no right to use his power for selfish ends, self-love facilitates the creation of ethical bonds.

The master link of Bruno's bonding chains is beauty in its widest Platonic sense. Beauty is a secret communication that has nothing to do with "prescribed proportions of limbs," as one might read in treatises on architecture and painting in the Renaissance.[22] As an attribute of God, beauty is one and unchanging. For this reason, it is a concept not appropriately applied to the divine. Rather, beauty corresponds to human multiplicity and difference; it encompasses change and responds to the manifold kinds of love present for mankind. The architect/magus is able to produce "beautiful" artifacts that are meaningful or seductive. To do this, a magus must remain continent while ardently desiring the subject of his magic: "The more saintly one is, the greater one's ability to bind others."[23] The architect must be obsessive about beauty in his work and compassionate about its purpose in the social realm. Thus, acts of wonder may be accomplished.

Modern transformations

Philosophy is written in this grand book—I mean the universe—which stands continually open to our gaze, but it cannot be understood unless one first learns to comprehend the language and interpret the characters in which it is written. It is written in the language of mathematics, and its characters are triangles, circles, and other geometrical figures, without which it is humanly impossible to understand a single word of it; without these, one is wandering about in a dark labyrinth.

Galileo Galilei, *Il saggiatore*

The Renaissance creator accomplished his deeds through faith and love, using embodied consciousness to align personal deeds with the divine will. The modern creator would depend increasingly on a rational ego. Modern science after Galileo and Descartes became dualistic. Drawing on an analogy with divine reason, it conceived human reason as purely mathematical and dismissed other aspects of human consciousness (such as the imagination and the senses) as potential distractions that might lead to errors in judgment. Empirical evidence was eventually replaced by quantitative experimentation. Truly hypothetical sciences, as in the writings of Copernicus and Galileo, bypassed embodied experience in favor of rationality, assuming that God, defined as omnipotent in the Judeo-Christian tradition, could have created the world in a way that is not apparent to our limited senses.[24] Thus, the "fact" that the earth moves takes precedence over our experience that the earth is fixed. As Copernicus states, God made the world "for us": not for our senses but according to "true reason," which is the unique characteristic of humanity.[25] The creator must therefore have made the universe with the greatest clarity, simplicity, and mathematical coherence, qualities not evident in previous geocentric theories.

During the seventeenth century many disciplines believed that God's creation was based on a geometric plan, a radicalization of Plato's story in

Timaeus. Magic began to transform into modern technology. For the new hypotheses to acquire the status of truth, they had to be demonstrated through experiments. Once the world's "text" was assumed to be mathematical, knowledge became identified with mathematical or geometrical know-how. According to Nicolas Malebranche's version of Cartesianism, only God, in his omniscience, knows how everything works. When we move a finger, for instance, we can grasp our mental intention and notice its effect on the finger, but we don't really know *how* it happens (with mathematical clarity). Therefore, we are not the "authors" or true cause of the movement. Only God is a "true cause" in Malebranche's sense. Consequently, the true creator is someone who knows *how* he or she makes things, with mathematical or geometrical certainty.

While the architects and magi of the Renaissance had been fascinated by perfect forms embodied in numbers and geometric shapes, they always acknowledged an insurmountable gap between the sublunary human world of change and decay and the immutable realm of abstractions. A number or line in the physical world, in buildings, and in perspective paintings was never *identical* to a number or line in the mind.[26] Early modern theory attempted to close this gap, as shown in Galileo's imaginary experiments on motion and inertia, as well as in architectural treatises by Guarino Guarini and Juan Caramuel de Lobkowitz. Instrumental knowledge acquired the status of truth. They believed that architecture (or music) could be formed as geometric ideas combined in the mind and then manifested physically in the world, in some cases almost regardless of the specificity of materials and means of execution.[27]

Although the seventeenth century sought instrumental theories, it remained an enchanted world. Baroque architects were motivated by the sensuous richness of God's created world, and faith was strong. God's presence was felt intensely, particularly through the metaphysics of light. Light, as the substance of baroque art, was the luminous energy of a *quadrattura* fresco and was the diaphanous matter of Guarini's dome casting a shadowy penumbra over the Holy Shroud of Turin. Endowed with simultaneity and ubiquity (or infinite speed), it was close at hand yet infinitely distant. Reconciling plurality into unity, light remained the epitome of the mathematical, a marriage of clarity with wonder. Furthermore, artists and architects were very serious about the genealogy and symbolism of artifacts. While baroque theories differed from those of the Renaissance in their self-consciousness about the importance of invention, new artifacts also celebrated the time of God on earth. For these reasons, material reality was never dominated by a geometrical methodology. Instead, baroque art and architecture represent a unique synthesis of the conceptual and the sensuous. As Guarini himself wrote in the opening passage of his *Architettura civile,* "Architecture depends on geometry, yet it is an art of seduction that would never upset the senses by means of reason."[28] In this period the most significant theological speculations occurred within science and philosophy, and in poetry, painting, and sculpture, mysticism was conjoined with eroticism.[29] Although Platonizing philosophers denigrated our mortal senses as causes of error and sin, Malebranche admitted that worldly things were also "in God." "We see in God only the pure idea of intelligible extension, the archetype of the material world"; thus, "when you contemplate intelligible extension [geometrized architectural space], you see the divine substance."[30] Not surprisingly, for the artist *erōs* (human love, motivated by desire) became equivalent to *agapē* (God's unconditional love for all his creatures). A creator was a geometrician, a vigorous lover, and a mystic.

It has been often observed that the Enlightenment's rational and taxonomic impulse progressively demystified the world.[31] When astrology, angels, and demons were reduced to figments of the imagination in the late seventeenth century,[32] and Newton demonstrated the almost perfect rationality of a universe governed by universal gravitation, the creative spark of genius became regarded as a supreme form of rationality. Thus, Denis Diderot placed the man of genius at the apex of a hierarchy of rationality. Although a well-educated man may understand the laws of creation and their application, he cannot actually produce anything—and production is the true capacity of a genius.[33] The creative man of genius was far superior and more rare than either "clairvoyant" or "enlightened" individuals.

A "genie" (*genius* in Latin) belonged to a class of demons. It is interesting that this definition was still present in the famous *Encyclopédie,* Diderot's most ambitious project. It tells us that genies were spiritual beings constituted from aerial substance, and that their purpose was to assist the gods and serve as intermediaries between them and humans.[34] This definition seems to resonate with Diotima's understanding of *erōs* as a *daimōn* or spirit in *Symposium,* but the *Encyclopédie* also provides a much more extensive explanation of the term in philosophy and literature. The author of the essay, M. Le Blond, defines genius as "the extension of the spirit, the force of the imagination, and the activity of the soul." The soul is affected by external objects through perception and memory. A man of genius, however, takes the imagination further by relating this memory to "a thousand other ideas" to create something with a much more intense feeling (*sentiment*). Although this process may resemble the modern "mechanism" of intellectual association, Le Blond distinguishes between a work that is generated by rules of "taste" and a work of true genius: "Taste is often distinct from genius. Genius is a pure gift of nature." Genius produces a work in an instant, whereas taste develops through time and study. Unlike genius, taste relies on a knowledge of many rules and it produces beauties that are based on convention. To be beautiful according to the rules of taste, an object must appear elegant, finished, and effortless; but in a beautiful work of genius there is a certain neglect and irregularity. Le Blond then associates genius with the "sublime." He insists that genius breaks rules "to take flight into the sublime, the pathetic, the great." Taste, on the other hand, is ruled by "the love of eternal beauty that characterizes nature, by a passion to conform its works to some kind of model which it has created."[35] Although these weak echoes of Plato's theory acknowledge the ineffable dimension of genius, the rational discourse of the Enlightenment is no longer able to fully grasp embodied erotic experience as the ground of artistic meaning. This limitation has led to serious contradictions in mainstream discourses on aesthetics and architectural ornament ever since.

Some years before the inception of the Enlightenment's rational genius, Giambattista Vico put forward an insightful critique of Cartesian epistemology. Writing in the early eighteenth century, Vico understood the implications of Cartesian philosophy, but he also sought to recover an understanding of embodied knowledge in mythical articulations of truth throughout history. From modern philosophy he grasped the intimate relation between the new science and experimental demonstrations. Ultimately, men know only what they make. Experiments frame experience and project mathematical reason into the world, and thus humans attain some certainties. These are mere hypothetical fragments, however, regardless of their scope. Since nature is not our creation, scientific certainty is ultimately unattainable in our understanding of the more-than-human world. Unlike the majority of early-modern thinkers, Vico concluded that the human mind was *not* identical to the divine. Humans, being mortal, are endowed with an embodied consciousness that does not enable us to fully understand the relationship between the mind and its products. Yet human making is not merely an intuitive, unreflective action; it is based on a practical philosophy and a meditative practice. For Vico poetry was a kind of metaphysics that gleans truths through the imagination (consciousness, body, and memory, all in one) rather than through scientific formulas. Humanity creates, makes poetry, architecture, and institutions, but in a way that is very different from that of God (or modern technology): "For God, in his purest intelligence, knows things, and by knowing them, creates them; but [humans], in their robust ignorance, [do] it by virtue of a wholly corporeal imagination, one liable to perturb in excess."[36]

Despite Vico's insight into meaningful making (which would be developed much later by phenomenology and hermeneutics), the dominant maker after the ancien régime was the engineer, the new aristocrat of the nineteenth century. As a technical specialist, he could plan, control, and transform the world by implementing instrumental theories. He was the builder of the modern megalopolis and the suburb. His new modes of production were fueled by a search for maximum pleasure, a misguided transformation of *erōs* into hedonistic values, and a rational, ahistorical ethic. Poetic, playful making remained viable through Romanticism, surrealism, and other artistic venues, but always as a strategy of resistance against the dominant force, which co-opted architects into its fold.

Friedrich Nietzsche was already confronting this predicament during the nineteenth century. In an unfinished book titled *Philosophy in the Tragic Age of the Greeks,* he proclaims the value of play, questioning Kant and offering a far more radical position than a Romantic philosopher such as Schiller could have contemplated: "In this world," he writes, "only play, play as artists and children engage in it, exhibits coming-to-be and passing-away, structuring and destroying [or in Heidegger's later formulation, revealing truth as *alētheia,* the world (order) and the earth (mortality) as the components of art], without any moral additive."[37] This kind of play is sensuous and is never subjugated by reason. Aesthetic man must conform only to the "inner laws" of his creation, standing "contemplatively above and at the same time actively within the work." Moreover, "necessity and random play, oppositional tension and harmony, must pair to create a work of art."[38] In his late writings, particularly in the fragments published under the title *The Will to Power,* we find an understanding of art as excess and intoxication, identified with the will to power itself—the sole activity capable of destructuring false ideological or scientistic values. In other words, art-as-play is the only way for mankind to find truth, in opposition to the "truth as correspondence" premise that modern scientific theories inherited from Descartes and theology and eventually applied to generate most artifacts in our technological built environment. Nietzsche's notion of play was radical, since he ultimately understood it through a cosmic (rather than human) disinterestedness. It was clearly beyond a conventional ethic of "good and evil"; and yet, as I will show below, it was not beyond an interest in the common good.[39] For Nietzsche, the artist is the epitome of the *Übermann;* he is a passionate lover, and the lover is always worth more.

Artists, if they are any good, are (physically as well) strong, full of surplus energy, powerful animals, sensual; without a certain overheating of the sexual system a Raphael is unthinkable— Making music is another way of making children; chastity is merely the economy of the artist—and in any event, even with artists fruitfulness ceases when potency ceases— Artists should see nothing as it is, but fuller, simpler, stronger: to that end, their lives must contain a kind of youth and spring, a kind of habitual intoxication.[40]

One is more complete when passionately in love, and Nietzsche rejoices at the heightened sense of one's personality when in this trancelike state: the ultimate affirmation of life. In fact, the ultimate effect of art is "to *excite the state that creates art*—intoxication. . . . [A]rt is essentially *affirmation, blessing, deification of existence.*"[41] His understanding of love is thus contrary to the experience of loss or "melting" that we find in the early Greek poets, and is closer to Socrates' recollection of Orphic Eros.

Orphic Eros in late modernity

All creation presupposes at its origin a sort of appetite that is brought on by the foretaste of discovery. This foretaste of the creative act accompanies the intuitive grasp of an unknown entity already possessed but not yet intelligible, an entity that will not take definite shape except by the action of a constantly vigilant technique.

Igor Stravinsky, *Poetics of Music in the Form of Six Lessons* (trans. Arthur Knodel and Ingolf Dahl)

Surrealism did not deny inspiration, an exceptional state: it affirmed that it was common property. Poetry requires no special talent but rather a kind of spiritual daring, an unbinding that is also an unwinding.

Octavio Paz, "Signs in Rotation" (trans. Ruth L. C. Simms)

After all of this, what can we say about contemporary architectural creation? Is inspiration a mere anachronism? Even in cultural contexts where design is highly appreciated, society may be suspicious of it. Recent scholarship is equally skeptical. Even when architects are aware that architecture is not merely about technical, social, or political interests, they tend to regard inspiration as a potentially dangerous force that challenges our democratic values and technological processes. Yet we can hardly claim that the status of certain cultural masterpieces is simply a prejudice of bourgeois society. In our experience, works of art stand apart from the products of mere hard work and from instrumental applications of theories and ideologies. Contrary to the logic of materialism and deconstruction, George Steiner and Elaine Scarry have argued that such differences are indeed real, pointing to our primary human capacity to experience beauty as meaning, which enables such masterpieces to reveal our own purpose as human beings within and across our cultures.[42]

Plato understood that the voice of the poet was not his own, and that is why he both admired and despised poets. The Homeric rhapsodist had brought forth truths that alphabetic writing and the language of philosophers could not render. By retelling and reinventing the old myths, the rhapsodist adjusted the story so that it would become appropriate to a new situation. The rhapsodist's voice was never his own; it was the voice of the world, the voice of the gods. The aesthetic distance that was created by the Greeks of the fifth century B.C.E. went hand in hand with the naming and identification of *erōs* and *philia,* the objectification of speech into phonetic writing, and the recognition of authorship in literary, artistic, and dramatic works. Not surprisingly, the earliest literary genre in our tradition was the love poem. The distance that opened up between the embodied reader and the written work was the very theme of those wonderful erotic works that still vibrate under our gaze.

After human works started to gain autonomy from nature, it became common for the artist-demiurge to experience "someone" interrupting his creative work and making him "do" things that he never intended. Such experiences, ranging from unexpected discovery to coincidence, continued to be acknowledged until the end of the eighteenth century. Only after Romanticism did this become a theoretical problem in art. Architecture, with its new rational paradigms, tended to disregard the "problem." As Octavio Paz has pointed out, some called this force a demon, muse, spirit, or genius; others named it work, chance, the unconscious, even reason. Some declared that inspiration comes from without, while others maintained that the artist is self-sufficient. All artists, however, are obliged to admit exceptions: inspiration appears when it is least expected.[43]

Inspiration irrupts into (and often disrupts) a work in progress at the precise moment of creation, subverting the expectations of rational planning. Does it really belong to the artist? The work of art weaves together a personal voice and the voices of the world. The Nietzschean augmentation is also a sacrifice, for "every mature art has a host of conventions as its basis—in so far as it is a language. Convention is the condition of great art, *not* an obstacle."[44] Thus it involves a sacrifice, a dissolution of the imagining self that enables the work to speak. Plato clearly understood the poet as a winged being, light and sacred, drawn by enthusiasm out of himself in order to produce his works. The origin of this inspiration was a transcendental other, whether the gods of classical antiquity or the medieval god of Christianity.

The advent of modern philosophy, particularly after Descartes, radically altered our idea of external reality. The dualistic structure of *res cogitans* and *res extensa* enabled us to conceive of external reality as a product of consciousness. Finally, after the French Revolution, nature ceased to be a living and animate whole. However, inspiration continues to exist, even though it challenges our intellectual beliefs.

The nineteenth century struggled intensely with this "problem," either by categorically denying its existence or by interpreting inspired Romantic art as an attempt to usurp the very function of religion. Sometimes the contradictions were perceived as insurmountable. To renounce inspiration was tantamount to denying the legitimacy of artistic pursuits, while affirming it might contradict how Romantic artists regarded themselves and the world. As is well known, positivism viewed delirium and inspiration with great suspicion, and artists often tried to avoid speculative contamination by working hard and efficiently. The work of art has never fit neatly the expectations of a capitalist morality, however. Often the greatest works of our artistic traditions are models of simplicity and effortlessness rather than painstaking labor. Furthermore, no amount of rational preparation or accumulated information can rival the inspirational power of sterility and drought, the sense of "lack" that, according to Rilke, lies at the origin of great poetry.

During the early twentieth century, surrealism articulated the "problem" of inspired creation by responding to insights from existentialism and phenomenology. It was a radical attempt to overcome the reduction of reality to the subject–object antinomy. It questioned both the status of the subject as a thinking substance and the status of the object as a quantifiable and unchanging substance. There is no reflective ego at one end of the creative process, and no completed and immutable work at the other end. There is instead a poetic force, initially directed by the poet-maker (perhaps at random or guided by his or her life project), but necessarily recreated by the spectator-participant. The poet in love is the only one who is capable of revealing the truth. André Breton is able to perceive the true Paris only through his love for Nadja—not the invisible but the utterly visible, in a state that is not reducible to either dreams or a banal reality.

The surrealist program placed inspiration at the center of a world vision, substituting it for both reason and religion as a "form of knowledge." According to Breton, inspiration is given in man and is part of his very being. As Giambattista Vico had already insinuated in the early eighteenth century, man is first and foremost a poet (a maker, from the Greek *poiēsis*), and poetically he must dwell. Despite the surrealists' well-known interest in Freud and his theories, Breton maintained that inspiration could not be explained by psychoanalysis. Surrealist artists often flirted with occult explanations and were fascinated by coincidence and chance encounters, which showed their acceptance of the obscure source of inspiration. The surrealists' conscious engagement of inspiration by deliberately stirring the forces of *desire* became a condition for authentic art and life.

Inspiration in contemporary *praxis*

Throughout modernity architecture sought the origins of creation in rational frameworks, such as programs understood as lists of spaces with quantitative notations, diagrams, and functional flow charts. Contemporary building design generally operates on the premise that in order to be socially responsible the process of planning must be thoroughly rational and, if possible, consensual and democratic. Indeed, following the heroic phase of twentieth-century architecture, inspiration was further discredited by critical theory's skepticism about our capacity to generate products that are both beautiful and ethical. A building project, furthermore, has to be substantially completed before construction can begin. In order to live up to these imperatives and yet be capable of innovation, some contemporary architects have sought to collapse "theory" and "practice" in new "algorithmic" processes of design that avoid subjective "judgment" and produce novelty through instrumental mathematical operations. Made possible by powerful computers and ingenious software, the new algorithmic magic creates novelty without love, resulting in short-lived seduction, typically without concern for embodied cultural experience, character, and appropriateness.

In *Phaedrus,* Socrates warned us against the deceptions resulting from the rationalization of the origins of love. Arguing against Lysias, who had written a powerful account of love that had impressed Phaedrus, Socrates associates the corruption of love with the power of reason. We are told in the dialogue how Lysias flaunts his self-control, mastering time and writing about love "from the end" of the relationship. In his story he is not truly affected by Eros, and this control enables him to dominate the relationship with his beloved and manipulate his "friendship" according to rational interests. From a certain perspective this may be a good thing. For Socrates, however, Lysias's story is inconceivable as a true account of love. Love and, by analogy, creation have their origins in the deeply felt experience of beauty itself, sometimes destabilizing and never in line with the principles of logic.

Recasting Socrates' insight for modernity, Nietzsche equated the artist with a vigorous lover. Existential philosophy recognized that man has no static essence. Rather, each one of us is a project and a story, like a beam of light in search of focus, always extending toward something other. Otherness is part of our essence, the void that we are and yet are not. This void ahead of us, something or someone that calls us to be ourselves, is inspiration. The very aspiration of the artist, a moving forward thrust of the imagining self, goes beyond itself to encounter itself, deconstructing the egocentric *I* in order to find itself engaged in a fuller wholeness. This is, of course, the voice of *desire,* the very voice of being that summons us beyond ourselves to the unknown. As in the story of primordial Eros, the beloved is one with the lover/creator, not at the end but at the beginning of the erotic process. The unknown, therefore, is familiar; and thus it is possible for us to know, with the knowledge of embodied memory, where inspiration comes from.

But this knowledge is a bodily knowledge, not a concept or an abstract idea. Inspiration cannot be grasped as a method or theory. We cannot wait for it passively; primordial Eros does not utter clearly articulated messages and is always encountered *in action.* Inspired work is usually prompted by other beautiful works. Beauty incites the act of replication; it brings copies of itself into being.[45] This is no mere theory but a fact that can be substantiated in history and through our own experiences. Inspired work appears in the process of making, as long as it retains a *playful* attitude toward creation and responsiveness to unexpected discoveries, quite at odds with the typical will to control the outcome by means of logical prediction, which is standard in contemporary building production.

2 Eros and Limits

Opening conversation

He seems to me equal to gods that man
who opposite you
sits and listens close
to your sweet speaking
and lovely laughing—oh it

puts the heart in my chest on wings
for when I look at you, a moment, then no speaking
is left in me

no: tongue breaks, and thin
fire is racing under my skin
and in eyes no sight and drumming
fills ears

and cold sweat holds me and shaking
grips me all, greener than grass
I am and dead—or almost
I seem to me.

Sappho, fragment 31 (trans. Anne Carson)

And this is a universal law: a living thing can be healthy, strong and fruitful only
when bounded by a horizon.

Friedrich Nietzsche, *Untimely Meditations* (trans. R. J. Hollingdale)

Plato calls Love a bitter thing. And not wrongly, because anyone who loves, dies.
And Orpheus calls him *gluchupichron,* that is, "bitter-sweet." Certainly, since love
is a voluntary death.

Marsilio Ficino, *Commentary on Plato's Symposium On Love* (trans. Sears Jayne)

Eros, spacing, and joints

According to Hesiod's *Theogony*, the castration of Ouranos and his separation from Gaia led to the initial bloody conflict among the primordial
Greek gods, followed by division and war in the world. At the same time,
out of Ouranos's loss, human love was born. The subsequent birth of Aphrodite gave us individual human beings, living in space-time, differentiated
by their gender and attracted to each other.[1] Aphrodite is accompanied by
her assistants, a reincarnated Eros and Himeros (Longing). Eros/Cupid is
no longer a force inside a single being that provokes its division into two;
instead, he provokes two gendered beings to engender a third. Hence, it becomes clear that only a god can reach without desire or, conversely, be
filled with endless desire. For humans, an ethical engagement with desire
always involves *limits*. Lack and fulfillment are never permanent and absolute in human existence. Such recognition enables one to grasp the sense
of reality as woven from pleasure and pain, limited by love *and* death.

The celebrated Canadian poet Anne Carson, author of an eloquent
study of Eros in Greek literature and philosophy, notes that the second incarnation of Eros is largely the invention of the early lyric and dramatic
poets. It coincided with the major cultural transformations that led to classical Greek civilization, including the inventions of philosophy and the
arts.[2] "Sweet-bitter Eros" represented for the lyric poets the paradoxical
convergence of love and hate, apprehended as a conflicted blend of action,
sensation, and valorization. Eros in Greek connotes *want* or *lack*. The lover
wants what he does not have. By definition it is impossible for him to have
what he wants: as soon as he has it he is no longer wanting.[3] This dilemma
is present in our Western cultural self-consciousness, from Sappho and
Plato to psychoanalysis and existentialism. Precisely because "no one ever
desires what is not gone," the Greeks invented Eros to account for this fundamental human condition in the Western tradition. The concept of *erōs*
as lack calls for *three* structural components: the lover, the beloved, and
the space-time that comes between them.[4]

Commenting on Sappho's fragment 31 (quoted above), Carson remarks that space *both connects and separates,* "marking that two are not
one, irradiating the absence whose presence is demanded by Eros."[5] The
points on the circuit of possible relationships among the three protagonists in the poem (including the narrator) "touch not touching." The space
of desire must be maintained for the sake of meaning. Foregrounded from
the confusion of everyday life by artworks of diverse genres, the space of

desire would allow readers and spectators to experience the site of a mean-ingful existence. In erotic narratives such as Longus's *Daphnis and Chloe,* this space was maintained with countless ordeals and rivals that separate the lover and beloved. In Greek vase painting, a favorite subject was *erōs* deferred or obstructed rather than triumphant.[6]

Carson observes that the reach of desire is defined in action.[7] Eros is intertwined with human, mortal time. Eros is indeed a twin of Thanatos. Renaissance authors would later observe that "the cause of death is love," quoting the Neoplatonic writings of Hermes Trismegistus. Desire, writes Carson, is beautiful in its object, foiled in its attempt, and endless in time. Eros requires boundaries, including the inevitable human boundaries of mortal time and spatial flesh. Any attempt to dissolve those boundaries would emphasize its impossibility.[8]

A number of scholars have pointed out the importance of alphabetic writing in the development of Greek culture.[9] Although the Greek alpha-bet was derived from other Middle Eastern forms of writing, it was the first to "freeze speech" by introducing a combination of vowels and conso-nants, representing their sounds by means of relatively arbitrary graphic signs. The Greeks developed a capacity to read the poetic image from such arbitrary speaking signs. Unlike prior writing systems based on the record-ing of images from the physical world, Greek alphabetic writing consoli-dated the "artificial" basis of human culture. The mute pictographic images of earlier civilizations had clearly expressed our human depen-dence on the more-than-human world.[10] Speech in oral cultures was a con-tinual communion among individuals and with nature. This communion with a mythical world, not encountered as an "it" but engaged as a "Thou," is difficult to characterize, but it is clear that individuals in oral cultures related differently to their environment, and conceived the body and the self differently, than do individuals in literate cultures. Once speech was recorded in phonetic writing, the unit of poetic thought was increasingly the word rather than the phrase. Greek phonetic writing was first rendered graphically as a continuous line, meandering from left to right and from right to left (*boustrophēdon*). Later, the words became sep-arated by a visual space, and writing developed the left-to-right format that is familiar to us. It is significant that consonants are "abstract edges" that cannot be pronounced without adding some "vocalic breath."[11] Not surprisingly, as Carson points out, some of the earliest uses of alphabetic writing were for erotic literature by the Greek lyric poets. This new writ-ten literature, as well as the new "graphic arts" such as painting, sculpture, and architecture, would make the articulation of erotic space a primary issue: not an objective geometric entity but the space of embodiment that separates *and* connects, and reveals its coincidence with cosmic place.

Before Greek philosophy and classical literature, the spaces between things were ignored. Writing in the late sixth century B.C.E., Empedocles still believed that breath, identified with Eros, was present everywhere and accounted for the diverse combinations of the four elements in all natural phenomena. Through breath, everything in the universe is capable of touching everything else. Wings and breath moved *both* Eros and words, in an inescapable bond.[12] In architecture, one might argue, buildings were perceived as natural features; the pyramid was a sacred mountain and the Mycenaean *tholos* was a sacred cave. The "artificiality" of architectural language both posited and occupied another space that Plato called *chōra*, to differentiate it from *topos*. Architectural writing in the form of *ichnographia* (plan) and *orthographia* (elevation) was simply not present in earlier cultures. In Greek architecture, space makes the edges visible; in language, vowels make the consonants audible. Erotic space also becomes the physical interval between the work and the new observer/participant, and between the architect and his work of *technē-poiēsis*.

Pythagoras is reported to have obtained great pleasure from tracing letters, "forming each stroke with a geometrical rhythm of angles and curves and straight lines."[13] In contrast to the Egyptians, who always used a brush, Greeks wrote letters with a reed pen; and after the fifth century, papyrus was the accepted medium. The pen, truly analogous to a cutting instrument, was crucial to trace the fine lines of the new letters, all ruled by sharp edges and based on geometry. Furthermore, there is an obvious connection between constructing letters for epigraphic inscriptions over geometrical guidelines and making architectural "drawings": both were inscribed in stone and evoked the perfection of mathematical ideas. In Euripides' *Theseus,* an illiterate man spells the name of the hero by describing the geometry of the letters on the sails of a ship. A comedy by Callias used chorus members personifying the letters of the alphabet to spell syllables for the audience, while Sophocles is said to have staged a satyr play in which an actor "danced" the letters of the alphabet. In Greek theater the dancing chorus usually left traces on the sand floor of the orchestra: a veritable *ichnographia* reminiscent of the labyrinth. A dancing platform and the labyrinth were the archetypal works of architecture attributed to Daedalus during his stay in Crete.

Given the importance of edges and limits, it is perhaps not surprising that Western architecture became obsessed with joints. The *daidalon,* the archaic architectural artifact that provided Daedalus's name, was a wonder-producing construction made of well-adjusted pieces. *Daidala* had different purposes and were very diverse in appearance: they included wooden and copper-plated sculptures so lifelike that they had to be tied down, as well as buildings, ships, defensive weapons, weavings, and famous deceptive devices, such as the Trojan horse and Pasiphaë's cow.[14] Yet they were all constructed of pieces well fitted together, a concept that philosophers eventually would use to characterize the human body and the universe. This characteristic became known as "harmony."

Indeed, harmony in both Greek and Latin was a key term in architectural treatises from Vitruvius to the Renaissance. As the fundamental quality of beauty (*venustas*), it is an arrangement of parts that seduces the user/observer and creates a significant space of participation. It is important to notice that *harmonia* initially had nothing to do with mathematics; it was a quality of embodiment (perfect adjustment) with the ultimate aim of love.

Harmonia originally meant "joining," "a joint," "agreement"; only later did it signify a concordance of sounds and the more general "combination or adaptation of parts, elements, or related things, so as to form a consistent and orderly whole."[15] The physician Galen (130–200 C.E.) wrote the most complete work on anatomical structure in antiquity, *On the Usefulness of the Parts,* in which *harmonia* refers to the union of two bones by mere apposition: a perfectly adjusted joint.

One of the most distinctive aspects of Greek classical culture was its interest in anatomy; dissection and the examination of entrails were applied for purposes of divination.[16] Indeed, this is the same culture that eventually established "organic" muscularity as a prime feature of the Western tradition in both anatomical treatises and works of art. Although other world cultures are equally observant, they never perceived a muscular body as it appears in Vesalius's *De humani corporis fabrica* (1543) or in the sculptures of Michelangelo and Rodin.[17] Of course, muscles are not really noticeable unless we work them out. Different representations of the body in Chinese, Indian, and Tibetan medicine indicate that our Western concept of the body is a construction. The muscular body inherited from Greek culture and our understanding of architecture as a *body* (recorded first by Vitruvius, ca. 30–20 B.C.E.) respond to this anatomical interest. This is an immense topic, quite beyond the scope of my present argument, but it is sufficient to note that Galen's work presents a mature understanding of muscles and their purpose, founded on observations made during dissection. Like Vitruvius examining the parts of a building almost two centuries earlier, Galen finds not only blood and entrails but also a divine design, an expressive assembly of parts that are perfectly adjusted to their purpose: "Everything is so well-disposed that it couldn't possibly be better otherwise." He dissected different kinds of animals to convince himself "that there was a single mind that fashioned them, and that the body is suited in all ways to the character of the animal."[18] Vesalius would later echo this thought in his *Fabrica,* which presents the dissected body as an admirable "microcosm" of the wisdom of God. As Shigehisa Kuriyama has aptly summarized, anatomical curiosity in the West is based on the premise that bodily forms express their creative purpose.[19]

Galen understood the muscular system as the "organ" of personal volition, distinct from mere flesh and sinews. By internalizing motion as the result of a personal will, he reinforced the differentiation of the self from the world that had started during the archaic period of Greek philosophy. In the classical period, however, there are no fully organic muscular bodies. Just as the word for "muscle" appears only sparingly in Hippocratic literature and not at all in Homer or Plato, so in classical sculpture and painting there are no muscles but only joints that articulate the parts of the body.[20] The Greek word for joints is *arthroi;* these are not joints in the modern sense, but divisions that articulate the form of the body. To be *anarthros* was to be debilitated, and it was believed that well-jointed feet and legs and sinewy bodies were signs of power and strong character.[21] *Arthroi* were also important in language: they were the words that *partitioned* the stream of speech by adding what grammarians call articles. What differentiates human speech from barking (the origin of the word "barbarian," according to Strabo) is "the articulation by means of the tongue."[22] Finally, the plural *arthroi,* when used by itself, did not mean joints but instead designated the male and female genitals, Eros's archetypal joint.[23]

Erotic space and the origins of Western culture

This initial characterization of Western cultural space as *fundamentally* erotic should be teased out further. Erotic space is not an a priori concept, nor an objectified geometric or topological reality. It is both the physical space of architecture at the inception of the Western tradition and the linguistic space of a metaphor, the electrified void between two terms that are brought together but kept apart. While this significant gap is the underlying subject of art (including love poems), bounded space is the underlying subject of architecture. It is the space for political and religious action and for theatrical performance, where drama produces *katharsis* and festival time occurs. It is *limited* space: in architecture, the creation of limits is crucial and cannot be reduced to material walls. Beyond the city wall of the Greek *polis* was a regional zone known as *chōra*,[24] a thick limit that was believed to be protected by specific divinities. This regional *chōra* is a quasi-homophone of the central *choros* or dance platform that mediated between the spectators in the amphitheater and the actors on the *skēnē* in a dramatic performance. In the *Iliad, chōrē* (the Ionian form of *chōra*) is a liminal space—for example, the narrow shoreline on which the Achaeans were left to fight, or the space between a horse and a chariot.[25] Once the Dionysian rituals were transformed into drama, this liminal space became architectural; it connected the spectators to the dramatic action but also separated them from it. Clearly, this charged erotic space is not identical to the isotropic space of our geometric or aesthetic world.

Given the inherently nondiscursive nature of architecture, it is helpful to delve into literature and philosophy to sharpen our understanding of erotic space in the Western tradition. In addition to the writings of lyric poets such as Sappho and philosophers such as Plato, there exist four ancient Greek novels, other fragments, and a number of Latin texts (from the first century B.C.E. to the fourth century C.E.) that could be considered early romances. The plots, not surprisingly, keep the lovers apart until the last page. This genre of writing and the epic genre originate the great forms of Western narrative. Aphrodite plays a crucial and paradoxical role: she both incites and blocks love's fulfillment. The novelist aims to convey both pleasure and pain.[26] This purpose is evident in Longus's *Daphnis and Chloe* (second century C.E.), the most famous work in this genre, and in later treatises that deal more directly with architecture, such as the *Hypnerotomachia Poliphili* (1499).

Daphnis and Chloe merits special mention. It was deemed by Goethe a major literary accomplishment that "you should read anew each year to learn from it over and over again and be influenced by its beauty."[27] *Daphnis and Chloe* links the natural forces of *erōs* to ways of learning, both innate (*physis*) and acquired by skill (*technē*). For the two "naïve and inexperienced" protagonists, love is more than a force that draws them together: it is the guide to knowledge and a strategy for teaching others (*paideia*).[28] Nature is transformed into culture as it becomes erotic space. The reader/spectator can share the experience as a witness and understand something of the essence of human reality. At the apex of the triangle linking the reader/spectator with the two peasants in love emerges the space of architecture.

The novel starts with a traditional *ekphrasis* (a rhetorical description of a painting or another work of art) as a prime motivation for story-telling.[29] This paradigm is significant: beauty reproduces itself, the experience of beauty motivates creation, and the poetic image in one medium is translatable to others. Erotic space is common to painting, literature, and architecture, thus linking language to other forms of making at the limits of language. Indeed, the disclosure of narratives in works of art had a profound impact on architectural discourse. Although there are significant differences between the Renaissance *Hypnerotomachia,* Jean-François de Bastide's *Petite maison* (1758), Nicolas Le Camus de Mézières's *Le génie de l'architecture* (1780), Claude-Nicolas Ledoux's *L'architecture* (1804), and even my own twentieth-century *Polyphilo,* a common thread runs through the primary tradition of Western architecture. The narrator of *Daphnis and Chloe* tells us that one day he was hunting on the island of Lesbos and found "the most beautiful sight," a seductive natural grove for the nymphs that was ornamented with an even more remarkable painting depicting a story of love. The skill (*technē*) of the painter and the story about *erōs,* evoked in him wonder (*thauma*) and an uncontainable desire to achieve the same result in writing. Art provided inspiration, a mimetic yearning, a desire for desire.

This story recalls Pliny's account of the erotic origin of drawing, in which the lover traces the beloved's shadow and invests the tracing with desire after the beloved has departed. In *Daphnis and Chloe* the pastoral couple go on a journey of sexual discovery and deferral of fulfillment, a temporal equivalent of the space made by the painting that both links and separates the spectator and the work. Metaphors, ruses, and subterfuges bring erotic space to life. The novel maintains this charged experience over many pages, presenting a *locus amoenus,* an enclosed and desirable pastoral space, that the reader wishes to penetrate without violating. Like the space of satyr plays, it is a place between culture and nature. Culture is finally contemplated in the form of the *paradeisos,* a prominent formal garden with a Dionysian temple at the center. The clear geometric order and disposition of this place evoke both the ideals of *theōria* and the classical theater. Dionysos was both an Olympian and a rustic divinity. He appears at social occasions of collective work (such as winemaking) and collective play (ritual festivities and tragedy).[30] Of course, this is also the place of architecture and a back stage for the comedic intrigues in which society legitimizes the lovers' pursuit. Eventually Eros returns to the grassy meadow facing the cave of the nymphs where Chloe as a baby was exposed, and the lovers consummate their marriage in the privacy of a bedchamber.[31]

Erotic architectural space in the *Hypnerotomachia Poliphili*

Poliphilo's "strife of love in a dream," the *Hypnerotomachia Poliphili* published in Venice by Aldus Manutius in 1499, is perhaps the most explicit articulation of erotic space in architecture, in the tradition of *Daphnis and Chloe*. The *Hypnerotomachia* is also one of the most beautiful books ever produced. While the book had a significant influence in philosophic, artistic, and even alchemical circles well into the eighteenth century, its impact on architecture is more difficult to ascertain. In France, for example, it was translated almost immediately and published in 1546 by Jean Martin, the same scholar who translated the texts of Alberti and Vitruvius. It was republished in 1551, 1554, and 1561. Transformed French versions with different titles appeared in 1600, 1657, and 1772. Free translations appeared in 1803, 1811, and 1883, and some have been reprinted in the twentieth century. The images represented monuments, gateways, sculptural details, hieroglyphs, fountains, festivals and processions, plans of buildings and gardens, geometric shrubbery, and ritual objects. They were sources for ephemeral and permanent buildings in Europe for at least 300 years.

In modern Europe, however, architects were suspicious of the esoteric tone of the text. The *Hypnerotomachia* generally has been excluded from standard histories of architecture and considered less important than the works of Alberti or Palladio.[32] In a recent dissertation on the topic, Tracey Winton has argued convincingly that the central aim of the book is to demonstrate Ficinian Neoplatonism at work, with its overtones of theurgic magic: the narrative follows the philosophical ascent of the soul, pursuing pictures from the mind's eye, and therefore is less concerned with the exoteric problems of architecture.[33] Regardless of its intended objective, the text is unique in presenting the poetic experience of ancient architecture through narrative. The reader participates in the space of human desire through precise descriptions of sensuous components and geometrical lineaments that elaborate on the beautiful woodcuts that accompany the text.[34] Indeed, by presenting the reality of architectural space as erotic and limited, the *Hypnerotomachia Poliphili* suggested potential alternatives to the technical emphasis that was already becoming explicit in other Renaissance architectural theories.

Dreaming about being in a threatening dark forest, Poliphilo encounters many things in a veritable "strife for love." He describes ancient marvels "deserving of a place in the theater of memory," architectural monuments, and ruins of classical buildings in his search for Polia, his beloved. He portrays a great pyramid surmounted by an obelisk and reports the precise measurement and characteristics of columns, their capitals, bases, entablatures with diverse architraves, friezes, cornices, and their respective moldings and ornaments. He also describes a forceful winged horse on an ornamented pedestal, and visits a crypt under a magnificent elephant containing the tombs of a king and a queen. Walking inside a hollow, half-buried colossus, he reports medical information attached to the organs, and realizes that lovesickness cannot be cured. His attention is seized by a triumphal gateway with its harmonic measurements and ornamentation. The iconography throughout this passage concerns good and bad fortune. Human destiny is ultimately in the hands of Fortuna Primigenia, the mother goddess identified with nature, Venus *physizoa* or *generatrix*. Human artifacts must be devoted to good fortune, engaging Venus, who, in the words of Lucretius, "alone gives life and governs the nature of things."[35]

After suffering a major scare at the threshold, passing the test of a frightening labyrinth, and being brought back to life by a wonderful encounter with the five senses in the form of five nymphs, Poliphilo quenches his thirst by drinking tepid water springing from a stone nymph's breasts and deciphers mysterious hieroglyphs. He is then taken by the nymphs to a sumptuous bath. They disrobe and he is teased by the five senses, making him realize that his beloved is always elsewhere. Eventually they arrive at the palace of the queen, the embodiment of free will, where he is invited to a splendid meal. He expresses his admiration for the variety of precious stones and materials worn by all present, and describes a game of chess performed as a dance and other harmonious choreographies. After the festivities, he is taken to visit three gardens: the first made of glass, the second of silk, and the third in the form of a labyrinth, a symbol of human life. In its midst was Trinity itself, expressed through hieroglyphs, from sacred Egyptian sculpture. Poliphilo then comes to a crossroads and encounters three doors with inscriptions, one of which he must choose. Behind the central door he meets Polia. She carries a lighted torch and they walk together. Neither realizes the meaning of their physical proximity as they walk hand in hand and admire the four triumphs of Jove: four processions whose chariots and artifacts celebrate the stories of the classical poets explaining the effects of various kinds of love. Then they witness the triumph of Vertuno and Pomona and the ancient sacrifice of Priapus. Eventually they enter a magnificent temple of great beauty where the sacrifices of miraculous rites and ancient religion once took place. It is here, in a most perfect circular temple devoted to Venus/Aphrodite, that they fully acknowledge their loving encounter. Under the dome, an eternally glowing lamp and a well designate the *axis mundi* where a priestess of Venus performs rites for a miraculous germination of life, while Poliphilo extinguishes Polia's fiery torch in the water.

Poliphilo tells how he and Polia left the temple and arrived at the coast to wait for Cupid at a ruined site that she had persuaded him to explore in search of admirable ancient monuments. Among many enlightening epitaphs of unhappy love, he describes a mural depicting hell for those who offend *erōs* through either promiscuous excess or abstinence. Scared again and reminded of death, he returns to Polia just in time to meet Cupid, who has arrived in his ship propelled by beautiful rowing nymphs. Both climb aboard, and Cupid uses his wings as sails. Sea gods, goddesses, and nymphs pay tribute to Cupid, and the vessel arrives triumphantly at the island of Cytherea: a perfect circular island where even the topiary is geometrical. Poliphilo then describes the forests, gardens, fountains, and rivers on the island, as well as the procession of triumphal chariots and nymphs in honor of the blindfolded Cupid, who guides them. In the center of the island, the final place of arrival, he describes the fountain of Venus with its precious columns and the loving embrace that takes place after the appearance of Mars. This highly erotic scene is followed by a visit to the innermost enclosure containing the tomb of Adonis, where the nymphs tell the story of the hero's death and the commemoration each year by a weeping Venus, his lover. These two scenes are related in the narrative, and seem to occupy the same space: love is bittersweet, even for the goddess Venus.

Finally, the nymphs ask Polia to tell her own version of the love story. She provides a genealogy of her family, explains her initial inclination to ignore Poliphilo, and details the ultimate success of their love. Following Polia's account, Poliphilo concludes by describing their embrace in the happy place of dwelling . . . until he is awakened, sad and alone, by the song of the nightingale.

The story is a sensuous and obsessive search for love that is *not* fulfilled. Throughout the book Poliphilo reminds us of his painful and delightful longing, and Polia remains absent at the end of the story. This battle for love is also a search for wisdom, but what truly matters is the search itself. Eros is not only the "weaver of fictions" *(mythoplokos),* as Sappho calls him,[36] but also a sophist—a professor of wisdom, in the words of Socrates. Furthermore, in a surprising move, Socrates collapses the two into one. Twice in the Platonic dialogues he speaks of his search for wisdom and asserts that his knowledge is nothing but a knowledge of "erotic things."[37] Without defining what he means, we can understand better his famous statement about his own modest wisdom: "I do not think I know what I do not know."[38] Properly human truths, truths that matter, can be grasped only by acknowledging limits.

The space of architecture *appears* throughout the *Hypnerotomachia* in descriptions of sites, materials, proportions, procedures, and specifications: obviously a lesson for an aspiring architect. However, the architecture *evokes what is missing;* it is the engine of the imagination. This recalls Aristotle's remarks about the function of the imagination (*phantasia*). *Phantasia* is what prompts creatures to reach out for what they desire, to use metaphor to bring near what is far. The story must always distinguish between what is present and known and what is not. Orientation is the crucial role of architecture in the narrative of the *Hypnerotomachia*. The ideal is not *in* this world; the perfect garden/city/architecture remains otherworldly but provides a utopian vector for the imagination by construing the good life in our here and now.

The *Hypnerotomachia* demonstrates that architectural meaning is neither intellectual nor aesthetic in a formal sense, but originates instead in our embodiment and its erotic impulse. Our inherent "lack," the need to quench our thirst, is the existential condition that humanity can reconcile only within the cultural realm of *poiēsis* and its metaphoric imagination. Indeed, Poliphilo is thirsty throughout the story. When he comes upon classical buildings and monuments, he first experiences their overwhelming luminosity, the color and texture of their materials, and the perfect adjustment among their parts; only secondly does he measure their proportional relationships. Light and music precede geometry. In his sensuous narrative, this secondary discovery of *mathēmata* is always combined with a recollection of love; the effect of architecture transcends the purely visual or theoretical by evoking both the memory and expectation of erotic fulfillment in a thick and vivid present. The harmony of architecture is always tactile and "mater-ial" (referring to the mother of all). The formal exactness of numbers builds on the sensuous qualities of materials, and this experience of wholeness is enhanced even further by the beautiful melodies that often accompany Poliphilo's encounters.

"Poli-philo" is indeed the lover of Polia. She is constantly evoked. Her face awakens in him a desire for wholeness and illuminates his ascent toward self-knowledge, the supreme coincidence of beauty and justice, which Plato suggests in *Symposium* is a ground for ethical action. While this voyage concerns the human soul, Plato's universe and its rendering by Renaissance writers is never dualistic. Polia is the absent woman whose name stands for the city (*polis*) and perhaps also for multiple knowledge (in the biblical sense of carnal knowledge). Architectural meaning, like erotic knowledge, is a primary experience of the human body and yet takes place in the world, in that prereflective ground of existence where reality is first "given." It can never be reduced to pure objectivity or subjectivity. Thus, Polia/architecture is represented as the missing sixth sense in the episode of the bath. Love and architecture are sensuous but also transcend the senses, with a wholeness underscored by alchemical themes of fragmentation and union that structure the narrative and propel the soul toward enlightenment. The space-time of human culture in *Hypnerotomachia* is mortally bounded yet pierced by an arrow of infinite desire, suggesting that the reader/architect/pilgrim, like Poliphilo, may embrace this purposeful tension and travel this path.

For Plato, Eros can reveal beauty "in the one moment of man's life that is worth living."[39] This is the same power of revelation that appreciates the products of human craft (*technē-poiēsis*) and enables our potential wholeness through the experience of a work of art or architecture. Poliphilo encounters this possibility at the crossroads. The two nymphs who accompany him, Logistica (Reason) and Thelemia (Desire/Will), cannot persuade him to take either the right or the left door. Poliphilo does not choose *vita contemplativa,* a life of contemplation associated with classical metaphysics and theology, in which architecture is a liberal art and science; nor does he choose *vita activa,* a life of action and production in the medieval sense, in which architecture is a mechanical art. Rejecting both sexual abstinence and the cycle of toil, reward, and endless disillusion, Poliphilo chooses the enigmatic middle door: *vita voluptuaria,* a life of desire in which fulfillment is not the ultimate aim, yet is never far away. Through recollection and projection, it involves ethical responsibility and requires respect for the beloved. As he crosses the threshold Polia approaches with her lit torch. They hold hands, together and yet not aware of their identity; they journey through a protracted delay while being initiated into the mysteries of love. This, we learn, is the life that the good philosopher/lover/architect must pursue.

After the couple's mutual recognition and "marriage" in the circular temple of Venus, they acknowledge the delightful wholeness and fruitfulness that love brings, but discover that happy endings are delusions. To fulfill their desire, the couple still must cross the sea of death. After leaving the circular temple, Poliphilo alone must visit a cemetery under a ruined temple, where he finds poignant funerary architecture with epitaphs that describe the tragedy of lovers separated by death. Overtaken by anguish, Poliphilo returns to the coast to find Polia, just in time for them to board

Cupid's ship. It is no coincidence that Cupid plays the role of navigator and becomes Tecton, the mythical carpenter, shipbuilder, and pilot, the Homeric ancestor of the architect. Cupid's wings become the sails of the ship, recalling the archaic myth of Daedalus and Icarus, in which the architect and his son escape from Crete by inventing, in different versions of the story, either wings or sails.

On the other side of the sea, on the island of love, Polia and Poliphilo are finally together, but only after being metaphorically blindfolded by Cupid. At a privileged central place described as a classical theater, *theatrum mundi,* the two lovers witness an ultimate ritual of love performed by the immortal gods. There they endure the last painstaking delay in their quest for love. But at the end of Polia's story, Poliphilo finally awakens from his dream to discover that he is alone yet complete in the presence of an architecture that anticipates the fulfillment and wholeness that, however weak, ground us as purposeful beings in the universe.

Chōra as erotic space

I wish to show that space-time is not necessarily something to which one can ascribe a separate existence, independently of the actual objects of physical reality. Physical objects are not *in space,* but these objects are *spatially extended.* In this way the concept of empty space loses its meaning.

Albert Einstein, *Relativity: The Special and General Theory* (trans. Robert W. Lawson)

I have already suggested a fundamental analogy between erotic space and Plato's concept of space in *Timaeus.* To conclude this chapter, I will further unpack this relationship and some of its consequences for the history of Western architecture.

It has often been observed that *Timaeus* marks the origin of our Western scientific tradition, and even foreshadows the geometric concept of space that would underlie classical physics and the technological world after the eighteenth century. *Timaeus* is the first systematic explanation of the universe and its origin, departing from the cosmogonic myths of Hesiod that I paraphrased in chapter 1. Turning his gaze to the heavens and contemplating its orderly motion, Plato imagined a geometrical universe that would inspire subsequent cosmological orders in the Western world until Newton. Plato's Demiurge based the world on a perfect geometric prototype; so human poets, craftsmen, and architects would embody similar mathematical proportions in their artifacts. By harmoniously taking measure of time and space, and by framing institutions within a universal order, humans could propitiate Fortune (destiny) and lead a virtuous life.

Though it was subsequently misread, Plato's articulation of reality was not a simple duality of immutable Being (the ideal realm of heavenly motions) and becoming (the concrete realm of mortal life). His first, unshakable observation was that the two realms were autonomous: there is nothing purely ideal in our mortal realm, which is always undergoing change. As Aristotle would write a few years later, the physical realm is not compatible with mathematics, yet both he and Plato believed that these two realms were related in some way. Aristotle's interpretation of forms, as things that the eye could see, helped carry the transcendental speculations of *Timaeus* into the natural sciences. Through Stoicism, this view would become the source of mainstream architectural theory, as evident in Vitruvius. Aristotle wondered about the organization of the world we experience and observed perfection in living creatures. He often used *eidos* (idea) and *morphē* (form) interchangeably.[40] In his *On the Parts of Animals*, Aristotle acknowledges the disgust one experiences when the human body is dissected, but insists that blood, flesh, and bones are not what anatomy is about. The anatomist does not focus on the immediately sensible stuff of the body, but instead seeks Nature's purposive design *(theōria).*[41] The first book of Vitruvius's treatise identifies the *theōria* of the physician with that of the architect, and declares that this is what the visible body of architecture signifies.[42]

At the same time, form remained *distinct* from matter, with an ambiguous relationship that has been studied by many historians of philosophy. This tension was also evident in architectural theory until instrumental thought became dominant in modernity. The very notion of a relationship between *eidos* and *morphē,* combined with Plato's impatience, led to considerable confusion, particularly after Galilean science proposed that the celestial realm and the physical realm were homogeneous, thus clearing the way for modern quantitative physics. Plato, however, revised his initial "dualism," starting in *Timaeus* 48–49. Observing the relationship, connoted by the word itself, between the ideal chair and a specific chair in front of him, Plato decided that reality could not be articulated as a mere duality: there is both a link and a distance between the "ideal" a word's usual meaning. This opaque relationship coincides with the space-time of human experience. Plato's third term, *chōra,* is distinct from *both* the ideal realm of Being and the natural realm of becoming. Plato introduces it in distinction to both "pure" geometric space and *topos,* the natural place of differentiated bodies. This word had been used before. In

Homeric literature it appears in several forms that refer mainly to place: in its masculine form it was linked to combat, and in its feminine form it was associated with dance. Plato, however, gave it a wholly original sense.

Let me emphasize: *chōra* is properly *human* space. It is the space of human communication that is *inherently* bounded and ambiguous. As Plato acknowledged, *chōra* can be grasped only with great difficulty; it is like the substance of our dreams, and we may conceive it only indirectly, through spurious reasoning. Yet without it, we simply cannot account for reality. There is a profound affinity between the erotic space of the lyric poets and this Platonic term in *Timaeus:* like love, *chōra* grounds all relationships and makes knowledge possible. "In general terms, it is the receptacle and, as it were, the nurse of all becoming and change."[43] However, Plato's concept encompasses even more. He compares the receptacle to a mass of neutral plastic substance and speculates on the fundamental substance that underlies all creation, of which fire, earth, water, and air are only qualities. He then proceeds to associate *chōra* with the primordial material of the craftsman (the *prima materia* of the Demiurge). The *prima materia* has no definite character of its own but is the ultimate reality of things. Plato associates it with semen, composed of "smooth and unwrapped triangles." Genetic misconceptions aside, this *prima materia* is androgynous, a receptacle of all "visible and sensible things" that is itself "invisible and formless, all-embracing, *possessed in a most puzzling way of intelligibility, yet very hard to grasp*" (*Timaeus* 50–51; my emphasis).

Thus Plato concludes that there must be three components of reality: first, "the unchanging form, uncreated and indestructible, . . . imperceptible to sight or the other senses, the object of thought" (Being); second, "that which bears the same name as the form and resembles it, but is sensible, has come into existence, is in constant motion, . . . and is apprehended by opinion with the aid of sensation" (becoming); and third, *chōra,* "which is eternal and indestructible, which provides a position for everything that comes to be, and which is apprehended without the senses by a sort of spurious reasoning and so is hard to believe in—we look at it indeed in a kind of dream and say that everything that exists must be somewhere and occupy some space, and that what is nowhere in heaven or earth is nothing at all." Plato then identifies this receptacle with the space of chaos, "a kind of shaking implement" that separates the four basic elements out of itself to constitute the world as we know it (52–53). Linked etymologically to the Indo-European *chasho,* chaos is understood as a primordial gap or abyss as well as a primordial substance. Plato thus describes *chōra* as nothing less than the space of human creation and participation, the orienting hyphen between natural place and cosmic space. It is a distinct reality at the crossing, the *chiasma,* of Being and becoming. It enables the creation of human artifacts through *technē* and is also disclosed by them. *Chōra* is also the underlying substance of human crafts. It contradicts the common distinction between contained space and material container, which dates from only the nineteenth century and has contributed to misleading separations among the arts. Most importantly, it points to an invisible ground that exists beyond the duality of Being and becoming and that permits the creation of language and culture. The problem, as Plato emphasizes, is that its presence can be grasped only indirectly, through spurious (literally, "bastard," *pothos*) reasoning.

Before Plato there was no awareness of this third realm mediating a dichotomy. Indeed, its absence characterizes the world of myth. In this primarily oral, thoroughly unified world, space and movement were articulated through the paired qualities of the goddess Hestia and the god Hermes. Of the six major divine couples who appear on the base of the great statue of Zeus at Olympia, only Hermes and Hestia are not related by genealogy or blood.[44] This is a *paradoxical* pair that represents the space of desire but remains unaffected by it. Together, they interweave realities of space and movement, center and path, immutability and change. While Hestia represents femininity, domesticity, the earth, darkness, centrality, and stability (i.e., qualities of interior space), Hermes represents masculinity, mobility, thresholds, openness, and contact with the outside world, the light, and the sky (i.e., qualities of external spaces of action). This pre-philosophical space-time could not be grasped as an abstract concept. It was a concrete experience of the world as a living "Thou" rather than as a scientific or philosophical "it." It is difficult for us to imagine a personified, willful, and unpredictable external reality that needs constant propitiation through human actions to ensure the survival of the world from one instant to the next. Nevertheless, that is precisely the world of myth and ritual.

The famous historian of Greek culture Bruno Snell described "the discovery of the mind" and associated it with the emergence of Eros/ Cupid, who could block fulfillment and turn the subject into itself.[45] The self-consciousness that we associate with the birth of philosophy, science, and architectural theory is inconceivable without the awareness of a distance between the mind and world that is revealed through desire. Unlike its previous articulations in a mythical horizon, desire began to be perceived in relation to an understanding of death as something that happens to the *self,* enabling immortal thoughts. Love is the cause of death, and both reveal the limits and purpose of human life, which they generate. This is the same distance that Aristotle eventually described in his *Poetics* as the space of drama. Replacing the older mythopoetic narratives (such as those of Homer and Hesiod), Greek tragedy sought to understand the will of the gods and their significance for humanity. It also replaced the undifferentiated space of Dionysian rituals by opening up a space between actors and spectators that is analogous to the space of Eros. This distance between the spectator in a Greek theater and the play performed by the chorus and the actors made possible the reflective understanding of the plot and the *katharsis* that takes hold of the spectators, enabling them to understand the purpose of tragic destiny,[46] and thus to recover their spiritual "wholeness" and find their bearings amid the disorienting events of everyday life.

Aristotle provides a clue about the rituals in ancient Greece that would become the historical precedent for Western art and architecture. He states that both tragedy and comedy originated in the dithyramb, a spring ritual dedicated to Dionysos.[47] The word *dithyrambos* meant a leaping, an inspired dance, and in its original form was an invocation to bring life back, a rising up or calling up that was brought about by *drōmena* such as song and dance.[48] The great tragedies of Aeschylus, Sophocles, and Euripides were performed in Athens during early April, at a spring festival in honor of Dionysos. As the ritual origin of the Western work of art, the Greek theater holds many lessons for architecture. The dramas probably were performed not on the stage but in the orchestra or *choros,* particularly in the early phases when the *drōmenon* was developing into drama. The chorus, a group of dancing and singing men who often lamented destiny, was always at the center of the action. To someone who is familiar only with modern theater, the role of the Greek chorus seems somewhat enigmatic. The focus of the event was the circular dance platform named *choros* or *orchēsis* after words originally designating a group dance. Roman texts from the second century C.E. indicate that such events combining poetry, music, and dance (the triune *choreia*) were believed to have a cathartic effect. In fact, both *katharsis* and *mimēsis* are concepts that were employed quite early in art. *Katharsis* meant a purification or a reconciliation between the darkness of personal destiny and the light of divine destiny (*dikē*) as expressed in the tragedies.[49] *Mimēsis* meant not imitation but the expression of feelings and experiences through movement, musical harmonies, and rhythms of speech: an acknowledgment of the body's intermediate location between Being and becoming.

This dramatic event was framed by the theater, one of the most cosmologically resonant building types in antiquity. First we should recall some pertinent aspects in the myth of Daedalus.[50] One of Daedalus's major projects was to design a *chōra,* a dance platform in Knossos.[51] This followed his more famous commission to build the labyrinth, which was also a site for dance and drama. The form of the labyrinth, an explicit combination of path (Hermes) and space (Hestia), became a privileged symbol of cities (and architecture in general) in the Western tradition; the same combination is implicit in the *chōra* or dance platform. The labyrinth was a condensed symbol of human life (one entry, one center) and also a symbol of the presence of order despite apparent disorder. It originated in the Trojan games as a dance that, according to Virgil's *Aeneid,* was performed in Troy on two occasions: to celebrate the founding of the city and to honor the dead.[52] The labyrinth is therefore a frozen choreography that remains implicit in the circular orchestra of the Greek theater.

The space in between the amphitheater and the stage, the circular dance platform occupied by the chorus, was the focus of the spectators' attention. Upon this most perfect form, dancers would leave labyrinth-like traces on the sand. In the Greek tradition there are explicit instances in which the labyrinth is reconciled with the circle. It is significant that the foundations of the *tholos* or circular temple in Epidaurus, dedicated to Asclepius, the god of healing, are in fact labyrinthine. In antiquity Epidaurus was well-known as a place for healing. The famous theater in the sanctuary at Epidaurus played a most important role in restoring psychosomatic stability to the patients, who could also undergo a dream cure in the *abaton.* In the rare circular temple, the circular form of the heavens (and the chorus) was physically reconciled with the labyrinthine form of the underworld, where the three sacred serpents associated with the ritual of Asclepius resided. Here, the function of architecture is analogous to medicines: it was to enable order to appear or, if lacking, to be restored. The theme of the labyrinth as the foundation of architectural order was seldom realized as literally as at Epidaurus, but it remained a pervasive idea during the Middle Ages and in Renaissance and baroque architectural treatises.

Whereas ritual enabled primitive humans to propitiate divinities and dwell in the world, Greek drama performed a similar task, now in the realm of art. The introduction of the amphitheater acutely illustrates the gap that begins to open with the arrival of Eros/Cupid and the advent of philosophy. The theater is a place to understand the world by seeing and hearing. This distant contemplation of the epiphany had the same cathartic effect on the observer as direct participation in primitive ritual. The relationship is equally embodied. Here, in Greek theater, there is no Cartesian separation that would equate thinking to a disembodied gaze. This distance, let me emphasize, is akin to the theoretical distance introduced by the philosophers, which enabled a discursive participation in the universe that would disclose the *logos* in the triangular space presented in Sappho's poems. Only in the seventeenth century would this distance become an insurmountable gap or an isotropic geometric space in which the world turns into a scientific "picture," observed by an instrumental or even pornographic gaze.

Emphasizing the importance of a healthy site for the spectators, Vitruvius writes: "When plays are given, the spectators, with their wives and children, sit through them spellbound, and their bodies, motionless from enjoyment, have their pores open, into which blowing winds find their way."[53] The classical Greeks were also aware of this condition of vulnerability, but they personified external forces and emotions as demons and divinities. As Ruth Padel has shown, the Greeks perceived what was inside them as a complex seat of consciousness, made of the same fabric as the physical universe, with parts analogous to the earth and qualities mirroring divinities that were dark and ultimately unfathomable.[54] This analogy is at the root of medicine, anatomical divination, and architectural theories such as Vitruvius's. Yet what came from the outside was always regarded as more aggressive and frightening. In the theater, spectators came to make peace with the world, to find points of coincidence between *phrenes* (or mind) and madness, to try to understand "the terrible as good."[55]

The human voice of the actor, continues Vitruvius, is "a flowing breath of air" that moves "in an endless number of circular rounds, like the innumerable increasing circular waves which appear when a stone is thrown into smooth water." Its flow requires the architect to perfect the ascending rows of seats in the theater by means of "the canonical theory of the mathematicians and the musicians." In the design of the theater the architect must apply his knowledge of harmony, and here Vitruvius introduces musical modes and intervals, followed by tetrachords. He also recommends placing bronze sounding vessels under the seats (examples of which have never been found) to enhance the building's harmonic resonance. The plan of the theater is designed in accordance with the geometric essence of the sky, starting from a circle and inscribing four equilateral triangles, "as the astrologers do in a figure of the twelve signs of the zodiac, when they are making computations from the musical harmony of the stars."[56] Although Vitruvius is describing a Roman (not a Greek) theater, his account of it as a cosmic place for tragedy is clear enough. It is here that architecture discloses an order that is both spatial and temporal.

This poetic image is irreducible to a mere aesthetic appreciation. Framed by architecture, the tragedy is an epiphany of the Platonic *metaxy*—a conception, as Eric Voegelin has noted, of human existence not as a given, static fact but rather as "a disturbing moment in the in-between of ignorance and knowledge, of time and timelessness, of imperfection and perfection, of hope and fulfillment and ultimately of life and death."[57]

Therefore, one's involvement in the drama is important because it enables participation in a movement with a direction to be found or missed. This sense of direction grounds human meanings and self-understanding. Drama is experienced as a tight weaving of temporality and spatiality aligned with the purposeful movements of the cosmos. Its effect comes from the single poet's narrative rather than from the plural voice of traditional myths. *Katharsis* recognizes the presence of Being in the events of everyday life but does not rely on ordinary language (prose). Greek drama is a poetic language that we recognize as metaphoric. It maintains a high-tension gap that is analogous to erotic space, in which the audience encounters the nearness of distance and other universal coincidences. In his *Poetics,* Aristotle posits *mimēsis* as the basic function of art; rhyme, rhythm, eurhythmy, and harmony are merely attributes of what the spectator recognizes as a universal ground in the plot of the tragedy. A "plausible impossibility" is always new and striking, yet uncannily familiar.

Thus, we may start to understand the nature of *significant* architectural space in the Western tradition. The receptacle *chōra,* a homophone of the dance platform in the theater, takes its shape through *mimēsis* from Being and becoming. It encompasses diverse characteristics: it is at once the material building and the space, its ground and its lighting, the truth unveiled by art, and the gap between word and experience. It is a space for both contemplation and participation: a space of recognition. It is my contention that the ever-present "origin" of Western architecture exists in this understanding of architecture as a space for the dance, for the poetic motility that distinguishes human beings from other animals, for the narrative language of "choreography."

Renaissance incorporations

For more than 2,000 years the theater was a metaphor for the world and a model for Western architecture. In multiple forms, framed by urban places or by ephemeral structures, the theater presented the space of desire as common ground, providing a site for existential orientation. In the Renaissance the theater was fueled by an interest in *perspectiva artificialis:*

the stage was framed more deliberately by a proscenium, acquiring a mysterious yet mathematical depth ruled by proportionality and luminosity. This perspectival depth in both painting and theater was qualitatively different from anything in embodied experience; it was an ontological disclosure, a window framing space ruled by transcendental mathematics. Despite theological arguments against Aristotelian cosmology that had been around since the late thirteenth century, for Renaissance culture infinity was an attribute of God, not a location in our world of experience.[58] Architects who were concerned with *scenographia* or *perspectiva artificialis* applied their talents to the design of theatrical spaces, stages for urban celebrations, and the re-created *skēnē* of theater buildings such as Palladio's celebrated Teatro Olimpico in Vicenza.

In addition, the theater became the site for the newly recovered practice of human anatomy. Anatomical amphitheaters were established in major European cities. Highly ritualized functions were organized in these institutions, often taking place after public executions and involving members of the general public. Dissections were undertaken in theaters that invoked a cosmic order, in both the outside world and the dissected cadaver. In fact, as Jonathan Sawday has pointed out, the positioning of the body in the "three-dimensional matrix" of perspective space is a key to the new anatomical understanding.[59] Yet sixteenth-century medicine did not abandon Galen's humoral theories for a mechanistic physiology. At stake was a "traditional" erotic knowledge, quite unlike modern science. Even the inanimate body remained a privileged object of contemplation and wonder, consistent with the traditional expectation of Aristotle: to discover *theōria* beyond the repugnant mass of putrefying organs. In the famous frontispiece of Vesalius's *De humani corporis fabrica* (Basel, 1543), the anatomist (Vesalius himself) invites his enraptured audience to contemplate the open female uterus, the matrix or *chōra,* at the center of the image, on the axis of a semicircular amphitheater and under the spell of mortality in the form of a hovering skeleton.

Renaissance architects, patrons, and writers such as Giangiorgio Trissino, Daniele Barbaro, his close friend Andrea Palladio, and Sebastiano Serlio (to mention only a few) believed that the theater had a special revelatory power. Evidence of this belief is provided by Trissino's patronage of the Teatro Olimpico, by Barbaro's discussion of the theater in his edition of Vitruvius, and by Cesare Cesariano's eloquent plate in the 1521 edition of Vitruvius, where the theater is represented as the cosmic building par excellence: a centralized, freestanding monument with a labyrinth on the circular surface of the orchestra. Some spectators in Cesariano's woodcut look into the dramatic action, while others stand framed by the structure of the building—they gaze into the distance, transformed into actors for the architect meditating on the building's significance.[60] The humanist tradition grasped the definition of the work of art given by Aristotle in his *Poetics,* one that still reflected a pre-philosophical common ground among the arts understood as *poiēsis* (calling something into existence that was not there before).[61] Referring in particular to drama, Aristotle defined the work of art as a *"mimēsis* of *praxis,"* a "representation of ethical human action" in the form of plots or stories.[62] Despite some misunderstandings motivated by the technical interests of the Vitruvian tradition, Renaissance architecture retained its fundamental ethical purpose, understood as decorum. But in the theater the representative content of architecture appeared most explicitly: it is the space of human action in which the morally good is nothing else than a harmonious fulfillment of human nature, which becomes part of the beautiful manifested in the staged event.[63]

Despite its well-known interest in geometrical figures and proportions, Renaissance architecture never conceived of space as a geometric, isotropic entity. Plots were always at work as the programmatic backbone of architecture. Thus, the perceptually exciting depth of the painting, the stage, and the building was never subjected to just one viewpoint and was incomplete without the *storia,* the poetic narrative that Alberti discusses in *Della pittura.* These narratives also provided themes and allegories for the *tableaux vivants* in urban celebrations. The fascinating depth introduced by *perspectiva artificialis* was still perceived as erotic space, an incarnation of the original *chōra,* a space of distanced participation. Plato's third term of reality was represented by artists and architects of the Renaissance as a mysterious geometric depth, the light of God in the world of man.

Chōra could be disclosed by art and architecture, and until the end of the Renaissance it remained distinct from *topos,* Aristotle's natural place. *Topos,* the sublunary realm, was the site of most things human with reference to the predominant presence of a living, more-than-human world. In Aristotelian physics, movement was not a "state"; becoming, a property of life, implied movement and change. Indeed, objects changed their being when they moved; an ontological difference existed between rest and movement. Within this common understanding of reality, *chōra* could still operate as both a separation and a link, a space of contemplation that was a mode of participation. The ideal was elsewhere and yet present, in a vertical structure, here and now. All Renaissance architects insisted that the physical point or line that we can trace with our instruments *was not* the ideal point or line in our minds. For John Dee, for example, the operations of Euclidean geometry take place "betwene thinges supernaturall and natural"; they are "thinges immaterial and neverthelesse, by material things able somewhat to be signified."[64]

All this changed with the advent of modernity, when *chōra* began to be concealed by modern geometric space. A key figure was Galileo Galilei, whose thought experiments on motion led to the discovery of the laws of inertia that were eventually taken up by Newton.[65] Inertia implies that motion and rest could be conceived as "states" incapable of affecting being. Despite his traditional sources and theological motivations, Galileo imagined a physics that differed greatly from Aristotle's. In Galileo's world the ontological difference between the supralunar heavens and the sublunar world was obliterated. It became a homogeneous, geometrical void in which bodies, both celestial and terrestrial, were objectified and described using the same mathematical laws. By bringing ideal geometric space from the heavens down to the earth, Galileo implicitly questioned the legitimacy of erotic space (as the site of human truths) and presented humans with an irreconcilable dichotomy. As mathematics became authoritative, linguistic and artistic works were eventually confined to the hazy realm of subjectivity. By the late seventeenth century, Leibniz could declare poetry and poetics a form of knowledge inferior to science (*gnoseologia inferior*), best known through Baumgarten as aesthetics.[66] In philosophical terms, Galileo's new concept of reality allowed for the eventual reduction of Being to the purely ontic—that is, to a re-presented world of objects. Thus, his natural philosophy created the conditions for the instrumental and technological culture that would proliferate in the Western world after the Enlightenment.

The second major protagonist in the transformation of *chōra* in early modernity was Giordano Bruno. As is well known, Bruno was accused of heresy and burned at the stake in Rome in 1600. Like Galileo, Bruno unified celestial and terrestrial physics and put forward a coherent argument against Aristotle, but there are important differences between them—especially in Bruno's concept of space as it emerges in *Cause, Principle and Unity* (1584).

Unlike traditional cosmologies that emphasized ontological difference, Bruno's vision incorporated Being and becoming within the One. In his view, there is nothing outside the realm of human experience, but human experience is much more than what appears to our senses. Bruno believed that there is no matter without form, and that forms (ideas) do not exist in a separate realm, apart from matter. There is no world of pure bodiless essences. The divine is not totally distinct from the human; on the contrary, divinity is present in everything, including us. Its presence enables humans to become powerful magicians. Some of Bruno's Renaissance predecessors shared this belief, but his cosmology made it more feasible. Retrospectively, from our technological world in which humans have become all-powerful, we can understand the potential dangers associated with this awareness. For Bruno, it entailed the development of an acute sense of ethics that was posited as a necessary love for the Other. In his essay "A General Account of Bonding" ("De vinculis in genere," 1588), Bruno discussed the power of seduction and love in all areas of human culture, even the possibility of psychic and mass manipulation.

Bruno's universe was thoroughly animated. Like Copernicus, he thought that the world moved. Unlike Galileo, however, Bruno's universe is paradoxical, incomprehensible in logical terms, and closed to mathematical reason. In his *Ash Wednesday Supper* (1583) he carefully portrays a world without mathematics and impenetrable to perspective. He describes our participation in a dark infinite universe, like a penumbra, in between light and shadow. For Bruno the earth moves because it is alive and motility is a property of the flesh. Even objects that seem inanimate share a spiritual substance. Many of his concepts resemble those of pre-Socratic philosophers such as Anaxagoras and Parmenides. Despite the apparent differences in matter, there is an underlying *prima materia,* a "quality" and not a "thing," that is *also* space. The space of lived experience is a coincidence of opposites; this is its original truth, often concealed behind appearances: "The universe is one, infinite and immobile. I say that the absolute possibility is one, that the act is one; the form, or soul, is one, the matter or body, is one, the thing is one, being is one. . . . It is not matter, because it is not configured or configurable, nor it is limited or limitable. It is not form, because it neither informs nor figures anything else, given that it is all, that it is maximum, that it is one, that it is universal. It is neither measurable nor a measure. *It is limit such that it is not limit,* form such that it is not form, matter such that it is not matter" (my emphasis).[67]

Without further engaging Bruno's difficult language, we can detect a wish to eliminate a reality that consists of three distinct terms, as Plato had conceived it. Bruno also questioned the differentiated hierarchies of Being that had been constructed so carefully by Neoplatonic philosophers such as Ficino. Curiously, the space of dreams, art, and poetry that was *chōra* seems to be understood by Bruno as all that is. Denying an essential difference between what is present and what is not, between the ideal and the real, Bruno's conceptual space could potentially transform into the universal, infinite, and isotropic continuum of late modernity. His argument against geocentrism, imagining the earth occupying a generalized location in an infinite universe, has often been characterized as a step toward modern science. But Bruno's dark and shadowy space is not a mathematical entity and it abhors the void. Since the universe is thoroughly animated, humanity is moved by love.

Bruno concludes *The Heroic Frenzies* (1585) with a vision of the kingdom of God and paradise in which the human realm is transformed into the divine. This vision is the result of man's capacity to love; *erōs* is for Bruno intrinsic to humanity. Only the lover, projected to infinity by the imagination, comes to realize the coincidence between knowledge and love. Echoing Plato's original reflections in *Symposium* and *Phaedrus,* the lover is transformed into the object of love. Desire operates inside the One, but it is not driven by it. *Erōs* is therefore understood as desire for unity, for an alternative mode of being that explains real change in the universe.

Bruno claimed that his vision liberates us from the fear of imaginary, cruel divinities that look down onto a sublunary world from beyond the sphere of the stars. It is, however, not through the light of rational science but only through the revelation of *coincidentia oppositorum,* the very province of art and poetry, that humans may come to terms with the universe's unfathomable mystery. Such an understanding makes possible both baroque and modern art, with their rich qualitative distinctions, and eventually the phenomenological understanding of reality as *flesh*.[68]

Modern transformations

The theory of space has an entirely different place in knowledge from that occupied by mathematics[;] . . . space has a reality outside our mind and we cannot completely prescribe its laws.

Carl Friedrich Gauss (1830), quoted in Morris Kline, *Mathematics: The Loss of Certainty*

The Baroque brought about a new attitude toward architecture, landscape, and the city by expecting that the ideal would be manifested in the human world. The change is clearly shown in Juan Bautista Villalpando's graphic reconstruction of the Temple of Solomon, based on Ezekiel's biblical prophecy, and its incarnation in the Escorial, the new royal palace and monastery of Philip II, king of Spain.[69] Villalpando cited Christ's Incarnation—in which God becomes man—as the main argument for modern Christianity's desire to "build" the ideal temple in the world of humanity.

Incarnation was a Christian belief that had been difficult to accept literally before the Renaissance. This is not surprising, given the ontological separation of the divine realm and the human realm in Platonic and Aristotelian philosophy.

In the Judeo-Christian tradition, it was the original sin of Adam and Eve that opened up the space of human desire. Eating the fruit from the tree of knowledge, Adam and Eve discovered sexual love and encountered death. Through this knowledge they also came to understand good and evil. There is a remarkable analogy here with Socrates' concept, noted above, of human knowledge as an awareness of "erotic things." Expelled from paradise, humans had to toil and find the right way to act, cultivating the land for food and building architecture for defense against a threatening nature. Christ's incarnation and sacrifice liberated humanity from this original sin. In theology, the advent of the Messiah brought about redemption, implying the possibility of freedom from erōs/desire. Christ's sacrifice replaced erōs with agapē, God's unconditional love for all humanity, including his accusers and executioners.

For those in the Middle Ages, salvation was almost accomplished and the world of human affairs appeared insignificant in God's time. Apocalypse, associated with the second coming of Christ and with the instauration of Heavenly Jerusalem, was believed to be imminent. The Middle Ages also had difficulty accepting Christ as both divine and mortal. A papal bull in the late fifteenth century proclaimed Christ as being *truly* mortal. Holbein's remarkable sixteenth-century painting visualized for the first time a dead Christ, putrefying inside the sepulcher before his resurrection. These events culminated in the Baroque (after the Counterreformation) with a recognition of the Incarnation as unquestionable dogma. God had indeed become a man. Conversely, the human mind was illuminated by divine light. Since apocalypse and redemption now lay at an unforeseeable point in the future, modern Christians were called to contribute to the project of building the city of God on earth. *Erōs* and *agapē* could become totally coincidental, and this constituted the ethos of baroque artistic production.

Baroque architects set out to change the world, and they accomplished an exciting synthesis of the qualities of natural and geometric space. For the first time, the human world could be transformed into a self-referential cultural entity. However, within this human world they distinguished between points of epiphany (the perspective vanishing points in theaters and churches) and the rest of experience. It was at these theatrical points that a sacred or profane representation attained its supreme meaning. Man could now contemplate the space of God as a geometric entity.

Geometry was understood as a product of the human mind and yet was also believed to be analogous to a projection of divine light. This transformation of the world into a picture also sought *fulfillment*, rather than maintaining the space of *erōs*. Baroque works of art and poetry, as well as the meditation practices of the Jesuits, transformed the experience of orgasm into a mystical union, fusing human and divine love.

To reach this epiphany, however, humans had to disregard their bodies and their binocular vision to experience the vanishing point. This geometric "point at infinity" had arrived in the world of experience; it could be experienced externally when contemplating a garden or a church, or internally in the process of meditation. The space between the observer and the vanishing point was clear and transparent, miraculously represented through light and geometry. But it must be emphasized that in baroque architecture, rooted in the traditional concept of decorum, these epiphanies of transcendence still framed significant human action, particularly political and religious rituals.

Aristotle had identified space with place in his *Physics,* understood as the position of a body among others: "the [invisible] limit of the containing body, by which the container makes contact with what it contains."[70] Like most else in the physical world, place was qualitative and not mathematical. Rejecting the idea of the void, Aristotle basically identified space with matter, as Plato did in *Timaeus* with *chōra,* but without the rich ambivalence of Plato's concept. This interpretation prevailed in the Western philosophical tradition well into the seventeenth century. It entered Descartes's dualistic articulation of reality, and was then equated with a geometric "entity": *res extensa.* Descartes insisted that since nature "abhors a vacuum," space and matter are co-substantial and knowable only through mathematics. In baroque painting, however, it is the geometric gap, imbued with metaphysical light, that becomes the primary subject of representation. The paintings of Georges de La Tour are a prime example.

Descartes himself seemed uninterested in painting. In his *Dioptric* (1637) he praised copper engravings because they conveyed the objective form of things with precision. For him, color was secondary. Only line drawing could represent his concept of linear extension as the reality of existing things. Descartes was obsessed with constructing vision according to a conceptual model rather than through perception. Disembodied vision, appearing at the geometrical point of the pineal gland, was understood as the transparent organ of mathematical thought. Descartes must be held responsible for the thinning and objectification of space. To him, space was an autonomous geometric entity, independent of points of view.

The embodied experience of *chōra* was being replaced by an objective, mathematical space that Descartes believed would bring us closer to a divine and human understanding. Like the body, *erōs* was for Descartes merely a source of error and disorientation. As suggested by Maurice Merleau-Ponty, when *perspectiva artificialis* was consecrated as the prime epistemological model, *depth* (the bittersweet space of *erōs*) lost its status as the first dimension and became merely one of three dimensions, equivalent to length and width.[71]

Western culture gave up a bounded space, the bittersweet space of classical times, in search of a mystical union. The transformations of space in baroque art, as well as in seventeenth-century philosophy, science, and instrumental theories, were ultimately motivated by theological concerns with their roots in the late Middle Ages and in the Renaissance works of Nicholas of Cusa and other Neoplatonists. They believed that the human mind shared the light of the divine mind and could bypass the senses to fully understand a rational universe. This was an ethical stance that enabled baroque *erōs* to become one with God's *agapē*. The remarkable synthesis of sensuality and abstract thought in all baroque cultural productions relies on an understanding of light as a transcendental entity. In Ignatius of Loyola's *Spiritual Exercises,* the image in the mind's eye permits divine understanding only if the observer is removed from this act of imagining. After grasping the image with each one of the senses, the mind should evacuate all sensuous experience and eventually the self, and thus assimilate with the divine light and divine will.[72] A similar paradoxical, disembodied experience was intended for observers of *quadrattura,* the supremely sensuous amalgamation of architecture, sculpture, and ornament that particularly characterizes baroque Jesuit church interiors.

During the eighteenth century, urban culture became intensely theatrical. As Richard Sennett has shown, even the social conventions for public interaction in the large European cities emphasized the theatricality of everyday life.[73] Indeed, architecture and theater became almost equivalent. The boundary separating the stage from the space of real experience seemed to disappear in Bibiena's *Architettura civile* (1711).[74] His *perspectiva per angolo,* a simple substitution of two-point perspective oblique sets for the preferred one-point constructions of the baroque theater, was symptomatic of a significant shift. This "invention" signaled the democratization of the theater; there were no longer privileged points of view, and every individual occupied a place in geometric space. Perspectival perception became a truth that is accessible at all times to all individuals.

In the churches, the frames around frescoes began to disintegrate. The vanishing point was lifted so that it no longer coincided with a geometric construction placing the spectator at its focus. Sometimes the subject matter was not even religious, illustrating instead prodigies encountered in nature. Traditional miracles, such as St. George killing the dragon or the ascension of the Virgin, had to be portrayed through theatrical sculptural settings of such verisimilitude as to be almost hyperreal. As Karsten Harries has beautifully demonstrated in his study of the rococo church, this shift signaled the arrival of a truly modern aesthetic distance.[75] The *ambivalence* of true erotic space was difficult or even impossible to accept for a culture that valorized mathematical precision and transparency as both preconditions of knowledge and (after Newton) the true miracle of nature. In the rococo, the space between the work and the spectator became a true *separation*. The geometric space that had unified the baroque *Gesamtkunstwerk* and its observers now merely separated them. A spectator could either participate or not. Aesthetic experience might be divided into the "beautiful" and the "sublime," previously unimaginable as separate characters of artistic meaning. The spectacle of the fine arts is fundamentally different from the embodied realm of *erōs*. Its assumptions would be developed into the modern discipline of philosophical aesthetics, and eventually would be questioned by Romanticism, surrealism, phenomenology, and hermeneutics.

Rococo architects combined the traditional Renaissance categories of ornament and structure, potentially transforming their work into a subjective formal game rather than a frame for rituals that demanded appropriate ornamentation. After midcentury, neoclassical writers arguing against rococo and for a return to the classical orders and their simplicity would nevertheless draw on this concept, merely reversing its formulation. Thus, Abbé Laugier stated that the structure (the order of columns) was itself the ornament. The primitive hut, composed of columns, horizontal beams, and pediments, was put forward as the "essence" of architecture, while all else (including walls and openings) was declared license or abuse.[76] Since architecture could thereafter become decoration, the notion of decorum or appropriateness could no longer be taken for granted, and during the eighteenth century it became the central theoretical problem.

During the eighteenth century, humanity started to believe in the reality of geometric space and of linear, progressive time. Western culture supposed itself to be on the verge of constructing paradise in a utopian future, now following its old quest for transcendence through reason and technology. At times, when the vision of a delightful paradise in the present was sought, artists like Fragonard presented a spectacle through an insurmountable gap, the aesthetic distance at the origin of a new paradigm: art for art's sake. This geometric space was also Newton's void, an all-pervasive cosmic space, invisible except for the manifestation of impersonal laws that take place in it. Newton's a priori absolute space and time consecrated the intuitions of Galileo and Descartes, free of the encumbrances of subtle matter (Descartes) or any "necessary" circular motion (Galileo). Enlightened rationality finally rejected all traditional beliefs in witches, angels, and demons. Instead, it put forward the clarity and simplicity of nature, expressed in its mathematical laws, as the true *miracle,* the manifestation of a rational Creator. This development represented a turning point in the tradition of architecture as *thaumata.* Architecture had always conveyed wonder and existential safety through seduction and disorientation. Echoing Socrates' concept of human knowledge as founded on the disorienting effect of *erōs,* architecture overwhelmed embodied consciousness like love itself in the moment that ensured its potential meaning. By embracing linguistic analogies as the only alternative, most eighteenth-century architects demonstrated their incapacity to grasp this original reality.

Not surprisingly, the "erotic" experience sometimes associated with architecture was often voyeuristic. Once Claude Perrault had declared that positive beauty in architecture and the arts had to be explicit to anyone's vision, while assuming that the nature of vision was perspectival, architectural meaning could not depend on unmediated presence.[77] Meanings were assumed to result from associations in the mind, derived from impressions and memories. This conviction was underscored by the sensualist theories of English philosophers like Hume. Theories of architecture drew from linguistic analogies to understand expression as a cultural construction, and issues such as "character" became predominant. While loosening its traditional connections to human action and potentially becoming "conventional" decoration, the theatrical architecture of the eighteenth century still sought a metaphysical or scientific grounding. Thus it retained an obsession with precision, proportion, and geometry as it attempted to ground expression in absolute certainty. The topic of architecture as a social contract, which has become preeminent since the eighteenth century, will be examined in later chapters in relation to the concept of *philia.*

The birth of the discipline of aesthetics in the work of Baumgarten coincided with a new genre of literature, the "libertine" novel.[78] Its erotic drive generally was understood by writers such as Choderlos de Laclos,

Crébillon fils, Vivant Denon, and Denis Diderot as a purely physical phenomenon, avoiding any valorization of the beloved, whether freely inspired or forced by society. Under the scrutiny of reason, *erōs* was dissected and analyzed. Starting in the seventeenth century the subtleties and complexities of the bittersweet character of *erōs* became the very substance of drama (for example, in Jean-Baptiste Lully's 1682 opera *Persée*). Any erotic delays caused by external circumstances or social restrictions had to be negotiated. The many variations on this theme were intended to escape boredom or even melancholy due to unfulfilled love. Although these narratives exhibited a fascination with erotic tension, they were driven by a quest for rationalization, fulfillment, and gratification—a different intent than that of the early erotic novels such as *Daphnis and Chloe*. This literature explored philosophical arguments and criticized social conventions but would become assimilated into pornographic practices in the following centuries.

In architecture, Nicolas Le Camus de Mézières's *Le génie de l'architecture* (1780) presents a seductive theatrical experience in which a reader/spectator is taken through the rooms of a house, one by one, as the emotional and erotic intensity grows. The portrayal is modeled after *La petite maison,* a libertine novel by Jean-François de Bastide.[79] Bastide's short novel describes the power of architecture as a tool of seduction. Trémicour, an aristocratic host, and Mélite, his guest who has never taken a lover and has spent all her time acquiring good taste and knowledge, agree on a wager for her favors. She is taken through his house, decorated with such character and good taste that she slowly lowers her defenses and finally surrenders to him. According to Louise Pelletier, Le Camus's understanding of architectural meaning draws from this plot and yet keeps its distance from the libertine novel. In other lesser-known novels and plays, Le Camus was aware of the role that erotic distance played in artistic meaning.[80] In his architectural treatise he seems intent on recovering architecture as an erotic experience, related to questions of appropriateness. Rather than detailing the orders or the traditional problem of proportions, Le Camus decided to describe the spatial qualities of a house in great detail, prolonging the reader's journey over countless theatrical thresholds. Never before had an architect felt compelled to recover lost architectural meaning by emphasizing (in a theoretical text) spatial characteristics such as light and shadow, textures, colors, sound, and smell. Le Camus obviously believed that previous theories of architectural character, which were based on the codification of the architectural orders, were insufficient. Describing space qualitatively in the context of the Enlightenment was indeed an act of resistance. Despite an obvious theatrical and voyeuristic interest (there were even hidden passages in the house that allowed the owner to observe all activities within it), one could argue that Le Camus also kept his distance from Condillac's philosophy of sensations.[81] Experience is acquired from the senses, *partes extra partes,* in the hope of recovering meaning and generating true emotion. By emplotting this process while rejecting all instrumental applications of theory, however, Le Camus recovered synaesthesia as a ground of architectural meaning and with it the possibility of a poetic architecture.

After the French Revolution, artists and architects became divided over how the nature of their work related to the values of science and technology. Functionalist theory, especially in the work of Jean-Nicolas-Louis Durand, rejected eighteenth-century theories of character and assumed that meaning would simply follow the efficient solution to a pragmatic problem. Early in the nineteenth century, the Ecole des Beaux-Arts attempted to distance itself from this engineering approach by recovering architectural tradition, but it did not question the underlying premise of "art for art's sake." Positions during the nineteenth century were varied and often polarized.

The space of Western architectural representation became a secularized perspective depth, a mathematical entity that, in the wake of God's death, was no longer transcendental. Its structure was now fully dictated by optical considerations. In this context, the most insightful contributions to a renewed articulation of *chōra* came from the margins of architecture: for example, from Romantic poetry, the poetic philosophy of Nietzsche, the meandering universe of John Ruskin, and the literary works of Lewis Carroll.[82] Aesthetics was both elevated to a religious truth and denigrated as a chimera. Architecture tended to occupy either the transparent space of technology or the inaccessible space of art. In most cases it was conceived either as practical building or as applied ornament that was ultimately irrelevant or even ethically criminal (as Adolf Loos would proclaim a few years later).[83]

Facing this crisis, August Schmarsow set out to clarify the status of architecture as a fine art. He concluded that architecture, unlike painting and sculpture, is "the art of space." Schmarsow's papers, published in the early 1890s, marked the first time that this "obvious truth" had been asserted in architectural theory.[84] Architecture's raison d'être, according to Schmarsow, was the artistic manipulation of space.[85] Although he fell short of defining space as *chōra,* raising this question was a significant accomplishment. His intuitions led him to state positions that were not far from

Husserl's phenomenology. Despite his idealist framework, he realized that space is *more* than the isotropic entity described by geometricians.

In retrospect it is clear that Schmarsow's insightful declaration was made possible by developments in the earlier part of the century that conceptualized architecture as an instrumental operation in geometric space. Gaspard Monge's "descriptive geometry" had become the (often implicit) foundation for architectural design after the French Revolution. This led to a variety of new concepts and attitudes: attention to style and formal composition, the use of axes and the *mécanisme de la composition,* the concept of architectural experience as a voyeuristic building tour, theory as design methodology, and history as an evolution of building types. Architecture's newly discovered "essence" was eventually imagined as axonometric space, which is still characterized as the true modern space. Yet, stimulated by discoveries in cubist painting and cinema, early-twentieth-century architects and artists realized axonometry's capacity to work *against* a prosaic or illusionistic perspectivity. Eventually artists embraced insights similar to Schmarsow's and postulated space as irreducible to a geometric concept.[86]

The moment that faith in the divine light floundered—once *agapē* and divine justice were questioned by the *philosophes* of the French Enlightenment and Laplace could describe the laws of the universe without the help of God—infinite human space became problematic. The human will, strong like God's, became a will to power, assaulted by infinite yet meaningless possibilities. Early-modern culture had substituted an infinite, horizontal deferral into future progress, for the vertical idea, present yet absent for Socrates in the here and now (the ultimate goal of a loving soul). The impossible, unattainable goal of *erōs* would be eventually "resolved" by late-modern culture through unending consumption. Technological artifacts aim to please, always to the point of orgasm; they demand unceasing reiteration, never capable of quenching our thirst yet fueling our yearning for possession and control, while hiding humanity's mortal essence.

By contrast, erotic space is not transparent to instrumental reason and entails a mode of participation that does not require "fulfillment." Rather, the artist and the lover, participant and inhabitant, all want to face the beloved and not be destroyed, accepting the simultaneity of pleasure and pain, of life and death, the integrity of cultural memory. Erotic space is both lived space *and* aesthetic space, unlike the either/or conditions set by the work of art and by scientific epistemology in early modernity. The fundamental nature of this space is *lack* rather than the possession of plenitude. In more contemporary terms, this is not a space that merely enhances the present cultural delusions, transforming lived experience into "virtual" experience, with its sense of infinite "development" and evolutionary potential. It is not a space that entrenches systems of power, seeking perfect efficiency, comfort, and control over time. Rather it is a revelation of enigmatic depth, of density and uncertainty—a disclosure of the unfamiliar in the old, and of the familiar in novelty.

Indeed, once geometric space had become the locus of social and political life, there were always a few architects, artists, and writers seeking to crystallize truly erotic space, unwilling to give up their quest for the sake of mainstream practices. Piranesi and Ingres were precocious members of this group. Their pursuit was continued by artists in the twentieth century, such as Cézanne, with his obsession to abandon the external form of objects that preoccupied realism and impressionism in order to retrieve a new depth—a truly erotic depth—that traditional illusionism could not convey. Bridging the nineteenth and the twentieth centuries, Romanticism and surrealism partook of this interest, both in literature and the plastic arts. Works by Lequeu and Duchamp, Gris and De Chirico, Giacometti, Le Corbusier, John Hejduk, Daniel Libeskind, James Turrell, and Peter Greenaway, among others, exemplify the same quest. To paraphrase Merleau-Ponty, these works break the skin of things: they go beyond mere appearance and technological or aesthetic expectations in order to show "how the things become things, how the world becomes a world."[87] In these works limits are reestablished, depth is again mysterious and light recovers its qualities as *lux, lumen,* and *splendor* and is once again endowed with shadows; desire is exacerbated and, in its bittersweetness, is elevated to a way of life.

Erōs and time

In *erōs* we find not only a paradox of space but also a paradox of time. Lovers both hate to wait and love to wait. In fact, the erotic nature of human experience demonstrates the inextricable links between time and space, present in the Platonic concept of *chōra* and, more recently, even in scientific speculations about post-Newtonian "fields." Merleau-Ponty insists that our primary engagement with the world is through a living body, imbued with time in the form of motility. Thus the spatiality of the human body always involves a temporal dimension.

The temporal aspect of the erotic paradigm is complex in architecture. The experience of architectural works is always temporal, and in more than one sense. Even mere "contemplation" has a temporal dimension. When architecture frames a given ritual or proposes a new program, it is experienced through rhythm. While modern hedonism usually expects instant gratification, *erōs* creates delays to avoid premature revelations of things that must take time. Once one bites the apple the desire is gone; we cannot want that, and yet we do.[88] The challenge for the architect is to negotiate this reality, proposing useful spaces for life that are not readily consumed. As part II of this book will show, the use of narratives is helpful in accounting for how the proposed building may adequately and critically respond to issues of utility and cultural continuity while encouraging the delay intrinsic to a poetic image.

Time is the condition of both delight and decay.[89] In the past, ephemeral structures associated with all kinds of festivals in European cities were deemed of great importance. Festival time was obviously different from "normal" time. It dislocated and relocated human temporality, without resorting to banal linear time or a simple return of the same. This tradition lasted from the Middle Ages to the end of the ancien régime, and even festivals and world's fairs in late modernity may evoke similar experiences. Ephemeral architecture occupied the attention of great architects over long periods and was invested with the same symbolic connotations as more permanent structures. Although the results were short-lived, they "relocated" cultural values by reframing events such as triumphal entries of royalty, weddings, and funerals. Triumphal arches of canvas and wood, *tableaux vivants,* theatrical structures, firework displays, and mock naval battles were all *thaumata,* and they may have been admired more intensely because of their ephemeral nature.

What about the more permanent buildings of our tradition? The permanent nature of architecture has been often compared to writing. The Greek term *graphē* (trace, engraving) came to signify writing, painting, and also architectural drawing. Vitruvius used the term (as *ichnographia, orthographia,* and *scenographia* or *skiographia*) when describing the *ideai* used by the architect in design, today understood as vertical and horizontal projections.[90] Like writing, buildings possess a degree of permanence. While speech is transient, writing (and reading) permits temporal pauses and manipulation. Nevertheless, Plato warns us in *Phaedrus,* "Writing has this strange power, people who learn the art of letters come to believe that they can render things clear and fixed for all time" (275c, 277d).[91] This is, according to Plato, a dangerous delusion: true knowledge can be experienced only through speech; it is never gained forever and must always be reactivated in the present.

The architect may indeed be subject to the same delusions as a bad writer, particularly if he or she assumes a power to "communicate" clear and distinct meanings, collapsing the "now" and "then" of love. In architecture, the rituals and events framed by a building are transient, just as speech is and the experience of architecture is qualified by these events. In other words, the meaning of architecture, like that of a poem, is reenacted by the participant. It is surely different to "visit" a building as a modern tourist than to experience it through ritual, or to live and work in it. The building may be relatively permanent, yet at least a portion of its meaning is impermanent. The Parthenon is certainly not the same architecture for an ancient Greek participating in a procession in honor of Athena as it is for a modern visitor admiring its rich marble and fine detailing.

Socrates relates the delusions of writing to the delusions of love. He points out that a real lover should know what he wants of time. He dislikes Lysias's speech because the sophist "starts from the end" (*Phaedrus* 264a); he is in full control and nothing changes his friendship. The real lover, assaulted by *erōs,* desires no change and growth in the beloved; he wishes to stop time, and thus "the boy is most delightful to his lover just where he does most damage to himself" (239c). Writing also stops time, and when people read books they gain merely an appearance of wisdom, not true wisdom. Wisdom is alive; it is the "living, breathing word." Like painting, and indeed architecture, the written word fixes things in time and space, but the *logos* that is written down by a writer or architect only approximates the living organism in its interrelation of parts. This view anticipates Vitruvius, who echoed Socrates' description of discourse—it should be "organized like a living creature with a body of its own, not headless or footless, but with a middle and end fitted to one another and to the whole" (264c)—in his statement about the work of architecture.[92] In other words, just as the sentences in a text should not be interchangeable, so every part of a building should be in its proper place and should be disclosed with an appropriate rhythm.

For an architect to know what he or she wants of time is to acknowledge that the work is more than a physical trace or a volume, far more than the subject of a photographic spread in a glossy publication. Temporal experience is crucial, and meaning is bound by use in its most general sense, as ritual or modern function. This awareness of architecture as a representation of ethical human action was always implicit in Western practices until the end of the seventeenth century.

Socrates understood the paradox of *erōs,* but since his time it has often been rendered simplistically as a dilemma of *erōs* versus *philia,* and eventually of aesthetics versus ethics. He knew, like Lysias, that desire pulls the lover into paradoxical relations with time. Certain tactics toward the beloved may damage him. Yet Socrates considered Lysias's proud expression of control over the passions as a detached, nonloving attitude, a crime against *erōs*.[93] Lysias's insights on *erōs* are dispassionate: he is observing love from an "aesthetic" distance that cancels erotic space. Socrates, on the other hand, argues to accept the destabilizing power of *erōs,* for *erōs* is the ground of *logos,* the space of culture between two people in conversation. In short, the writer, like the lover and the architect, must aim to seduce, even if the attempt means a loss of control and a challenge to communication. In that moment we may catch a glimpse of reality. Despite all the dangers, engaging in the play of *erōs* is therefore fundamentally ethical.

3 Eros and the Poetic Image

Opening conversation

It is of "Winged Eros"
The mortal lover sings;
But gods prefer to call him *"Pteros"*
Who makes us all sprout wings.

Plato, *Phaedrus* 252b (punning on *pteron,* "wings," and Eros; trans. Benjamin Jowett)

Love is *"midway between wisdom and ignorance."* Moreover, love pursues things which are beautiful. The most beautiful of all things is wisdom. Therefore it seeks wisdom. He who seeks wisdom does not possess it completely. For who seeks things that he possesses? Nor also does he lack it altogether.

Marsilio Ficino, *Commentary on Plato's Symposium on Love* (trans. Sears Jayne)

In his *Rhetoric,* Aristotle associates desire with the imagination. Desire is a reaching out for a sweet delight. In the future as hope, or in the past as memory, desire reaches out with the imagination (*phantasia*).[1] The imagination activates the thick, vivid present that is the time of *erōs;* without it, the present indeed can be reduced to a nonexistent *punctum.* Both Aristotle and Socrates understood that *erōs* and knowledge are inextricably connected. While insisting that he knew very little, Socrates admitted a few times that he did know erotic things (*ta erotika*). He delighted in the process of knowing itself, the asking of questions and the careful unraveling of potential answers. To know "what he did not know" meant to understand the ever-present gap between the thinking mind and what it desires. Never content, the mind reaches out to grasp something of which it has an inkling, something separate from itself. The path of true wisdom is always a "leaping" across an erotic space between the known and the unknown.[2]

The imagination's quest through erotic space was thus understood as a condition of knowledge. Aristotle emphasized that it is natural for humanity to reach out to know, and to feel both delight in reaching and pain in falling short. Through Diotima's voice, Plato also explained this drive as our quest for immortality in various forms of creation: procreative, artistic, and intellectual. It is in this sense that Aristotle recognized the central role of metaphor for knowledge.[3] Through metaphor we can know nameless distant things via their resemblance to familiar local things. In both the arts and the sciences this leap or "transference" is crucial for knowledge and can be made only by the imagination; it is beyond the reach of logical identity. Metaphor was the very condition of natural (and mythical) language, and it became the domain of poetry and art after speech became normalized in science and philosophy.

Hans-Georg Gadamer has suggested that the poetic image is also *mimēsis* in its original sense, a representation of the "star dance of the heavens."[4] The philosopher and the architect are often possessed by a madness that enables them to recollect "those things by virtue of being close to which a god is divine."[5] This madness, which architects aim to share through their work, is the enthusiasm of recollecting ideal beauty when they see beauty on earth. Souls thus become winged and are eager to fly upward. This inspiration is often frustrated and castigated as madness, yet it is "the noblest and highest and the offspring of the highest to him who has or shares in it" (Plato, *Phaedrus* 249d–e). According to Socrates, every soul has beheld its true being, because that was its condition before passing into the form of man; however, not all souls are easily reminded of things in this other world by things on earth. Therein lies the difficulty of art and architecture.

In *Phaedo,* Plato characterizes virtue as a detachment from pleasure and pain, beyond the illusory exchange of one pleasure for another. Similarly, Diotima's description of the soul's ascent in *Symposium* is a liberation from its earthly attachments, a *katharsis,* that nevertheless does not deny *erōs*. While the philosopher may comprehend the cycle of illusions and come to love beauty itself, this trick is difficult for the common man who cannot recognize that the luminous world of ideal forms is the world as it truly *is,* shining through its earthly appearances. The common man needs the poet to disclose "not a vision of the sphere, but a vision of the sphere incorporated in the image," such as Dante's *Paradiso*.[6]

Similarly, architecture (as *poiēsis*—the bringing into existence of something that was not already there) discloses incarnate beauty through playful making. It is an act of seduction that employs "cunning intelligence" (*mētis* in Greek, *sollertia* in Latin) to disclose order (*agathon*), a sense both of wonder and of security. The order disclosed by poetic artifacts that "stand out as good" (*prepon*) is never "fully" present, for it would blind us; it is indeed a reflection of the luminous universe, which happens to be our human truth (*alētheia*—a revealing that is never totally acquired, and is therefore also a concealing). Capable of disclosing an order that is *also* our mortality, the poetic image in architecture generates a spark in the difference between the actual and the possible. In Western architecture a space must be maintained between the poetic image, called after Vitruvius the architectural idea (the images that are proposed by the architect, issuing from his or her mind's eye, originally named *ichnographia, orthographia,* and *scenographia* or *skiographia*), and the building. The challenge is to make both present while accounting for the temporality of lived experience. A spark of *erōs* moves across the space to activate delight in the inhabitant's mind. According to Aristotle, delight is a movement of the soul.[7] There has to be a difference between the actual and the possible for *erōs* to be engaged.

Origins

Love is not consolation, it is light.
Simone Weil, *Cahier VI* (quoted in Mark Z. Danielewski, *House of Leaves*)

Plato's demiurge, the maker of the cosmos, was replaced when Aristotle conceived Nature as an immanent force. Living bodies, in particular, were shaped by this force, enabling Aristotle to believe that the perfection of creatures might be evident to our eyes, to the theorizing gaze of the dissector. For Aristotle, particularly in his biology, idea (*eidos*) became often interchangeable with form (*morphē*) and was inseparable from matter. Stoicism took this notion further, elaborating Aristotle's reinterpretation of "forms" as something that the eye could directly see. In architecture, the circle could become potentially interchangeable with a *tholos,* for example, the circular temple in which the Greeks celebrated a feminine deity.[8] Lucretius writes: "Nothing can act or be acted upon without body, nor can anything create space except the void and emptiness. Therefore, beside void and bodies, there can be no third nature of itself in the sum of things."[9] As Dalibor Vesely points out, it was under the influence of this radicalized and, in a certain way, distorted Aristotelian understanding of corporeality that Vitruvian theory came into existence.[10] The reality of erotic embodiment as the primary mediation, *chōra,* became absent from the explicit theory of architecture at the origins of the Western tradition.

Indeed, Stoic philosophy profoundly influenced Vitruvius's understanding of architecture as a body, analogous to the human body. It also
enabled Vitruvius to describe the potential significance of architectural artifacts as a mere "semantic" pair of signifier-signified, ruled by proportion
and harmony. According to Gilles Deleuze, the Stoics reversed Platonism
by suggesting an essential continuity between things (as spatial entities)
and words (as abstract or ideal entities).[11] This initial fusion of the ideal
and the real was the original seed that would eventually transform architecture into a compositional technique and its theory into an *ars fabri-
candi,* or applied science. Stoicism "flattened" reality and transformed the
vertical axis of Plato into a horizontal geography. But Deleuze has argued
that this horizontal surface could remain mysterious, implying that the
most extensive and most tortuous labyrinth is the straight line, a distance
between the actual and the real.[12] This geography seems to correspond to
the space of dreams, suggesting an analogy to the original Platonic *chōra,*
which brought together Being and becoming but also kept them apart.
Rather than accepting a linear temporality divided into past, present and
future, Stoicism recognized the present as possessing real existence, with
the past and future dividing each present moment ad infinitum. Thus, the
space-time of desire became horizontal. In Stoicism the poetic image remained within the immanent realm of human experience. This view was
fully grasped by Giordano Bruno during the sixteenth century, and by a
number of poets, artists, and architects during late modernity.

From the Renaissance to the eighteenth century, the various commentaries on Vitruvius show the complexity of the problem. Deeply
rooted in culture, architecture could not be reduced to a semantic opposition. Theory was never an autonomous "technique," and practice required
the architect to participate in the oral traditions of culture. For Vitruvius,
optical correction, a species of *sollertia,* was the most significant technique
for embodying precise ideas (poetic images) in a real building. Because human perception, particularly vision, depended on the body's position in
the world, the essential proportions and geometry of a building needed to
be "adjusted." Doing so enabled the ideal order to appear in the real building, both bridging and celebrating the gap between "matter" and "form"
present in all other areas of human experience. Until the end of the Renaissance, architects sought in their works to embody beauty, understood
as self-evident value. Seeking *venustas,* the beautiful as a quality of Venus,
the architectural *ideai* (the images proper to architecture) excluded "perspective." They were never that which is merely apparent. The poetic images of architecture, "written" by the architect in the space of desire, were

present yet absent in buildings until the crisis of representation in early modernity.[13] Space, truly the erotic spatiality of the body, joined and separated the ideal and the real.

In the late seventeenth century, when Claude Perrault's architectural theories (and his own commentary on Vitruvius) incorporated Descartes's epistemology and psychology, it was the "scientific" dimension of Vitruvius that came to be appreciated. Although optical correction had been present in all treatises and commentaries in the Western tradition, Perrault regarded it as a mere justification for errors of craftsmanship, hiding a faulty application of the rules of proportion. The purpose of theory was to provide a simple rational technique, easy to apply, that liberated practice from the uncertainties of *sollertia*. After Perrault, the erotic gap acknowledged in optical correction was generally dismissed as nonexistent. Similarly, Perrault regarded beauty as a relative value that depended on the tastes of different human societies rather than as a self-evident absolute that came from a higher order (nature, God, the cosmos).

Marsilio Ficino and the poetic image in the Renaissance

The form cannot desert matter, because it is inseparable from it, and matter itself cannot be deprived of form, but I have proposed that it is light which possesses of its very nature the function of multiplying itself and diffusing itself instantaneously in all directions. . . . Therefore light is not a form subsequent to corporeity, but it is corporeity itself.

Robert Grosseteste, *On Light* (trans. Clare C. Reidle)

In the fifteenth century Marsilio Ficino recovered the tradition of Neoplatonism, one that had been critical of Stoic materialism. This tradition, which had been fused with Christian mysticism and theology during the late Middle Ages, culminated in the optical speculations of Robert Grosseteste and Roger Bacon. Ficino asserted the impossibility of knowledge without images (*phantasmata*). His commentary on Plato's *Symposium* reiterates some of the topics now familiar to us, while sharpening their significance for modernity. Ficino explains that our spirit can use the senses to grasp images of external objects. Given that the soul is incorporeal, unlike our own body or perishable objects, these images cannot be perceived directly. In other words, our consciousness can contemplate the images of objects (grasping what Husserl might call their essence) "reflected in it as in a mirror," because it grasps not "objects" but "images." It is through images that we can appraise objects.[14] In one of his books on magic, from 1588, Giordano Bruno also emphasized the importance of the image.

Magic action occurs through indirect contact involving sounds and images.[15] Images can inspire all emotions—particularly sympathy and an-
tipathy, the conditions of desire. Through sight and hearing, the magician,
often an architect, can introduce "chains" and lure the soul through the
imagination. The chain has to pass through the imagination (*phantasia*),
for "there is nothing in the intellect that was not previously perceived by
the senses, and there is nothing which, coming from the senses, can reach
the intellect without the intermediary of the imagination."[16]

Plato observed that the quest for love is never fulfilled and that sexual union cannot be the ultimate aim of desire. Therefore, beauty cannot
be reduced to the material. Love is associated with beauty because beauty
is not merely aesthetic perfection but total perfection, including all that is
valuable and thus meaningful. In the Sixth Tractate of the First Ennead
"On Beauty," Plotinus (204–270 C.E.) developed this theme. Criticizing
the popular Stoic definition of beauty as "the symmetry of parts towards
each other and towards a whole . . . [together with] a certain charm of
color," he wonders how "one face, constant in symmetry [meaning 'commensurability'] appears sometimes fair and sometimes not."[17] His conclusion is that symmetry itself owes its beauty to a more remote principle:
"What symmetry is to be found in noble conduct, or excellent laws, or any
form of mental pursuit? What symmetry is to be found in any form of abstract thought?" He declares, "All the loveliness of this world comes by
communion in Ideal-Form." To further explain the relationship between
material and "that which antedates all Matter," Plotinus uses architecture
as an example: "On what principle does the architect, when he finds the
house standing before him correspondent with his inner ideal of a house,
pronounce it beautiful? Is it not that the house before him, the stones
apart, is the inner idea stamped upon the mass of exterior matter, the indivisible exhibited in diversity?"[18] Marsilio Ficino recovered this Neoplatonic understanding and emphasized beauty's affinity with the image.
Engaging a medieval cosmos, organized vertically with the heavens above
and the earth below, Ficino's *Platonic Theology* and his commentaries on
love are crucial to grasp the role of the poetic image in architecture, operating in erotic space.

Departing from the theocentric Middle Ages, the Renaissance had to
wrestle with humanity's newly acquired freedom. God was no longer to
blame for all calamities; there were other forces at work, including intermediary spirits, both good and evil. The church emphasized both the mortality of Christ and the immortality of the human soul. Both emphases
were novel, and Ficino was directly responsible for promoting the latter.

Although his work was profoundly rooted in Christianity, it had two central objectives. First, he proclaimed the potential of man to become a magus, who could exert power over a nature filled with sympathies, hidden ciphers, and signs. Instead of merely waiting for the second coming of Christ, he advocated transforming the earthly world by producing artifacts and buildings to propitiate Fortuna and obtain a good life for all. Second, Ficino sought a way for the soul (that is, embodied consciousness) to reach a realm of pure Mind and Will, Knowledge and Love, through a poetic, amatory, and even priestly ascent. Both aims were shared by Renaissance painters and architects who generated poetic images and proposed places for a good life, engaging desire while trying to avoid being enslaved by desire, by the demons ever present in nature.

Ficino read Plato's *Symposium* through his own Christian beliefs and added notions from Platonic and Neoplatonic philosophy. His *Commentary* describes the cosmos as a hierarchy of being that emanates from God (unity) and extends down to the physical world (multiplicity).[19] Every level in this hierarchy comes from the level above it, and desires to rise again to this level above. This desire to return to one's source is called "love," and the quality in the source that generates this desire is called "beauty." The human soul, situated exactly halfway between God (now a Christian God) and physical things, is involved in the same process. However, the immortal human soul, with its mortal body, is polarized between two kinds of love. The desire to procreate inferior beings is called "earthly love," and the desire to rise to higher levels of being is called "heavenly love":

Venus is twofold. One is certainly that intelligence which we have located in the Angelic Mind. The other is the power of procreation attributed to the World Soul. . . . When the beauty of a human body first meets our eyes, our intellect, which is the first Venus in us, worships and esteems it as an image of divine beauty. . . . But the power of procreation, the second Venus, desires to procreate a form like this. On both sides, therefore, there is love: there a desire to contemplate beauty, here a desire to propagate it. Each love is virtuous and praiseworthy, for each follows a divine image. (53–54)

In both of its phases, descending and ascending, human love is part of the natural cosmic process that all creatures share. Human love is therefore a good thing and must be cultivated. Architecture and art enable the cultivation of love; through them the splendor of beauty contributes to reconcile multiplicity into unity.

Indeed, for Ficino, concupiscence is at the root of all things. Love is the fundamental power of the world, the energy of nature: "Love accompanies chaos, precedes the world, wakens the sleeping, lights the dark, gives life to the dead, gives form to the formless, perfects the imperfect" (40). This is a natural love that impels some to study literature, music, or painting; some to pursue virtue or the religious life; some to make money; and many to seek the pleasures of the stomach and the flesh. This fervor is both immortal *and* mortal: immortal because it is never extinguished and it transforms rather than dies; mortal because it does not always concentrate on the same object but seeks new pleasures, owing to a change in its own nature or to having experienced too much of the same thing. It is immortal also because a figure that was once loved is always loved. Although the beloved's features are not present to the mind's eye at all times, they remain fixed forever in the breast.

For Ficino, love is our desire for beauty, and beauty is a grace that originates most often in a harmony of several things. It may be perceived in three ways: souls are known through the intellect; bodies are perceived through the eyes; and sounds are perceived through the ears. An appetite that follows the other senses is called not love but lust or madness, and it may lead to intemperance and disharmony. This claim is not merely an expression of Christian values or a denigration of the body; the problem with smell, taste, and touch is that these senses perceive "simple forms, whereas the beauty of the human body requires a harmony of different parts" (40–41). While Ficino affirmed the immortality of the soul, he also believed that human consciousness is embodied and not merely a mental phenomenon. His concept differed both from the original Greek understanding of the soul as the vital principle of a mortal body and from the dualistic mind-body split that would become prevalent after the seventeenth century.

Ficino also remarks that the passion of a lover is not extinguished by the sight or touch of any one body. In some measure, desire may be quenched by possessing what is desired. Certainly, hunger and thirst are satisfied by food and drink. Yet love is not satisfied by seeing or embracing a body. Therefore, love does not seek "any nature of a body," though it certainly seeks beauty. "Whence it happens that it cannot be anything corporeal[;] . . . for those who are aroused by love and thirst for beauty it is necessary, if they wish to quench their burning thirst by drinking this liquid, to seek the very sweet humor of this beauty . . . elsewhere than in matter[,] . . . quantity, shape or any colors" (89). The lover does not desire this or that body, but he admires, desires, and is amazed by the splendor of the celestial majesty *shining through* bodies. "For this reason lovers do not know what they desire or seek, for they do not know God Himself, whose secret flavor infuses a certain very sweet perfume of Himself unto His works. By which perfume we are certainly excited every day. The odor we certainly smell; the flavor undoubtedly we do not know. . . . Hence it also happens that lovers *fear and worship* in some way the sight of the beloved" (52; my emphasis). While this passage expresses Christian orthodoxy through Neoplatonic negative theology, it also conveys the original understanding of beauty as artistic meaning, an understanding that would continue until the separation of the beautiful and the sublime in eighteenth-century aesthetics.

Ficino emphasizes that even if the beauty of a body were in some way corporeal, "in the sheer density of its body," it would not please the beholder by virtue of being corporeal.

For the beauty of any person pleases the soul not insofar as it lays in external matter, but insofar as an *image* of it is comprehended or grasped by the soul through the sight. That image cannot be a body, either in the sight or in the soul, since both of these are incorporeal. For in what way could the small pupil of the eye take in the whole heaven, so to speak, if it received it in a corporeal way? In no way, obviously. But the spirit receives in a point the entire breadth of a body, in a spiritual way and in an incorporeal image. The soul likes only that beauty which it has taken in. Though this beauty may be an image of an external body, it is nonetheless incorporeal in the soul. (88)

Starting with a notion from Plotinus and adding more contemporary elements from the Christian metaphysics of light, Ficino criticizes those who think that beauty actually comes from a certain arrangement of parts: in his terms, symmetry, proportion, and agreeableness of colors. Because an arrangement of parts exists only in composite things, no simple things could be beautiful. "Now pure colors, lights, a single voice, the splendor of gold, the gleam of silver, knowledge, the soul, all of which are simple, we call beautiful. In addition, the proportion of the whole construction arises out of all the parts. Whence something very absurd follows, that things which are not beautiful of their own nature give birth to beauty. . . . [Therefore] we should consider beauty to be something other than the arrangement of parts" (88).

Ultimately, beauty can be conveyed only by an image, and an image relies on light. "Beauty is a certain lively and spiritual grace infused by the shining ray of God[,] . . . a grace which through reason, sight, and hearing moves and delights our souls; in delighting carries them away, and in carrying them away, inflames them with burning love" (95). This is the divine medieval light (*lumen*) that also becomes human light (*lux*) in the Renaissance, which portrays the poetic images of the new painting, *perspectiva artificialis*. Ficino says that the eye sees nothing but the light of the sun, since the shapes and colors of objects are never seen unless they are illuminated with light. "They themselves do not come to the eyes with their matter. . . . And so the one light of the sun, imprinted with the colors and shapes of all the bodies illuminated by it, presents itself to the eyes. The eyes, with the help of a certain ray of their own, perceive the light thus imprinted: they see both the perceived light itself and all the things which are imprinted in it." Therefore the world is perceived not as matter but as light, devoid of body. "The light itself cannot be a body, since it fills the whole world instantaneously from east to west, penetrates the whole body of air and water everywhere without obstruction, and is nowhere soiled when it is mixed with filthy things. . . . Whence it happens that all this beauty of the World, which is the third face of God, presents itself as incorporeal to the eyes through the incorporeal light of the sun" (91).

In a paragraph that is particularly important for painters and architects, Ficino adds that this splendor cannot shine through matter unless it has been appropriately prepared. Preparation demands three things:

Arrangement, Proportion, and Aspect. Arrangement means the distances between the parts [an interval between incorporeal lines], Proportion means quantity [or rather the boundary of quantity, without thickness or depth], and Aspect means shape and color [not in matter but the pleasing harmony of light and shadows]. Although they exist in matter, these three characteristics cannot be any part of the body. Beauty is so alien to the mass of body that it never imparts itself to matter itself unless the matter has been prepared with the three incorporeal preparations. (93–94)

In Ficino's theory, love is both the process and the effect. Love is a magician, since the power of magic relies on love. "The work of magic is the attraction of one thing by another because of a certain affinity of nature. From this common relationship is born a common love; from love, a common attraction. Therefore the works of magic are works of nature, but art [and architecture] is its handmaiden. For where anything is lacking in natural relationship, art supplies it through vapors, numbers, figures, and qualities at the proper times" (127).

Ficino says that architecture seduces and inflames us with love. Although architecture possesses a geometric body, its true beauty comes from incorporeal light.

In the beginning the architect develops a Reason or Idea, as it were, of the building in his soul. Then he builds, as nearly as possible, the kind of house he has conceived. Who will deny that the house is a body and that it is very much like the architect's incorporeal Idea, in the likeness of which it was built? Furthermore, it must be judged as being like the architect, more on account of a certain incorporeal design than on account of its matter. Therefore go ahead; subtract its matter if you can (and you can subtract it mentally), but leave the design. Nothing of body, nothing of matter will remain to you. On the contrary, the design that came from the artist and the design which remains in the artist will be completely identical. You may do the same in any body of a man. You will find that its form, corresponding to the Reason of the Soul, is simple and devoid of matter. (93)

The poetic image in Renaissance theory

Although the philosophical speculations of Ficino diverged from writings on architecture by Leon Battista Alberti, Francesco di Giorgio, Filarete, and Andrea Palladio, Ficino's sophisticated meditation on beauty elucidates the meaning of architectural *lineamenti*. First described by Alberti in the opening paragraphs of his *De re aedificatoria* (1485), and generally understood as his main contribution to the modernization of architectural practice, *lineamenti* referred to the essential geometric "idea" that issued from the architect's mind, took the form of a drawing, and guided the production of architecture. For Alberti and his successors architecture was not a mechanical but a liberal art, a product of the soul's intelligence. Ficino had taken from Plotinus a distinction between the soul's "contemplation" and the soul's "intelligence." While the soul's contemplation is forced to change from one object to another, fragmented by the multiplicity of the "lower life," intelligence may be capable of embracing the whole intelligible world in a single, timeless vision.[20] This characteristic may explain the early desire to encompass the "whole building" in a drawing, and even the tendency to lift the point of view and generate "military perspectives" in parallel projection.[21] These drawings were intended to be prophetic, not as a systematic representation of a future building but as poetic images that are truly mantic (a term derived from *mania,* or "madness"): an architectural promise of the future, a divination in search of the good life.

There has always been a madness in the architect's work because of the uncertainty of construction. We simply cannot predict the outcome of an architectural enterprise, owing to the gap between a project and a building, between the architect's intentions and the public's reading of the physical place. Nevertheless, as Plato knew well, both truth in prophecy and excellence in poetry arise from madness: the greatest good comes to us from madness (*Phaedrus* 244a–b) although poetic words and oracular declarations are never entirely clear. The Renaissance still cultivated this quality of the architect's work.

During the Renaissance, *imagines* or *graphice* were constructed with lines; they included some scaled drawings by architects and sketches in the margins of manuscripts by Francesco di Giorgio and Filarete, for example. In an evocative account, Francesco tries to understand the nature of architectural drawings by interpreting the famous passage in Vitruvius's first book (chap. 2, para. 2), describing the plan (*icnografia*) as the able use of the compass and ruler to delineate forms and intervals in a horizontal plane, the elevation (*ortografia*) as the front and figure of the future building, and, most significantly, *scenografia* as the foreshadowing or adumbration of the front and sides of the building as they respond to the center of a compass.[22] The last corresponds to the function of the gnomon or shadow tracer, a *daidalon* that oriented humans in space-time and that inaugurated cities and buildings. The projection of shadows and the imagination of a future building are acts of prediction and propitiation. Consequently, Francesco had to be mindful of the site's astrological alignments. He believed that all parallel lines of heavenly light meet at the center of the earth, so alterations to the earth's surface matter greatly.[23] Buildings could make a site more or less fertile, more or less auspicious for human life. He never failed to consult astrologers before building his many fortifications.

Being *linear,* architectural images resemble geometrical figures, and thus are easily reconciled with the eye's light and the mind. Recollected in the time of experience by the inhabitants of cities and buildings, they are the goal of desire, always unattainable yet present in the work. When exposed to the soul's contemplative gaze, these erotic spaces become perspectives (*perspectiva artificialis*), like the magic engravings of the *Hypnerotomachia Poliphili* or the seductive paintings of Uccello, Carpaccio, and Botticelli. Tracey Winton has shown that the *Hypnerotomachia Poliphili* is indeed the Renaissance work that best reflects Ficino's concept of the Neoplatonic poetic image in architecture.[24] The proportional relationships governing the image express the ideal goal—the possibility of reconciling multiplicity into unity, somewhere else and yet visible in our world, in the epiphany disclosed by the mind's eye, the picture frame, or the proscenium arch.

The Neoplatonic distinction between the soul's contemplative and intellectual modes was the basis for the theoretical argument that perspective has little to do with architectural *ideas,* as well as for the affinity between architecture and painting during the Renaissance.[25] Both were based on geometry and light. Linear perspective (*perspectiva artificialis*) revealed a clarity (*claritas*), a transcendental light that had been absent from the earlier understanding of depth. Alberti believed that painting and mathematics were the only crucial disciplines for the architect, in sharp contrast to Vitruvius's plea for an encyclopedic theory of architecture. He sought to create a "charmed" (and charming) space (a term derived from the Latin *carmen,* "incantation"), a seductive depth that could make our consciousness aware of its potential wholeness.

Modern transformations

In one of his early works, *De umbris idearum* (1582), Giordano Bruno portrayed the "shadows of ideas" as linear and geometrical diagrams, and associated them with magic. He explains how magic works by paying attention to the sun's shadows. Shadows of ideas are archetypal images in the heavens, closest to the divine mind.[26] By incorporating Nicholas of Cusa's "coincidence of opposites" and questioning both Ficino's vertical hierarchy of being and Christian orthodoxy, Bruno proposed a magical memory system whose reliance on the powers of the subject rendered it an effective instrument of transformation. For Bruno, nothing exists outside experience and yet the magus knows archetypal reality beyond earthly appearances. This is precisely the power to conceive architecture. According to Frances Yates, Bruno had in mind the famous statement in the *Corpus Hermeticum* (a collection of early Christian gnostic and Neoplatonic apocryphal texts, attributed to Hermes Trismegistus and translated by Ficino in the fifteenth century), in which Pimander exhorts the magus to make himself equal to a God. To understand God, the magus made himself grow "to a greatness beyond measure," rising above all time, becoming Eternity, imagining all things at once: times, places, substances, qualities, and quantities. For Bruno, the manipulation of images works by God's light, and yet the human imagination is primarily productive instead of reproductive. Since the image is immanent in the world of experience, it could be more readily identified with the object, a notion that eventually led to modern instrumentality.

Contrary to the premises of standard aesthetic theory since the eighteenth century, the notion of beauty in the Western tradition had always been infused with erotic experience. Beauty, in its original sense, produced wonder, in *both* fear and admiration. This was the purpose of the *daidala* that were described by Homer and Hesiod, attributed to Daedalus, and embodied during the Renaissance in mechanisms and buildings of war and peace. Although we would seldom associate fortification design with aesthetic emotion, emphasis was often placed on the poetic image of defense, from Francesco di Giorgio to the seventeenth century. The towers and ramparts of fortified cities evoked fear, but the emotion was always ambivalent: marking the limits was always an issue of existential safety. As Machiavelli taught his prince, fortifications typically are useless for practical purposes, and can even damage the credibility of a sovereign with his own people. During the seventeenth century scores of treatises on fortification were written by architects, soldiers, and Jesuit priests, and all of them placed an inordinate emphasis on tracing regular polygons as poetic images that symbolized safety, the divine mind, and the shape of paradise. These geometric cities and fortifications were seldom built, and their effectiveness was finally discredited at the end of the baroque period by the first modern military engineer, the Maréchal Vauban.[27]

It was perhaps Michelangelo Buonarroti who first embedded the poetic image, with its full erotic force, in the mortal flesh of modern experience. Understanding Christianity as *kenosis,* emphasizing the diminution of God's alien power through Christ's Incarnation, he reconnected it to the classical tradition. Michelangelo's explicit love of embodied beauty contrasted with the long-standing ambivalence toward earthly beauty in medieval and Eastern Christianity, and was eventually criticized during the Counterreformation. The "real mortality" of personal consciousness led him to embrace *erōs* as suffering, transforming love into a creative madness rather than avoiding it as an illusory craving of the ego. Believing that this passion is the essence of the human condition, he celebrated our self-conscious living on our death as a precious divine gift, the fire that motivates one's work. *Disegno,* like light, was a continuous flow drawn from the human figure in various degrees of abstraction, from painting and sculpture to the androgynous body of architecture, the mother of the arts. Eroticism, for Michelangelo, was never tender; it was always incandescent and keenly bittersweet, the "figure" of the present in the "ground" of temporality, our Being *as* becoming.

Michelangelo, like Giordano Bruno, did not believe that perspective representation, the geometric *costruzione legittima,* has anything to do with truth. Michelangelo criticized Dürer's book on human proportions, with its objectification of bodies (male and female, young and old, at various stages of development), for disregarding the reality of the body in growth and motion. In *Ash Wednesday Supper* Bruno elucidated optical phenomena to explain the eclipse of celestial bodies and noted that visual perception cannot be mapped onto geometry. "It takes a fool to believe that in a physical division of a finite body one may go on to infinity."[28] The human eye *is* and *is not* a mere point.

Unlike most of his colleagues during the Renaissance, Michelangelo had no interest in architectural *lineamenti*. He worked out his building projects mostly with sketches and models. In the related text of Vincenzio Danti, *Libri delle perfette proporzioni per il disegno* (1568), purportedly based "on Michelangelo and God," proportions are conceived as relationships in motion, as the inexplicable "coming to be" of human life. They are not merely the form or structure of a work but a revelation of nature's purpose in forming something the way it was meant to be: not *a* meaning, but "sense." Michelangelo's *contrapposto*, "unfinished work" (such as the famous "Slaves"), and the serpentine compositions anticipate what is not yet present, manifesting *erōs* as delay in human temporality.[29] In his architecture there is always a tension between the actual process of construction and the apparent formation of the building from *prima materia,* in which beauty is perceived as the force or energy within a healthy life. For Michelangelo, the poetic image is immanent to the work; it is futile to try to render it in terms of objective numbers or geometry.

Building on the realizations (and the inner struggle) in Michelangelo's work, the baroque period pursued a paradoxical separation of eroticism and religion. The Council of Trent sought to purify Christian dogma from pagan contamination by emphasizing the Incarnation and mortality of Christ while avoiding "lewd" representations in religious subject matter. Yet the most convincing expressions of religious faith came from San Juan de la Cruz and Santa Teresa de Avila, who initiated a long-standing debate between the *logos* of theology and the ecstasy of mysticism.[30] The mystical process is analogous to the mania of falling in love. The meditating subject starts by excluding all objects from his conscience. As he empties his mind, an impersonal mental space appears, one that is no longer a personal mind. Thinking "nothing" reveals mental space. It is no longer *his* mind, but a universal space: vision becomes a compassionate crying vision, and the meditator is overtaken. Both San Juan and Santa Teresa make explicit that the aim is to let go, to void the mind and keep nothing. The mystic assures us that once the mind has been evacuated God will become present, as expressed in Eckhart's "silent desert of God" and San Juan's "dark night of the soul." As Ioan Couliano has shown, this process is common to all shamanistic practices, in which the purpose is usually an ascent, a healing communion with other worlds.[31] One experiences not an object of thought but a superlative union, comparable only to a human orgasm. This is expressed vividly in Bernini's sculpture *The Ecstasy of Santa Teresa,* now in S. Maria della Vittoria in Rome, in which the saint floats in the light of God, mouth agape, and is about to be pierced by the final golden arrow of God's love, held by a smiling angel who is ready to disrobe her. This state of grace is shared by the mystic and the person in love. Life loses weight, we smile, and our gaze relaxes. This is the state that irritates theologians and technocrats—understood by Socrates as an authentic glimpse of truth, despite its dangers. Although this state may threaten historical rationality and even deontological human action, the unknowing it reveals to our experience is crucial for the construction of any truth: the seductive power of the poetic image is the foundation of signification.

The Jesuits took the dogma of the Catholic Church to all corners of the world, teaching the word of God through theater, sensuous experience, and architecture. These militant soldiers of Christ promoted their new *logos,* which integrated the revelations of Christianity and the discoveries of the new science. Since then, the Jesuits' intellectual accomplishments around the world and in all fields have made them a formidable theological and political force for Catholicism. It is significant that their founding text, Ignatius of Loyola's *Spiritual Exercises,* came from the mystical tradition of the Iluminados, a Spanish sect that advocated meditation and the elimination of sensual experience to attain emptiness and thus align the personal will with the will of God.[32] For Ignatius, as for Bruno, the image is the shadow of God's light; yet the scenes of meditation in the *Exercises* were meant to be visualized as realistic theatrical perspectives that helped one contemplate questions of redemption through inner dialogue.

Juan Bautista Villalpando came from the Jesuit tradition and was the first writer to propose the *identity* of perspective images and parallel projections in architecture, such as plans and elevations.[33] Combining medieval optics with a baroque identification of light as God's wisdom (the Holy Spirit), he believed that the light of God (the sun) generates parallel projections that are like shadows with a perspective geometry that is projected to infinity. His argument is expressed in a commentary and reconstruction of Ezekiel's vision of the Temple of Solomon, a project described in the Old Testament that was communicated directly to the prophet by God's light. Villalpando's work is significant in associating the images in an architect's mind with God's modus operandi, producing precise "projections" that describe a future building, which can be measured and eventually executed. It is also important to note that the description of the prophet's vision would be realized in the monastery and palace of the Escorial. Although Villalpando's premise would eventually be transformed into the reductive and prescriptive practices of modern architectural representation, the project for the Escorial by Juan de Herrera and Philip II came from a profound interest in magical practices and the symbolic power of the cubic figure.[34]

Two major alternatives for artistic *praxis* thus emerged during the baroque period. On the one hand, the ideal poetic image could be "realized" literally, risking the annihilation of the erotic distance. On the other hand, the poetic image could retain its "otherness" through an association with light, believed to be at once infinitely distant and everywhere present—its mystery both a divine attribute and a scientific enigma. Baroque architects argued vehemently about the appropriateness of perspective representation in architecture. At one extreme, Jesuits such as Andrea Pozzo advocated *quadrattura* that could dissolve "real" space into a pictorial space of religious apotheosis, disclosing the projective qualities of God's light (always mysteriously distinct from the "real" light of the church) through perspectival compositions of paint, sculpture, and architectural ornament. At the other extreme, Guarino Guarini emphatically rejected *quadrattura* frescoes in churches because they revealed too much, all at once, unlike the infinite light of God. Baroque architects such as Borromini and Guarini explored a newly found human capacity for *productive* imagination—in contrast with the more literal *mimetic* imagination of previous times—that transformed geometric figures into architectural "projections" and cast them into light. Unlike Renaissance material traces (*vestigia*), the novel images generated by Guarini, Neumann, and Fischer were imbued with a rhetorically mysterious light. The result was a remarkably new architecture that explicitly engaged the temporality of human experience in its disclosure of poetic images.

Kepler's *Ad Vitelionem paralipomena* (*Supplements to Witelo*) of 1604 was the first modern book on optics. He painstakingly explained how all the light from a point in the visual field enters the eye and is focused onto a point on the retina.[35] Kepler was the first to demonstrate that an inverted picture (which he called *pictura*) is projected onto the retina as in a *camera obscura,* independently of the observer's will. This geometric phenomenon, however, cannot fully explain what we see or how we actually perceive an image. Kepler avoided the question of "post-retinal transmission" but endorsed medieval optics on the existence of a "visual spirit" affected by qualities of light and color.[36] "Vision," he writes, "occurs in the spirits and through this impression of species on the spirit. However, this impression is not optical but physical and mysterious (*admirabilis*)."[37]

Indeed, when Kepler discusses light he sounds more like Robert Grosseteste in the thirteenth century than like any modern writer after Newton. For him, light was the most excellent part of our corporeal world; it is the origin of animal faculties and, most significantly, the link between the worlds of matter and spirit. Coming from the sun, it is also heat, contained in all life and potentially in all matter: he believed that one day we should be able to see the little flashes produced by a beating heart. Color and light have similar natures, as shown when sunlight strikes an object and liberates its color. Kepler claimed that every material is transparent, even brick. Not surprisingly, baroque architects often spoke of a diaphanous architecture, both literally and metaphorically. They thought that our inability to see through dense material was due to its angular texture, which reflects and refracts light rays in different directions.

This concept of light accounts for Kepler's notion of the image as a physico-mental construct that travels along invisible geometric lines. While putting aside the old Aristotelian debates about light, Kepler left the door open for later theories that would recognize the mysterious qualities of light as they pursued its quantitative characteristics, including its speed. In contrast, Descartes did not elaborate further on the nature of light but did make an analogy between vision and a blind man's cane, implying a quasi-tactile relationship between mathematical thinking and seeing. For Kepler what we perceive is *not* simply an optical phenomenon, but direct vision became an epistemological imperative for Descartes. In fact, Descartes regarded pictures in perspective as the only genuine way of seeing, since consciousness at the pineal gland provides "true" vision. In Kepler's optics the poetic image was understood as the inner light of embodied consciousness; it was not identical to a geometric retinal image. Descartes, on the other hand, was afraid of ambiguity, including phenomena such as anamorphosis, the perspective distortions that challenged the absolute veracity of the geometric image. He thought that images should be present to the *ego cogitans* without the delay of bodily experience, free of illusion, and devoid of color and shadows.[38]

Claude Perrault assimilated Cartesian epistemology and optics into architectural theory, and was the first to reduce architectural meaning to communication, which he believed could contribute to the refinement of civilized society. Under the aegis of Cartesian reason, he clarified the social function of architecture and purged it of all mystical resonances. Beauty had to be visible to be beauty at all. Even its more subtle aspects (such as proportion) acquired its rules based on common use and common values (by association with symmetry, grandeur, and excellence in execution—the qualities of beauty allegedly self-evident to all people). Human architecture was not analogous to God's universe; it was instead analogous to language, expressing historical cultural values. For Perrault, theory had to become an efficient instrument to produce exactly what the architect intended. This was the explicit intention of his revision to the rules of the classical orders. His theory recognized no difference between the retinal image and embodied experience. Any formal adjustments had to be motivated by explicit expression. Perspectival vision was the mode of "reception" on which all decisions were based.

Perrault, like Lysias, was suspicious of seduction because of its destabilizing power. In architecture he sought full rational control to further the golden age of Louis XIV and preserve its accomplishments for posterity. Socrates' *erōs*, however, was never far away, often disguised as the genius of reason itself. In this guise it appears as a *daimōn* with a flaming head and pointing to the primitive hut in the famous frontispiece of Laugier's *Essay on Architecture* (1753). For Laugier, the original architecture of Nature was the poetic image that any good architecture should evoke. Of course, too much civilization could also be boring, so the eighteenth century sought as well playful destabilization in works of art. Some Enlightenment architects and theoreticians attempted to synthesize architecture's social vocation with its traditional poetic calling. Without invoking either cosmology or science, the eclectic teacher and writer Jacques-François Blondel advocated the development of decorum (*la bienséance*).[39] Although Blondel, in his encyclopedic vein, often reduced this concern to formal typologies and also repeated traditional arguments about architecture imitating nature, guided by the proportions of the human body, his work is a good example of how the poetic image could be sought within the history of the discipline itself and not just through a direct *mimēsis* of the natural world. Because architecture was analogous to *spoken* language and other arts, such as painting and music, it could learn how to express poetic truths.[40]

Edmund Burke's well-known distinction between the "beautiful" and the "sublime" became a dominant concept in aesthetics, but a few artists and architects resisted this simplistic polarization. Burke, writing in 1756, already presumed the new aesthetic distance that protected the spectator from irrational upheavals of *erōs*. At the inception of this new consciousness in the eighteenth century, Giovanni Battista Piranesi, the famous disciple of Carlo Lodoli, sought erotic meaning through historical reference. His tactics of engaging the poetic image in architecture are especially evident in his series of etchings titled *Carceri* (*The Prisons*).[41] Piranesi produced a first series of prints showing various imaginary spaces, based on the two-point perspective method of the Galli Bibienas (*perspectiva per angolo*). The spaces include complex theatrical constructions of masonry and wood and frightening machines of torture. Although these spaces are threatening, they are still rational, derived from a geometry of plans and elevations.

In a second version of the etchings, however, Piranesi exploded this geometry by introducing a new sense of temporality that the Russian film-maker Sergei Eisenstein would later identify with filmic temporality, en-abled by montage. The spaces in this second series present a different quality of depth than either the Galli Bibiena or subsequent perspective systems with an objectified "third" dimension. Piranesi obsessively dark-ened his etchings, often adding ink with his fingers. The spaces became highly seductive to the imagination, yet impenetrable to the physical body. It would be impossible to construct such spaces literally, deducing a cohe-sive three-dimensional geometry from the image. These spaces, in short, are paradoxical.[42] Piranesi's *Carceri* invite existential orientation by con-fronting darkness, the very darkness that humans ultimately cannot es-cape, at a time when Western culture had opted for the exclusive light of reason. Piranesi always insisted on his title as "architect," despite his cen-tral métier as a printmaker. Implementing a strategy of *delay,* his poetic spaces are implicitly critical of a banal architecture objectified in the shad-owless light of three-dimensional perspective.

In his engagement with the poetic fragment Piranesi also departed from the majority of his contemporaries who sought an ideal, rational model in history. His historical engravings often proposed poetic narratives through the juxtaposition of fragments, while his practice as an imagina-tive "restorer" of ancient pieces could produce wondrous, original arti-facts. His conception of history is described in his writings on the "magnificence of the Romans," and illustrated in his treatment of ornament in later works such as the *Camini*.[43] The fragment, a *symbolon,* evokes a missing whole and an object of desire that is *both* present and absent.

Like Piranesi, the insightful eighteenth-century philosopher Giam-battista Vico found that scientific reason was helping to purge the world of a poetic dimension that he considered fundamental for the survival of culture. Unlike philosophy, which addresses cultivated men and considers important matters in abstract ways, poetry and art can reach most men di-rectly through sensuous experience. Artists and poets "invent" their sub-ject matter, and therefore may depart from conventional reality to pursue a more constant, more abiding order.[44] He also thought that the solipsis-tic Cartesian mind promoted distrust of our shared world of experience, leading men to become wild beasts in "a deep solitude of spirit and will," scarcely able to agree on anything, and seeking their own pleasures and caprice. This "barbarism of reflection" would blind us to the wisdom of the senses and would legitimize only actions to obtain "the sheer necessi-ties of life." Thus, thought Vico, this "pragmatism" would lead men to engage in destructive wars that would eventually turn "cities into forests and forests into dens and lairs of men."[45] Nevertheless, Vico could still believe that divine providence might allow a new beginning, a return to primitive simplicity, poetry, and truth.

For Vico, human institutions originated not in a rational golden age, somehow derived from nature, but in a mythical age that was poetic and free from intellectual presuppositions. The first wisdom of the gentile people was a metaphysics not "rational and abstract like that of learned men now, but felt and imagined as that of these first men must have been, who, without power of ratiocination, were all robust and vigorous imagination. This metaphysics was their poetry, a faculty born with them."[46] The questions were all *ta erotika* (erotic things) that addressed the fundamental issues of the human condition. The Jewish God (Vico also included Christianity, probably to avoid trouble) may have access to a pure *logos,* for God knows things "in his purest intelligence," and by knowing them can create them. Only for God does the word coincide with the deed and the object. It is for this reason that humanity's operations of technical mastery and planning are always limited and provide only partial truths. Vico's profound knowledge of cross-cultural myths corroborated his commonsense awareness that human consciousness could not exist without corporeality: the dualistic concepts of Cartesian philosophy were obviously flawed. We—for gentile humanity includes not only the first men but all of us moderns—can use our corporeal imagination to create, despite our "robust ignorance." Poetry, which Vico traces to its etymological sense of "creation," includes the making of poetic objects and words, and therefore has three functions: "(1) to invent sublime fables suited to the popular understanding, (2) to perturb to excess, with a view to the end proposed: (3) to teach the vulgar to act virtuously, as the poets have taught themselves."[47]

Vico had carefully studied Cartesian philosophy but sensed that something had gone wrong in the age of reason. The rationality of mathematics and physics could be known, since it was a human creation, but it was either too abstract or not general enough. To know clearly and distinctly, he states, is like seeing at night by lamplight: the object in the foreground can be seen but the background is cut off. When seeking truths that may orient human action, we should look for the daylight of a higher order (divine providence) through the opacity of bodies in the world.[48]

Vico believed that Cartesian epistemology could not provide humanity with a discursive framework for action, offering only a probable mechanical description of a natural world that we will ultimately never know, since we have not made it. Instead, he called for a historical rationality that could account for the disclosure of truths in the myths, art, and poetry of world cultures. This is the first instance of historical hermeneutics, a weaving together of philosophy and philology. His *New Science* thus proposes a history in which there is *real* change: the present is *truly* different from the past, a premise quite unlike the eternal return in cosmological epochs. Nevertheless, a *ricorso* is also possible: history follows a helicoidal path between past and future that provides a higher (critical) vantage point to later eras. For Vico, *poiēsis* was the origin of all nations (meaning all human cultures): poetic images were the true "universals," incarnated differently in every culture to constitute a civil order and ethical imperatives.

This philosophical framework also seems to underlie Piranesi's highly imaginative work. For Piranesi, poetry was the key to history, and memory coincided with the imagination. Although he thought it was inappropriate to conceal the structure of a building, its ornamentation (the fragment) should add to its mystery and promote a sense of awe. In other words, ornament, like dress, helped open up an erotic distance, generating pleasure through fear and even extravagance. Such ornamentation required originality from the architect, who nevertheless should recognize his work as constitutive of a tradition and contributing to a political order.

Piranesi had a great influence on architects north of the Alps, although they were usually attracted by his formal ideas and dismissed his polemical writings. Vico's books remained almost unknown until well into the nineteenth century. In a subsequent chapter I will touch on the theories of Jean-Louis Viel de Saint-Maux, whose position resonated with that of Vico and Piranesi. Most French and English architects of the eighteenth century acknowledged the historical roots of architecture and the recent theories of character, while continuing to work within a frame of reference based on a miraculous yet rational Nature that had been set in motion by a rational Judeo-Christian (and theistic/freemasonic) God. The poetic imagination of the eighteenth century was influenced by Newton's symbolic mathematics (implicit in his theory of universal gravitation) and particularly his *Optics,* with its "musical" theory of light.[49] However, the same scientific mentality inevitably led to a suspicion of poetic meanings and a growing interest in instrumentality.

The influence of Newton's *Optics* on architecture was acknowledged by architectural writers as diverse as Bernardo Vittone (a disciple of Guarini, working in Turin), Charles-Etienne Briseux (in Paris), and Robert Morris (in England). Although light was no longer associated with the divine mind, an analogy between the seven colors of the rainbow and the seven notes of the diatonic scale in music was extended into ideas about the poetic image in architecture. Often this analogy was interpreted as a demonstration of harmony in the visual realm, leading to a renewed interest in proportion and resulting in contradictory instrumental theories.[50] The best example is Nicolas Le Camus de Mézières's book *Le génie de l'architecture* (1780), in which the author rejects instrumental and quantitative concerns and describes instead how qualitative spaces in the *hôtel particulier* contribute to its seductive character. Le Camus relied greatly on the modulation of light to convey an architectural experience of seduction. The spaces, which had started to lose their cultural *genius loci,* were expected to express a sequential experience, not simply as a linear visit but as a thick temporal poetry, culminating in a surrender to the work and intimate participation. Le Camus's book describes how the spaces of the house engage the participant in a theatrical experience, through their lighting, color, texture, and even smell. Louise Pelletier has noted a parallel between Jean-François de Bastide's *La petite maison* and Le Camus's sequence of spaces.[51] In *Le génie,* the long enumeration and description of rooms in the *hôtel particulier* ends in the riding school, a place to win wagers, and a final boudoir. In Bastide's novella it is in the final boudoir that Mélite, the young girl being seduced by Trémicour's "little house," finally surrenders her virtue to the overwhelming beauty of the experience. In Le Camus's boudoir, light envelopes the architecture voluptuously, producing sharp contrasts between protruding and receding parts that weaken self-consciousness and incite the imagination. The narrative is like the script for a very long filmic shot: linear temporality dissipates, as we are drawn into the work and seduced by light and shadow, delayed fulfillment, and an extended threshold that open up an architectural space of desire.[52]

Compromises were always possible during the eighteenth century, but nineteenth-century culture polarized a debate between positive reason and emotive understanding. The new applied sciences dismissed the Socratic insistence on embodied *erōs* as the ground of human knowledge. Instead, positive science sought clarity and precision, enshrined planning as the only legitimate model for human making, ignored the inherent limitations of human knowledge, and left the erotic tradition to be taken up as an act of resistance by Romantic philosophers and writers.

Romanticism recovered the self as the playful center of existence, with all of its complexity and its conscious and unconscious layers. It rejected Descartes's notion of a rational ego, as well as the impersonal anthropology of English empiricist philosophers such as Hume. The Romantic self is not transparent to scientific reason; it is neither constructed by sensory impressions nor dissolved by temporal change. The self, as the pure presence that remains throughout our lives, is a primary reality that enables us to contemplate eternity, according to Schelling. This most intimate and authentic experience is our only way to know that anything *is* in the true sense of being; everything else is merely appearance. On the other hand, Schelling believed that all of our knowledge comes from direct experience by our embodied consciousness. Consciousness is synaesthetic and its primary knowledge is *given*. When we stop thinking of ourselves as subjects of scientific experimentation and identify with an object of contemplation, we are no longer *in* time; instead, "pure eternity" is in us. By abolishing distinctions between the body and the mind, the outside and the inside, physiology and psychology, Romanticism privileged erotic experience as the supreme form of knowledge: an intimate sense of wholeness. Poetic language and the poetic image showed how the incarnated conscience could reach this truth by facing the abyss of the *Ungrund,* a positive nothingness. Rather than being nihilistic, Romantic philosophy recognized that human truth is *not* an absolute truth, in the sense of science and theology. The human condition is the origin of truth, so all truth relies on human analogies, and all real sciences are "human sciences." Consequently, all serious Romantic philosophers looked to the creative imagination as their source of truths.

Gérard de Nerval praised excessive love and its temporal delay as the very meaning of the work of art: the space of desire. Nerval's insight was profoundly admired by other nineteenth-century writers and critics such as Baudelaire and Lautréamont. Love was also important in Nietzsche's poetic philosophy, one that in retrospect was far ahead of its time. He believed that art comes from erotic desire and is the supreme form of a significant will to power that expresses our human need for stories. Although some interest in fiction and the Romantic poetic image was apparent in nineteenth-century architectural theory (for example, in Ruskin's writings), the new technological imperatives of the industrial revolution led architectural practice to adopt the framework of positive reason. At the beginning of the century, Durand denied any link between architecture and the fine arts. It sufficed for architecture to devise an efficient solution to a practical program; spiritual questions could only be subjective. This situation was illustrated in declarations about the secondary status of ornament applied to the primary structure of a building. Subsequent discussions about architectural form were usually framed in terms of "style," a new term that differed from "character" in its emphasis on syntactic questions and that revealed a further reduction of architecture to the domain of decoration. Discussions about the expressive potential of style focused on discursive communication rather than poetics. Even art remained divided, often invoking scientific reason and transparent communication to explain developments such as realism in painting and literature, and even impressionism.

This ambivalence was the product of the imperative of participation. As I have already suggested, eighteenth-century aesthetics legitimized the autonomy of art (art for art's sake), and aesthetic experience *opposed* erotic participation. To avoid solipsism, the new artists generally emphasized discursive communication; nineteenth-century painting, for example, would aim to replicate a retinal image. The artistic imagination during the next two centuries would have to contend with the same dilemma: How could participation again be activated, given an acceptance of the immanence of visibility, the imperative of making a world increasingly more emancipated from theology? Attempts to wrestle with this problem led to a new concept of art and to new institutions to house it, such as the museum and the gallery.

While a concern with participation to secure the social relevance of art would never disappear, it was again more broadly integrated with issues of poetic expression only during the twentieth century. Painters became aware of the limitations of retinal art. Particularly after Duchamp's revolutionary oeuvre, radical questions were raised that touched the very nature, site, and location of art. Installations, performances, land art, and artifacts that don't fit the traditional categories of the old fine arts are only a few instances that emerged out of this awareness. Avant-garde artists recognized that addressing this question was a key to the cultural relevance of their work. In the case of architecture, the fact that a building was capable of *fulfilling* a practical or social function, an increasingly dominant dimension of the discipline since the Enlightenment, has been simplistically thought to address the issue of participation. After Durand declared architecture's primary utilitarian function, this question could indeed be easily dismissed. In most theoretical debates, in books and journals over two centuries, formal and functional questions have been kept separate ("art" versus "engineering" or "social planning"), and the importance of aesthetic autonomy versus social relevance has been discussed and framed in these antithetical terms. The blind spot, at the crossing, has usually been ignored, and the real issue of participation has been missed.

The poetic image in modernity

The great weakness of contemporary thought seems to me to reside in the extravagant reverence for what we know as compared to what we do not yet know.
André Breton, *Mad Love* (trans. Mary Ann Caws)

Everything in the spiritual realm, as well as the natural, is significant, reciprocal, correspondent . . . everything is hieroglyphic . . . and the poet is merely the translator, the one who deciphers.
Charles Baudelaire, *L'art romantique*

And perhaps man's real name, the emblem of his being, is Desire. For what is Heidegger's temporality or Machado's "otherness," what is man's continuous casting himself toward that which is not he himself, if not Desire? If man is a being who is not, but who is being himself, a being who never finishes himself, is he not a being of desires as much as a desire for being? In the amorous encounter, in the poetic image and in the theophany, thirst and satisfaction are joined together: we are at once fruit and mouth, in indivisible unity.
Octavio Paz, *The Bow and the Lyre* (trans. Ruth L. C. Simms)

The twentieth-century avant-garde recovered the poetic image in a more self-conscious way and extended its meanings beyond eighteenth-century aesthetics. In architecture, Adolf Loos's writings on ornament transcended the debate between "essential structure" and "contingent ornament" that had been raging throughout the nineteenth century. Loos understood that ornament for mere aesthetic appreciation was meaningless and inappropriate, but also knew that a building could not simply express its system of production. Architectural meaning and cultural relevance depended on participation. Loos was aware of architecture's capacity to touch and seduce. While traditional symbolization was out of the question, the building could still be understood as an object of desire, whose dress and spatial qualities unfold in time to suggest the presence of something that is not fully apparent. Slowly, throughout the century, architectural practices would pay more attention to surface and cladding,[53] but, more often than not, it would be merely an aesthetic applied to a functional solution.

At the same time, phenomenology radically questioned Cartesian dualism and returned to human embodiment as the ground of meaning. While much of this reflection is too technical to paraphrase here, Edmund Husserl wrote a beautifully simple page on the immobility of the earth, questioning the nature of truth in Copernican theory. In our experience the earth does not move and the universe is organized vertically. This is no illusion but a primary reality. It enables us to think and to theorize various cosmologies, from Ptolemy to Einstein. Maurice Merleau-Ponty developed Husserl's insights and recovered embodied consciousness, engaged in the world through motility and *erōs*, as the origin of meaning.[54] In his late philosophy, he even put forward the concept of "flesh" as the "first element" of reality, describing it in terms very similar to the Platonic *chōra*.[55] For Merleau-Ponty, our bodies can recognize and understand, despite our so-called scientific common sense and its Cartesian isotropic space, the wisdom embodied in a place, in a culture—its profound, untranslatable expressive qualities. This understanding is made possible particularly by works of art, capable of disclosing places that speak back to us and resonate with our dreams, opening up the space of desire that allows us to be at home, while remaining always incomplete and open to our personal death. Contrary to the assumptions behind contemporary culture, even binary spaces could not appear to resemble reality if we were not first and foremost mortal, erotic, self-conscious bodies *already* engaged with the world through orientation and gravity. According to Merleau-Ponty we don't merely "have" a body, we "are" our bodies.

Surrealism picked up threads from Romanticism and phenomenology, transforming them into a lucid poetic theory that sought to recover the original depth of *erōs* in artistic practices. In *Mad Love,* André Breton associates the beauty of art with erotic pleasure: "I confess without the slightest embarrassment my profound insensitivity in the presence of natural spectacles and those works of art which do not straight off arouse a physical sensation in me, like the feeling of a feathery wind brushing across my temples to produce a real shiver. I could never avoid establishing some relation between this sensation and that of erotic pleasure, finding only a difference of degree." Breton uses the word "convulsive" to describe "the only beauty which should concern us."[56] This experience of desire involves a gap that is temporal, spatial, or both, such as the time between the moment when navigators first sight land and the moment when they finally set foot on it.

All feeling of duration [is] abolished by the intoxicating atmosphere of *chance*—a very delicate flame highlights or perfects life's meaning as nothing else can. It is to the recreation of this particular state of mind that surrealism has always aspired, disdaining in the last analysis the prey and the shadow for what is already no longer the shadow and not yet the prey: the shadow and the prey mingled into a unique flash. . . . Independent of what happens and what does not happen, the wait itself is magnificent.[57]

For the surrealists, desire denoted forces within man that are normally repressed by reason, power, personal inhibition, and other social circumstances. Their first aim was to raise desire from instinct to full consciousness, eventually fulfilling subjective desires in objective terms. In surrealism there is no difference between delay and fulfillment; the two moments are related in fluid transition, but both should always be present. This coextension distinguishes a poetic object from a technological artifact that promises instant fulfillment. According to Breton, desire should be cultivated by developing confidence in perception, reversing the scientific understanding that characterized bodily experience as a source of delusion. Once the gaze is polarized by desire—during a walk through the city in search of love, for example—perception reveals analogies to the artist that he can use to disclose both mystery and order in the given reality. These are not concepts imposed on the objects of perception but rather appear on the surface of things. Through this operation the unconscious transcends the ego of the artist and reveals the deepest truths of the human condition. Like our dreams, the work becomes "unoriginal," yet truly eloquent and significant.

Rainer Maria Rilke, one of the greatest poets of the twentieth century, was also an authority on modern love. Rilke spoke frankly about sex and expressed its enigmatic reality, avoiding physiological and hedonistic reductions. Although it is "difficult," like many things with which humans have been charged, human sexuality is our "best possession" and must be managed through one's own personal experience, never relying on convention. In one of his many letters on love he wrote: "Physical pleasure is a sensual experience no different from pure seeing or the pure sensation with which a fine fruit fills the tongue; it is a great unending experience, a gift, a knowing of the world, the fullness and the glory of all knowing. . . . [T]he bad thing is that most people misuse and squander this experience and apply it as a stimulant at the tired spots of their lives and as distraction, instead of rallying toward exalted moments." Sex, therefore, should never be taken lightly; it is our access to a higher understanding. Rilke asks us to be more

reverent toward [its] fruitfulness, which is but *one*, whether it seems mental or physical; for intellectual creation too springs from the physical, is of one nature with it and only like a gentler, more ecstatic and more everlasting repetition of physical delight. . . . In one creative thought a thousand forgotten nights of love revive, filling it with sublimity and exaltation. And those who come together in the night and are entwined in rocking delight do an earnest work and gather sweetnesses, gather depth and strength for the song of some coming poet, who will arise to speak of ecstasies beyond telling. . . . Do not be bewildered by the surfaces; in the depths all becomes law. And those who live the secret wrong and badly, lose it only for themselves and still hand it on, like a sealed letter, without knowing it.[58]

In his introduction to *The Bow and the Lyre,* Octavio Paz brilliantly articulates the essential characteristics of a poem, whether it be made of words, paint, or stone.[59] Poetic artifacts obviously belong to a specific time and place, and thus have a style, like other utensils and human works such as philosophy and customs. Style is not an illusion. However, true poets transcend language by turning it into unrepeatable poetic acts. The poet "feeds" on styles, but while styles are born and die, poetic works endure. Indeed, a true poem is unique. As Giordano Bruno knew well, "there are as many true rules as there are true poets."[60]

It is important to note the differences between a poetic work of architecture and a mere utilitarian building, between a poem and a utensil. One difference concerns the act of creation. Though a poetic work may be created by a technique, this technique is not automatically repeatable. Thus, when an architect gradually acquires a "style," he or she risks forsaking poetry and becoming merely a constructor, regardless of how fashionable the work might be. When others imitate this style, the risk is even greater.

Paz notes that no human work escapes language. The ultimate reality of language eludes us. It is indivisible and inseparable from man. It is a condition of our existence and not an object, an organism, or a conventional system of signs that we can accept or reject (*The Bow and the Lyre,* 21). Whatever man touches is tinged with intentionality. The world of humanity tolerates ambiguity, even madness and confusion, but not lack of meaning. Despite important differences between spoken or written languages and other "plastic" or even "musical languages," they are all endowed with a communicative force. Because the poet cherishes the ambiguity of the word, poetry is closer to spoken language than to prose. While the prose writer imprisons language, the poet sets language free. Likewise, while technology uses up matter to make utensils, poetic making sets matter free. Poetic matter has color, rhythm and texture, yet it is always something else: it is *image.*[61]

A poetic work is a peculiar form of communication. Without ceasing to be language, it transcends language. A building will also be a poem if it expresses something other than its parts, its materials, its construction process, its ideology, or the identity of its owner or inhabitants. Paz notes that a characteristic of modern poetry since the nineteenth century is that it cannot be reduced to direct symbolization. Indeed, the creation of poetic architecture begins with violence to conventional ways of building, to the technological and formal "language" of architecture. Unlike the craftsman, the architect is not served by the tools used; instead he or she serves them to recover their "original" nature. In architecture, tools involve both conception and construction. This is the complex, sometimes contradictory operation that produces the poetic architectural image.

Architecture is typically conservative; a future archaeologist will have no trouble dating our artifacts, even if they are as wild as our dreams. The architect/poet wrests elements from their habitual state: lines and surfaces, walls and openings all become unique. While the imperative of cultural participation is always present, the modern poet, according to Paz, does not speak the language of the dominant technological culture. A characteristic of modernity since the early nineteenth century is that the poet cannot share the values of civilization (*The Bow and the Lyre,* 32). The poetic object of our times cannot escape articulating a critical dimension, often addressed to a particular audience of individuals or groups. Perhaps in this limitation lies its future fecundity. More optimistically, Paz also observes how poetic language, however sophisticated, seems to recover the original sense of the spoken word, a plurality of meanings. Thus, the poetic artifact seems to deny the very essence of social language: the expression of more or less univocal meanings. Indeed, poetic architecture may be polysemic and yet often invites silence, in the most eloquent of significations.

Paz argues that poetic creation emphasizes rhythm as an agent of seduction. Rhythm is the root of life and culture, and is inseparable from our human condition: "It is the simplest, most permanent, and most ancient manifestation of the decisive fact that causes us to be men: the fact that we are mortal, and always thrown toward 'something,' toward the 'other': death, God, the beloved, our fellow-men" (49). The experience of architecture is also rooted in rhythm. When Vitruvius wrote about the nature of architectural order, he invoked eurhythmy from music and the dramatic arts. Rhythmic experience is like an incantation that transforms ideal geometries into living places. Rhythm also enables linear time to dissolve into festival time, when we participate in a higher, paradoxical order. Juhani Pallasmaa has eloquently described how the architectural imagery used by film directors such as Michelangelo Antonioni and Andrei Tarkovsky evokes and maintains a full range of human emotions, usually absent from technological building.[62] Indeed, film and literature have the capacity to sculpt time, sharply revealing the importance of rhythmic modulation in the experience of a poetic architecture.

Operating as it does at the edges of language, the poetic image in architecture can be grasped only as a faint echo or evocation. It does not reside simply in a representational system, in working drawings, or in a material building. It is never possible to say definitely what it *is,* for a poetic work can never be paraphrased. In the complex process of architectural production, the poetic image may exist in diverse incarnations that are always specific to the means of representation. At its most universal, it is about the coincidence of opposites; it presents such coincidences as a *fact,* while we know that whatever coincides in this experience would be contradictory in the world of linear logic. Think, for example, of the constant presence of water in the architecture of a Tarkovsky film, or the way in which light becomes darkness in a Gothic cathedral, or in Le Corbusier's La Tourette monastery. In literature and drama, the poetic image can be a character that brings together contradictory realities, like Segismundo in Calderón de la Barca's *Life Is a Dream.* In Segismundo, sleep and waking are bound together in a mysterious, indissoluble way: "La vida es sueño, y los sueños sueños son" (quoted in *The Bow and the Lyre,* 85). While science can demonstrate that an orange held at a certain distance from our eyes appears to be the same size as the sun, only a poet can state that the crepuscular sun *is* a blood orange.[63] In La Tourette we recognize a monastery with a cloister and ambulatory, yet we experience the cloister as inaccessible and the ambulatory as a labyrinth. Ultimately, the poetic image is the key to the human condition: it enables us to grasp the sense of our mortality and experience the coincidence of life and death in a single, incandescent moment out of time. Through the rhythms of architectural experience, we can recognize the work and its elements for what they are *and* as new and unusual. The heavy is light, and yet the heavy is also heavy.

A poetic work proclaims the dynamic and necessary coexistence of opposites, and also their ultimate identity. This was Baudelaire's discovery, also taken up by surrealism. Parmenides' original distinction of Being and nonbeing eventually allowed for the "occultation of Being," in Heidegger's terms. Building on this distinction, Western philosophy and science followed a quest for truth as "clear and distinct ideas." The poetic image in mysticism and poetry, operating in the seemingly contradictory space of *erōs,* did not suffer the characteristically Western horror of what at the same time is and is not. Eastern philosophies, including Hinduism and Buddhism, have taken the opposite path and affirmed that opposites are relative. In Taoism, "There is nothing that is not this; there is nothing that is not that. . . . Life is life in relation to death. And vice versa. Affirmation is affirmation in relation to negation. And vice versa. Therefore the true sage rejects the this and the that and takes refuge in the Tao."[64] Eastern sages say that to think is to breathe; they know that holding one's breath stops the circulation of the ideas. This void enables being to appear. To think is to breathe because thought and life are not separate vessels. As Paz eloquently states, the ultimate identity between man and the world, consciousness and being, being and existence is man's most ancient belief and the root of science and religion, magic and poetry (89). Though cultures seek to close these distances through either technology or meditation, Western poetry attempts to preserve the distance while affirming the identity of opposites. In Eastern philosophy there is a point at which lead and feathers fuse, but the challenge for the Western poet/architect is to proclaim *both* identity *and* difference.

Eastern philosophies speak of difference as being only a truth in the relative world, while identity is a truth in the absolute world. As inheritors of the Western project, we don't have the luxury of this distinction. The Western poetic strategy preserves the imagining self as the irreducible ethical agent and celebrates the *delay* that is life. But we can learn from the Eastern project that words can be used to express the inexpressible: not through discourse but through the poetic utterance, as in the aphorisms of Tao and the haiku verses of Zen Buddhism. Language can return to the silent place where names are superfluous, to the realm of architecture.

To convey a moment of insight, a prose writer describes it. A poet, in contrast, evokes an experience, with all its contradictory qualities. Similarly, the architect uses rhythm, light and shadow, to re-create our first encounter with depth, the wondrous place of human dwelling that cannot be conveyed through descriptive geometry, a photograph, or an illusionistic reproduction. The experience is always surprising, like a clearing in the forest that we identify with a place in our dreams. The image is never reducible to the object that contains it and that we recognize as belonging to a culture or typology. The image explains itself (*The Bow and the Lyre*, 94). It cannot be paraphrased; nothing except it can say what it tries to say.

The experience of the poetic, like sexuality, jolts us and can change our life. Just as every love is a self-revelation through absolute alienation, so participation in a poetic event brings together absence and presence, silence and word, emptiness and plenitude. Unlike conventional religions and contemporary technological artifacts, however, modern poetic works do not conceal or take away our death. They disclose our original and permanent condition, they affirm our constitutive *lack* of being. Architecture, through its engagement with life-enhancing programs and its use of image and rhythm, can also affirm the strange and the uncanny. The image/ rhythm of architecture can propose, like sexual experience, a glimpse of the indissoluble unity of opposites—life and death, the ephemeral *and* lasting nature of culture and the human condition. Rejecting both the eternal life of religions and the absolute death of nihilistic philosophies, poetic works of architecture frame a living that implies and contains dying.

From Lequeu to Duchamp

Eroticism is a very dear subject in my life and I certainly applied that liking or that love to my Glass. And in fact I thought it was the only excuse for doing anything, to give it a life of eroticism which is completely close to life in general and more than philosophy or anything like that. And it is an animal thing that has so many facets that it's pleasing to use it like a tube of paint, so to speak, to inject in your productions. It's there stripped bare. It's a form of fantasy. It has a little to do also . . . the stripped bare probably had even a naughty connotation with Christ. You know the Christ was stripped bare, and it was a naughty form of introducing eroticism and religion.

Marcel Duchamp, from *Marcel Duchamp: Work and Life* (ed. Pontus Hultén)

The Bride does not refuse this stripping by the bachelors, even accepts it since she furnishes the love gasoline and goes so far as to help towards complete nudity by developing in sparkling fashion her intense desire for orgasm.

Marcel Duchamp, *The Green Box*, Edition Rrose Sélavy (from *Marcel Duchamp: Work and Life*)

My rewriting of the *Hypnerotomachia Polyphili*, titled *Polyphilo or The Dark Forest Revisited* (1992), was a story of delay and fulfillment that celebrates our human condition, neither perpetually fulfilled nor perennially lustful, characterized as "bittersweet" by the Greek poets who invented Eros/Amor.[65] The story presents the nomadic condition of modern technological man, suspended between a fully carnal body and a homogeneous mental space, always in transit, always crossing a threshold, traveling for the sake of the trip rather than to reach a clear destination. Because the modern nomad lacks a traditional sense of place, his body is the site of meaning, a body that flies along the horizon in a technological artifact that seemingly goes nowhere and simultaneously is still able to dream about flight—a vertical body that must be reconciled with gravity. To the primary reality of embodied consciousness, architecture speaks in the medium of the erotic, as poetic image. This story is thus also a theory of architecture as poetic image, presenting alternatives to instrumental practices. On its journey through the architecture of resistance it passes through

Romanticism and surrealism, gathering artifacts at all scales and in various media that are normally not included in typologies of architecture. Since the eighteenth century the traditional divisions among the fine arts have been subverted, with the result that many poetic works that are significant for architecture are not full-scale buildings. *Polyphilo* visits some of these works and evokes their ephemeral truths to the man in transit. The works of Jean-Jacques Lequeu and Marcel Duchamp are prominent among them.

Indeed, a link between Lequeu and Duchamp has been traced by Philippe Duboy in his speculative critical commentary on Lequeu's manuscripts.[66] Early in his life Duchamp worked at the Bibliothèque Nationale in Paris, where he probably became familiar with Lequeu's drawings and writings. Lequeu was born in Rouen in 1757, the son of a cabinetmaker. He worked as a draftsman during the day, and at night created a spectacular, hallucinogenic collection of projects and drawings that he later donated to the Bibliothèque. In his work and in his life, Lequeu cultivated erotic distance. He was a cross-dresser, with a feminine alter ego, and lived on the top floor of a brothel. Like Piranesi, he looked at history as a collection of meaningful fragments that could lead to imaginative innovation. In his projects he associated ornament with dress and emphasized the craft of drawing.

Lequeu's architecture sought to recover a space of participation for a culture that, during the Revolution, was about to give it up. For him, the origin of architecture was not a hut or a shelter but the theater, which he associated etymologically with *theōrein*—implying the gap of theory and contemplation, which is related to the clearing in the forest and the grove. Architecture was thus the space of appearance, a public space that he associated with the gap of erotic seduction. Recognizing the limits of ancien régime politics, he devised highly imaginative erotic rituals for his architecture: a submerged Indian cabinet of delights, surrounded by a pool and lazy fish; a barn in the form of a cow; temples of love inspired by the *Hypnerotomachia* and analogous to lewd figures; an anthropomorphic gateway, always humid, sited in the Elysian fields; a collage house at Bellevue as a place of encounter for voyeuristic activities. Although coordinated sets of plans, sections, and elevations would become the norm at the Ecole Polytechnique and the Ecole des Beaux-Arts, he drew almost exclusively in elevation, rarely in plan and never in perspective. For him, poetic meaning was concentrated in the "face" of architecture, dressed and "made up" for seduction. Erotic depth, enabling public participation, resided in the vertical profile. He used the latest techniques of descriptive geometry and shadow projection, but he transformed them into ironic mechanisms and imaginative readings of the architectural tradition. He also added writing to the drawings, describing operations and materials with great precision, from the mixing of pigment to the composition of the earth. This ironic set of "specifications" celebrated not clarity but rather the unsayable: a coincidence of opposites.

As for Duchamp, it would obviously be impossible to do justice here to the richness of his artistic contributions. Among many other accomplishments, he introduced into mainstream artistic discourse the topics that obsessed Lequeu. Duchamp proclaimed the end of "retinal" art, by which he meant the aesthetic paradigm of the eighteenth century. He believed that participation in art is essential to re-create the work's poetic meaning. To this end, he acknowledged the split between appearance and apparition that marks modern consciousness. Yet unlike Descartes, who rejected anamorphosis as delusion, he used the technique (for example, in his painting *Tu'm*) as a device to engage the spectator and express a delay between appearance and apparition.

Commenting on the rigorous unity of Duchamp's work, Octavio Paz writes:

Everything he did revolves around a single object, as elusive as life itself[;] . . . his life's work can be seen as different moments—the different appearances—of the same reality. Anamorphosis in the literal meaning of the word: to see this work in its successive forms is to return to the original form, the true source of appearances. An attempt at revelation, or, as he used to say, "ultrarapid exposure." He was fascinated by a four-dimensional object and the shadows it throws, those shadows we call realities. The object is an Idea, but the Idea is resolved at last into a naked girl: a presence.[67]

Eroticism is the central issue in Duchamp's work. In his "ready-made" objects, for example, there is a deliberate disruption of fulfillment. Ordinary objects reveal their surprising, poetic potential. Duchamp was also a poet, and his singular use of language reveals the ambiguity of clarity. In his two major works, the *Large Glass* and *Etant Donnés,* the space of participation is activated through *erōs.* The *Large Glass* transforms the mechanical metaphor that underscores the modern world into a "celibate machine." "The Bride Stripped Bare by Her Bachelors, Even" discloses the supreme analogy of all that is, revealing the presence of the ineffable through the conceptual order of perspective geometry. In *Etant Donnés* the bride— naked on a bed of twigs, behind a heavy Spanish door—comes to inhabit a figural space. The space between the observer peeping through the door and the reclining girl exposing her pubes is tense and unbridgeable and yet, as Octavio Paz has pointed out, it is a space of participation. *Delay* enabled Duchamp to transform our visual mechanisms, framed within the perspectival tradition, into a new source of meaning, into a vehicle for the poetic image.

Frederick Kiesler's endless architecture

The coming of the Endless House is inevitable in a world coming to an end. It is the last refuge of man for man.

Friedrich Kiesler, *Inside the Endless House*

I quote an old Chinese poem
of Su Tung-p'o:
He who judges pictures by the likeness of shapes,
Must be thought of as a child;
He who hammers out a verse by rule,
Shows that he is not yet a poet.
Poetry and painting are rooted
in the same law,
The work of heaven and of the first cause.

Kiesler, *Inside the Endless House*

While living in New York, Duchamp became a close friend of the architect Frederick Kiesler. Kiesler was unique among twentieth-century architects for his explicit participation in the surrealist program, particularly after 1942. He wrote about Duchamp's *Large Glass* in architectural terms, emphasizing the connections between artistic and architectural "constructions." In the late 1940s he worked on the surrealist magazine *VVV* and designed a number of exhibitions and stage sets for the group. In his collaborations with Duchamp, he created optical devices to exhibit the artist's work and heighten erotic desire. In 1950 he built the first model of his Endless House, a project that would incorporate the insights of surrealism into architectural work.

Throughout his life Kiesler was involved in many projects for the theater, and he became best known as the architect of the poignant Shrine of the Book in Jerusalem, the repository for the Dead Sea Scrolls. His extraordinary theoretical project for "endless" human space, however, has been often misunderstood. Kiesler appreciated the surrealist critique of technology's dehumanizing dimension, associating the misuse of technology with banal gridlike architecture. Yet he sought to use technology to create a poetic dwelling by "correlating" art and science. Formally, his Endless House proposed perforated egg-shaped shells with uninterrupted flowing spaces and walls that transformed into ceilings and floors. Kiesler regarded these flows as a critique of the banal division of space into cubicles, "growing into tumors of skyscrapers."[68]

Despite this polemic, which has tempted contemporary critics to read his work as precedent for computer-generated "blobs," Kiesler's main concern was not stylistic innovation. His aim was to make a human dwelling that would be responsive to dreams, acknowledging both a given, if remote, natural world and our capacity to "build" a cosmos. For Kiesler, architecture must be driven by an ethical imperative, not merely a formal one: "Which of us architects dares to assume not the aesthetic but the full moral responsibility of a building?" he asked rhetorically.[69] Form does not follow function, he wrote; rather, it follows vision and should seek a reconciliation between dream and reality. In itself, form is therefore "weak"; its space of interiority is wholly familiar, despite the presence of unfamiliar shapes. His house symbolized human dwelling in the widest sense, and its light and perceived dimensionality were intended to complement the inhabitant's psychic states. Kiesler imagined space as actually fluctuating, animated by change, imbued with temporality. His ultimate aim was to induce a heightened state of awareness to correlate the present and eternity. Indeed, Kiesler's often baffling "theory of correalism," which tries to reconcile disparate aspects of art, science, and the practice of architecture, is in essence a theory of the poetic image. In his diary he wrote that cathedrals and pagodas used "an architecture dedicated to death" to "pacify the unknown gods," but a reconciliatory architecture dedicated to life had never been proposed. In this Nietzschean spirit, the Endless House is a first attempt; both ironic and analogical, "it brings the sky down and the earth up."[70]

Daniel Libeskind's Jewish Museum

The breath of a house is the sound of voices within.
The house gains immortality when it becomes only a thought that ceases to exist.
When a woman smiles in a house, Death tries to imitate her.

John Hejduk, "Sentences on the House and Other Sentences"

In contrast to the self-sufficing act of building, architecture reveals the contours of an idea which goes beyond concrete forms. . . . There are hardly any buildings, with the exception of the *Carceri d'Invenzione* by Piranesi, which bear this double burden of representing both actual buildings and mental structures.

Kurt W. Forster, "'Mildew Green Is the House of Forgetting'" (on Daniel Libeskind's Jewish Museum)

Daniel Libeskind's first major building, the Jewish extension to the Berlin Museum, is perhaps the most accomplished recent work in the poetic tradition of his teacher John Hejduk, Le Corbusier's La Tourette, and Kiesler's Endless House. Much has been said about the unquestionable originality of this building. In this context, I invoke it as an important example to conclude my discussion of the poetic image in the Western architectural tradition.

Like Piranesi's *Carceri,* Libeskind's early drawings and projects (the *Micromegas* series, for instance) always denied expectations of objective space and shelter. A mysterious depth in these projects tested the limits of architecture and challenged the very possibility of poetic building in a world of "educational technicians and monetary utopias."[71] In his own words, these drawings explore the relation between the intuition of geometry as a grammar of the visible world, "as it manifests itself in a preobjective sphere of experience," and the formalization of geometry, "which tries to overtake it in the objective realm."[72] In the Jewish Museum, Libeskind takes up his own challenge in the world of economics and politics. He manages both to represent the inconceivable destruction of Jews in Europe during the Second World War and to construct an experience of hope and possibility for all, transcending ethnic specificity and resentment. Both finite, like our own lives, and endless as it unfolds in our experience, the museum is "difficult" as a place to take refuge and yet profoundly spiritual in the rewards it offers those who see *through* the anger and brutality of its fragmentation. After exiting one of the subterranean arms, one encounters the "Promised Land," a garden in honor of E. T. A. Hoffmann; but it too delays fulfillment as we experience not a lush paradise but an uncanny emptiness: a void that simultaneously resonates with the emptiness left by the Holocaust victims and is a playful figure of hope.

Libeskind's work, like that of his illustrious predecessors, is always much more than material form: it is the product of an ethos to ameliorate the human spirit. Libeskind writes: "Some sage said a long time ago that every day one should reach a higher spiritual level. If you do not, you are not really doing anything worthwhile. So everyone has to ask himself at night: have I reached a higher spiritual level today? If the answer is no, you are really in trouble. . . . One has to work not only in architecture, not only on objects, but also correspondingly always on oneself, to cope with things. Making it better means also to improve oneself spiritually."[73]

A similar ethical interest is present in Libeskind's (unbuilt) competition project for the Sachsenhausen concentration camp site. Most projects faced with this program would either erase the past or memorialize it, but his architecture discloses and remembers while instilling a sense of hope, growth, and healing. This reconciliation is crucial for humanity and can be accomplished only through poetry. Thus, for Libeskind, the city of the future is based on universal hope. This is a city driven by possibilities, yet checked by the gravity of history. It is a city of imagination, not logic; a city of desire, not fulfillment.

These projects by Daniel Libeskind cannot be reduced to categories such as style and fashion. Their poetic content is not reproducible in other similarly "deconstructed" architecture. They question the inherent tendency of buildings to become idols, representing a single meaning or ideology. Instead, they embody the significance of the human project *through* architecture, like icons revealing not the face or the gaze of a god, but the blind spot in our retina that nevertheless allows us to see and open ourselves to the gift of being human.

The poetic image in the contemporary world

Our world of great technological accomplishments, of inexhaustible pornography and seductive publicity, seems to have little use for the personal imagination. Great pleasure appears to issue from the instrumental applications of binary logic, always seemingly innovative, while personal knowledge and wisdom appear insignificant compared to the storage capacity of our supercomputers. The imagining self is often shamed by its inherent "limits," accused of bias or misjudgment. This capacity of technological plenitude to annihilate our humanity and blunt our sense of ethics is perhaps the greatest danger in our culture of hedonism.

In a passage expounding the role of *erōs mythoplokos* (the weaver of fictions), Anne Carson evokes a city where there is no desire.[74] In such a place, the inhabitants might continue to eat and procreate in a mechanical way, but life would be flat, truly "superficial" as if lacking a whole dimension. No promises would be uttered, no gifts given, and few would think to shun pain. The dead would be discarded and forgotten. Even fervent dreams would be ignored, and fiction would appear to be false. Seduction and beauty would become a perpetual game, yet lose their meaning. People could imagine only what they already knew. In a city with no imagination, architecture would be totally absent; only shelter would remain.

Such a place is so alien to human experience that it is actually very difficult to describe. Perhaps it is all a question of degree, and, as Jean Baudrillard might argue, a fair portion of depth in human desire has already been lost.[75] Although modern architects are generally uninterested in poetry, I would contend that the tradition is not be dead, only ailing. The challenge is to find ways to bring it forward. Despite the frightening power of modern planning to obliterate the past and create nightmarish environments, history is layered like a palimpsest in our cities, providing a vast store of enticing memories embedded in matter. The perennial questions still have to be answered by every generation in its present world, though; historical answers are only partial. Plato noted that "Eros makes of every man a poet" (*Symposium* 196e), a truth equally valid today. The fact remains, however, that for the moderns fulfillment takes precedence over *erōs,* the architect tends to oblige, and this impoverishes our lives.

I have suggested that a contemporary poetic architecture is possible and rests on a rich tradition. Activated through the poetic image, *erōs* reveals both our limits and our wholeness, the *sense* of being human. While in different historical times it may have had specific symbolic meanings, architecture fundamentally communicates not a particular meaning but rather the possibility of *recognizing* ourselves as complete, in order to dwell poetically on earth and thus be wholly human. Operating beyond discursive language, the poetic image can make us whole by offering an order that is often surprising and never obvious. The unity it offers is never *fully* attainable, like a classical problem of composition: in experience it unfolds and breaks up, as does life itself in its erotic essence. The poetic image overrides reality, like the "person" we fall in love with, which is both more real in its detail than in objective incarnation and also vastly less objective than what may be grasped by a "rational" gaze. The poetic image is not a copy; it augments reality. It is not a picture that we can paraphrase, yet it is given to our experience through the privileged senses of sight and hearing. Sight and hearing, however, are part of a synaesthetic complex given to embodied consciousness, rather than independent senses coming together at a point of association in the mind. This is a crucial difference. The poetic image does not *exist* but *is,* and in this sense it is also *nothing.* It subverts, upsets, and completes our selves; it appears and is always evanescent: it becomes memory *and* promise.

Let me emphasize: this *recognition* that poetic architecture makes possible is not one of semantic equivalence; rather it occurs in experience, and as in a poem, its "meaning" is inseparable from the experience of the poem itself. It is embedded in culture, it is playful by definition, and it is always circumstantial. These artifacts, *thaumata,* convey wonder, a form of beauty grounded in *erōs* (*Venus-tas*). The modern world challenged this concept. Magic was overcome by technology and rituals were sacrificed to democracy in the early nineteenth century. Nevertheless, Romanticism

and surrealism found a way to preserve the poetic image and its epistemological value. The poetic image became deliberately void of specific reference; it signified "nothing" in its quest to preserve its original truth.
Even though the utilitarian dimension of architecture may be co-opted by
political or technological power, the capacity of architecture to touch and
transform through its erotic power remains. Through the poetic image we
recover the spiritual dimension of the world, appearing not beyond but on
the surface of things, never imposed by theology. The miraculous eloquence of the poetic object invites a recollection of being and an opening
of vision through light and rhythm. These are the qualities that we find in
artifacts as diverse as Le Corbusier's La Tourette, the Catholic and Protestant architecture of Antoni Gaudí and Sigurd Lewerentz respectively, the
minimalist architectural objects of Juhani Pallasmaa, the books of John
Hejduk, and the luminous spaces of Steven Holl. The significance of these
works has *nothing* to do with style, and yet they have something in common that is worth exploring further.

What differentiates architecture from other forms of *ars* or *poiēsis*
concerns its intertwining with life itself in the form of significant action,
ranging from the founding of cities and waging of war to religion and politics. Thus architecture offers societies a place for existential orientation.
As representation of meaningful action, it contributes to an understanding of one's place in the world. Through its sense of decorum it opens up
a clearing for the individual's experience of purpose through participation
in cultural institutions. In addition, *modern* architecture *plays* with power,
setting forth programs for a better human life. It is radical orientation in
experience, beyond words. So, while its theory may be rooted in mythic or
poetic stories, philosophy, theology, or *scientia* during different times of its
history, architecture is none of these but an *event*: it is ephemeral, yet it has
the power to change one's life in the present, like magic or an erotic encounter. Thus, it can be said to embody knowledge, but it always offers
more than merely information; it is knowledge of the world and its sensuous materiality understood by the body: a carnal, fully sexual, and therefore opaque experience of truth. For this reason, its "meaning" can never
be objectified or reduced to functions, ideological programs, formal or
stylistic formulas. Likewise, its technical medium is open rather than specific (as are, say, building typologies); it includes all artifacts from diverse
media that make possible human dwelling and that by definition stand "at
the limits of language," establishing the boundaries of human cultures
within which other more properly linguistic forms of expression may take
place. Poetic architecture is the product of a *praxis* grounded not in vague

intuitions or a soft heart but in the rigor of process work and a modality of linguistic understanding: in a practical philosophy or *phronēsis—prudentia,* in Latin—evoking wisdom and soundness of judgment.

The nature of this wisdom that seeks not the exactness of numbers but an intuitive measure and moderation—proving itself in the concrete situation; standing within a living network of common convictions, habits, and values—will be a central topic of discussion in the following pages. Practical wisdom, a mode of rationality that is not reducible to theories or methods, is the capacity to *interpret* a situation and, once a personal understanding is reached, to propose appropriate answers that are adequate to such a situation. These answers cannot be had from a general orientation about good and evil in the same way as instructions are given for the use of a tool. Reaching an appropriate understanding happens in dialogue, through a profound comprehension of history and culture, and never simply through the application of specialized techniques. Only work grounded in such practical philosophy is capable of contributing effectively to cultural communication, becoming authentic innovation rather than mere fashionable novelty.

Interlude: *Erōs, Philia,* and *Agapē*

Erōs and recognition

[Some] people say that lovers are seeking for their other half; but I say that they are seeking neither for the half of themselves, nor for the whole, unless the half or the whole is also the good.

Plato, *Symposium* 205d–e (trans. Benjamin Jowett)

In Plato's dialogues on love, *Phaedrus* and *Symposium,* we find another powerful reason to cultivate the space of desire. Illuminated by beauty, this space enables humans to contemplate ethical aims emerging from their own experience, not from an externally imposed morality. For Plato, ethics and poetics are not antithetical, as is often emphasized by postmodern critical discourses. Modern interpreters of Plato, such as Hans-Georg Gadamer, John Brentlinger, and L. A. Kosman, argue that the contemporary misunderstanding is born in great measure from a historical shortsightedness.[1] The Socratic formulation provides important insights for architecture. If Socrates is right, the poetic and communicative dimensions of architecture are not at odds with each other. Architecture can embody a poetic image and function as communicative practice in the service of a community and as steward of nature. Socrates suggests that ethics is impossible apart from a concern with beauty.

The quotation opening this chapter is Diotima's answer to the story of the *symbolon,* introduced by Aristophanes in *Symposium.*[2] The tale, recounted by Plato in different places, accounted for the origin of desire in the human condition through the division of a whole into two parts. Aristophanes vividly describes the lovers' feelings. In the best case, when a lover meets his other half, "the actual half of himself, whether he be a lover of boys or a lover of another sort, the pair are lost in an amazement of love and friendship and intimacy" (192b–c). These lovers spend their lives together, yet "they could not explain what they desire from each other. No one could plausibly think that it is just sexual relations that makes them enjoy each other's company with such intensity; rather, the soul of each manifests a desire for something else, but what that is it is unable to say, and gives only obscure, oracular pronouncements of its wishes, and makes riddles" (192c–d).

Aristophanes imagines that Hephaistos, the divine master craftsman, could weld the happy pair together as they rest side by side, maybe even for eternity. No lover would be satisfied with this proposition, yet we all recognize in this "meeting and melting" our longtime yearning. The reason, states Aristophanes, is that the human constitution was originally one and "we were a whole, and the desire and pursuit of the whole is called love" (192e). God divided humans because of the wickedness of humanity, and ever since we became like half a token, the asymmetrical pieces of a broken knucklebone. "Each one of us is but a *symbolon* (half a knucklebone, half a sphere), forever pursuing our other half" (191d). *Symbola* were used as identity tokens for newborn children, or to identify a friend returning from many years abroad on whose necklace hangs the piece that completes the half kept by another. Aristophanes concludes that desire is directed toward our true being: *erōs* restores us to our native selves, to our true, good, and beautiful nature. Love recognizes the beauty of another and thereby calls forth the other's true virtue. At this moment *erōs* unfolds as affection and caring; it valorizes the other and has the potential to become "agapic" love.

Diotima's story does not answer all of Socrates' questions. He insists: Why is love of the beautiful? What would man gain by possessing the beautiful in some measure? It suffices to substitute "the good" for "the beautiful" to understand that what might be gained is happiness, answers Diotima. Indeed, adding a new dimension to Aristophanes' rendition, Diotima suggests that Eros does not move only horizontally, seeking merely the human "other half"; rather he aims toward the sky, redirecting the lover and beloved upward, in the direction of their true home. The lover contemplates beauty in the eyes of the beloved. On the physical level, love is "the love of generation and birth in beauty" (206e). The love between two beings consists in engendering a third. This is the most beautiful love, an essential impulse toward immortality, celebrated during "that instant that makes life worth living." Homosexual love finds its legitimacy only when transposed to the spiritual plane.[3] Through the experience of singular *beauty*, the splendor of light in the beloved's eyes, the lover experiences the multiplicity of beauty and realizes the limitations of loving the singular.

Eventually men come to appreciate and love all that participates in the Beautiful, the common good. The soul ascends and eventually reconnects with its essence in unity, a truly erotic experience of absolute, unchanging Beauty (210–211). *Erōs* is creative and affirmative, yet it reveals our personal dissolution.

In *Phaedrus,* Plato argues that beauty is a form of deeply shared cultural experience. Beauty, shining "in company with the celestial forms," comes to earth to be found through sight, "the most piercing of our bodily senses" (250d). Of course, there is a danger that in contemplating worldly beauty the soul may give itself over to brutish pleasure (250e). Once initiated, however, the soul will recognize in the face of the beloved the luminosity of something other. The experience of beauty is a vehicle for the soul to ascend toward truth. For Socrates, wings have natural roots in every human soul, and the beauty embodied in another person, in works of art, and in a coherent theory incites them to grow back. When we look upon beauty and are seduced, we fall in love amid painful and pleasant sensations; our soul sprouts wings, signaling the beginning of what we are meant to be (249d). While the lover gazes, wishing to sacrifice to his beloved, a "shudder passes into unusual heat and perspiration; for, as he receives the effluence of beauty through the eyes, the wings moisten and he warms." The *light,* which is beauty, causes warmth that "melts" the parts of the soul that had become rigid and out of which the wings grew. "As nourishment streams upon him, the lower end of the wing swells and starts to grow from the root upward," making the whole soul winged. During this process the soul boils and overflows, like the "irritation and uneasiness in the gums at the time of cutting teeth" (251b–c).

When we enter a *now,* the thick present of love, we remember what it means to be really alive. In the presence of beauty, made evident through art, poetry, and architecture, we experience (without fully understanding) the transformation of Eros into Pteros. For Eros, declares Socrates, "in the language of the Gods" is known as Pteros, meaning "wing-growing necessity" (252b). This is a language that mortals will never fully understand. Even though falling in love entails a loss in reasoning power, Socrates insists that this experience is the true and only road to wisdom and goodness. Transformed into *pteros,* love both dislocates and reveals a higher order, a sense of being in becoming: it opens humans to truth and fairness. On a final epiphany of earthly beauty, the soul receives a "surpassing overflow" and ceases from its pain with joy. Then the process is reversed, the orifices of the wings dry up, and the soul is "pierced all around and maddened and pained, but then in turn at the recollection of the beautiful one she is again delighted" (251d–e). The divine meaning of Eros is revealed only to those that lose their bearings, seduced by the beloved or by the awe-inspiring and wondrous power of a shocking poetic image. Socrates suggests that in this area, human reason *must* defer to experience.

This is of course not a simple matter for the founder of Western philosophy. Plato recounts different versions of the *symbolon* story in his dialogues. The space that opens up between the *symbola* separates and joins, and most importantly, it allows for *recognition*. This quality also defines the nature of "symbolic" artifacts, the products of *technē-poiēsis*, the mimetic products of craftsmanship that we call art. Unlike the copies of some higher reality that Platonic reason could dismiss, "symbolic" objects had the capacity to reveal beauty and enable an understanding of the good.

Indeed, art and architecture seem to awaken powers dormant in ordinary perception, demanding a different relationship with things. This observation may well be a universal truth. Gadamer, building upon the insights of Heidegger and earlier existential phenomenology, has discussed the relevance of the beautiful in the age of science, putting forward a theory of art that recovers a space of participation after eighteenth-century aesthetics. Gadamer reads Plato insightfully and uses the story of the *symbolon* as a point of departure for his argumentation. The symbol, for Gadamer, is especially a token of remembrance. The Socratic stories show that the experience of the beautiful in art is a form of knowing, the invocation of a potentially whole (and holy) order of things, wherever it may be found. This experience is more fundamental than the specifically linguistic meanings conveyed by a work, such as a painting's story, the plot of a novel, or the political program of a building.

Regardless of its origin, beauty is truth incarnated in the human realm, it is a trace of the light of Being that mortals never contemplate directly, it is the purposefulness of nature and culture mimetically reflected by an artifact. According to Gadamer, we can be deceived in this "world below" by what only seems wise, or fooled by what merely appears to be good; but even in this world of appearances all beauty is true beauty, because it is in the nature of beauty to appear. Beauty exemplifies, in Karl Jaspers's terms, reason incarnate in existence. Furthermore, beauty transcends the aporia of necessity and superfluity; it is both necessary for reproduction and crucial for our spiritual well-being. As Socrates noted, all these features make the beautiful distinct among ideas.

This reading of Plato by phenomenological hermeneutics seems easy to challenge in our epoch of cultural relativism. Indeed, it is not difficult to imagine taste as a subjective and ultimately relative matter, as a set of local, historically determined norms. This concept was itself historically determined in early modernity by the consecration of mathematical reason as the only legitimate instrument of knowledge. Late-twentieth-century philosophy has fundamentally questioned that belief. Once we move beyond eighteenth-century philosophical aesthetics, defined by the extrapolation of "truth as correspondence" from the natural sciences, taste must take its place among other forms of *phronēsis.* Aristotle used that term to denote a form of knowledge distinct from philosophy and science, a "practical wisdom" articulated in everyday language and based on the habits and values that we share with others. This is the discourse that frames ethical action, since it discloses values with utmost clarity and certainty. According to Gadamer and George Steiner, it is the rightful context of taste. There exists a tradition of poetic artifacts and stories valorized by our manifold cultures. Such self-evidence is no subjective fabrication. Its presence can become the basis of judgments that are no less rational for being grounded in *phronēsis.* Works of art and poetry are not only capable of moving and transforming us; they ground our existence through cultural identity. In this sense, aesthetics is indeed the mother of ethics.

Elaine Scarry shares many of these views on the relevance of beauty for ethics. In a remarkable recent book, *On Beauty and Being Just,* she emphasizes the connections between our experience of beauty, truth, and justice. To be *fair* means to be just and to be beautiful. This double meaning is significant at many levels. In the absence of justice, beauty is a necessary point of departure for critical action.[4] It is not that a poem or a painting may be "true" or just, but that the perfect adjustment of form recalls equality and "ignites the desire for truth by giving us with an electric brightness shared by almost no other uninvited, freely arriving perceptual event, the experience of conviction and the experience as well, of error." While its liability to error and plurality has given beauty a bad name, particularly in the wake of eighteenth-century aesthetics, the fact is that "our very aspiration for truth is its legacy. [Beauty] creates, without itself fulfilling, the aspiration of enduring certitude. It comes to us, with no work of our own; then leaves us prepared to undergo a giant labor."[5]

In experiencing beauty, Scarry argues, we have access to something that is sacred, is unprecedented, and has the capacity of saving one's life, whether it is manifest in artifacts or we experience it in nature.[6] Though destabilizing, the experience of beauty also invites deliberation. "Something beautiful fills the mind yet invites the search for something beyond itself"—something larger than or equal to it, with which it needs to be related. Even though today the claim to immortality may be gone, beauty retains its plenitude and inclusion. The metaphysical realm may have vanished, yet the beautiful girl, the small bird, or the sky, outside my window or in a painting by Matisse, still carry greetings from other worlds.[7]

Martin Heidegger writes that artistic meaning, in its most fundamental sense, rests on an intricate interplay of showing and concealing; it is the embodiment of truth as *alētheia*.[8] The work of architecture is no mere bearer of meaning, as if the meaning could be transferred to another bearer. Instead, the meaning of the work lies in the fact that it is there. Above all, Gadamer emphasizes, authentic artistic creation is not something that we can easily imagine being made deliberately by someone. In a profound sense, it belongs to the world. Its experience overwhelms us. Rather than simply meaning "something," art and architecture enable meaning to present itself. We recognize the meaning as new, as something unprecedented that is hard to name; we are invited to silence and yet must proclaim that what we witness is utterly familiar. Thus art and architecture, as cultural forms of representation, present something that can exist only in specific embodiments. This representative power is not reducible to replacement, substitution, or copy, nor is it linked to an ultimate meaning that could be recuperated intellectually. It distinguishes the work of art and architecture from other technical achievements. The work of architecture preserves its meaning within itself. It is not an allegory in the sense that it says one thing and gives us to understand something else. What the work has to say can be found only within itself, grounded in language and yet beyond it: this is the original sense of *mimēsis,* which explicitly has nothing to do with referencing an original as something other than itself, but means that something meaningful is there in itself.[9]

The confluence of ethics and poetics evoked by Gadamer is inconceivable if one disregards the primary evidence of beauty embodied in artistic artifacts throughout history. Modern reason can easily reduce artifacts to the category of homogeneous material traces. The erotic space involved in artistic *recognition* always refers to the primary gap between two speaking human beings. In contrast with Jacques Derrida's understanding of "writing" as an all-encompassing category, hermeneutics places wisdom and knowledge in a dialogical space, ranging from self-knowledge (I can only know myself through the Other) to textual interpretation. Dialogical space, the place of rhetoric, is at odds with the deferral/spacing evoked by Derrida. Erotic space and time cannot be reduced to a nonexisting *punc-*

tum between the past and the future: it has a thickness; it is the paradoxical chiasm articulated by Merleau-Ponty in his late writings, and by some recent commentators on his work in distinction to Derrida's *différance.*[10]

Socrates also criticized writing. He reminds Phaedrus that one would have to be very silly indeed to suppose it is possible to bequeath one's knowledge to posterity in the form of writing, "or to accept such an inheritance in the hope that the written word would give anything intelligible or certain, or to believe that writing can be anything more than a reminder to a person who already knows the subject" (*Phaedrus* 275c). Anne Carson adds that an erotic current seems to leap from the written page; the reader and the writer are like the two sides of a Platonic knucklebone, but neither achieves consummation.[11] The words we read and write never say exactly what we mean. Indeed, in language there is never a perfect match between what we say, read, or write and what we mean. Insofar as erotic space is in between, the two *symbola* never join seamlessly.

Texts and artifacts convey their meaning in a dialogical mode, as speech, thereby enabling them to reveal poetic truths rather than merely logical or mathematical propositions. Reliance on that mode is also the wager of modern hermeneutics as opposed to deconstruction. There never was and never will be a perfect match. The quest for such a match is a trap for written communication that has become a modern obsession. Architecture as a physical presence enduring through time may be understood as a form of writing under similar terms: the erotic space of architecture cannot be reduced to an issue of communication, yet it is *also* an issue of communication.

Our perception of both beauty and meaning are a function of the imagination, and the latter is inextricably linked with *erōs.* Erotic passion is impossible without imagination. The imagination, furthermore, is also crucial for ethical action. Richard Kearney, among other philosophers in the hermeneutic tradition, has addressed this question. Contrary to the belief in an irreconcilable contradiction between ethics (associated with democracy, rationality, and consensus) and the poetic imagination, Kearney convincingly shows that the lack of imagination may be at the root of our worse moral failures.[12] *Imagination is precisely our capacity for love and compassion, for both "recognizing"* (erōs) *and "valorizing"* (agapē) *the other, for understanding the other as myself* (philia), *over and above differences of culture and belief.* Imagination is both our capacity for truly free play and our faculty to make stories that partake of the language and vision of others.

Philia, ethics, and communion

Only the friendship (*philia*) of those who are good, and similar in their goodness, is perfect. For these people each alike wish good for the other . . . and they are good in themselves. And it is those who desire the good of their friends for their friends' sake that are most truly friends, because each loves the other for what he is, and not for any incidental quality. . . . That such friendships are rare is natural, because men of this kind are few. And in addition they [i.e., the friendships] need time and intimacy. . . . The wish for friendship develops rapidly, but friendship does not.

Aristotle, *Nichomachean Ethics* 1156b (trans. J. A. K. Thompson)

While *erōs* thrives on distance, *philia*—the term Aristotle uses for brotherly love—is all about solidarity: friendship and communion. It presumes the *intelligibility* of language in the form of oral speech. Since the emergence of the Greek *polis* and its institutions, architecture has framed *philia* and contributed to human solidarity at all levels. By drawing from its local traditions, it provided during many centuries a recognizable clearing for communicative action.

In his *Ethics* Aristotle presupposed a stable structure of norms and rituals; our situation since the eighteenth-century Enlightenment has been very different. At the end of the seventeenth century, in the wake of the scientific revolution, the old cosmic order was questioned. Galilean science and the Cartesian postulate about the thinking ego ushered in a profound change that would eventually define our modern consciousness. During the eighteenth century, the human subject became the agent of historical change, autonomous from divine will, and bourgeois social mobility in society became a fact of life. The imperative of *experiment,* to prove the new truths of Galileo and Descartes, became for Vico the imperative of all significant human products for embodied *experience:* what we know is what we make, and what we make is embedded in historical fragments and language.

This new human subject became the political agent of the new democracies after the French Revolution. Michel Foucault described this new agent as a panoptic voyeur, world colonist, and engineer: the "aristocrat" of the nineteenth century who conceived nature as nothing more than resources to be exploited, commodified, and controlled. Yet, almost simultaneously, the human subject *also* emerged as the Romantic self, who depended not on the clarity of reason, as did Descartes's *ego cogitans,* but on an intimate, synaesthetic feeling of existence, as in Rousseau's *Confessions.* Since we are ambivalent individuals, described by Nietzsche as being driven by both will to power and *amor fati,* Gadamer insists that we develop a rational discourse on self-responsibility. Rather than a set of norms, this discourse is case-specific and based in history, providing narratives drawn from the communicative character of our *praxis,* seeking deep solidarity and understanding.[13] This is crucial for all humans in specialized technical endeavors, particularly for the architect as a creator of public space. *In this sense, architecture is not only poetic; it is political, ecological, and intelligible.* During the past few decades, architectural historians have emphasized how building practices are based on regional traditions, despite the universal influences of formal styles. For the contemporary practitioner this realization has become more urgent amid globalization and technological proliferation.

It is important to trace the genealogy of our modern sense of self back to early modernity and to grasp the transformations in Romantic philosophy that led to contemporary hermeneutics. As we saw in part I, the human subject has a history in the Western tradition, but not until the seventeenth century was it believed to be the origin of reality. Romantic thinkers such as Schelling, Richter, and Novalis, who built on earlier intuitions by Rousseau and the Earl of Shaftesbury, insisted that the self is *not* the ego; the self is a fully embodied consciousness that incorporates memory, reason, and imagination. Today it has become fashionable to "deconstruct" the ego for all its potential dangers. Nevertheless, doing so sometimes leads to dangerous fallacies. We cannot (and should not, for ethical reasons) give up our modern responsibility to *make* history. While it may be wrong to assume that we fully control a utopian future, it is also wrong to pretend that the world organizes itself. Human cultures are not like "self-organizing" physical models; the personal imagination with its desire for a better world is the agent of culture, despite the dangers of self-destruction associated with power. Our main orientation comes from historical evidence, which we must learn to access properly.

While understanding the self as the center of existence, Romantic thinking also grasped our solidarity with all that exists. Later in the nineteenth century, Schopenhauer would recapitulate by suggesting that solidarity is timeless. Recalling mythical existence prior to the Greek "discovery" of the self, he noted that solidarity is not merely a relation between human beings, for the same will to live is present in all living things.[14] Echoing the Romantic insights in Schelling's *Essays* (1795) as well as in ancient Eastern wisdom, he insisted that the *principium individuationis,* the primacy of the individual, is just an illusion. Rilke expressed this later with poetic force: "The inner—what is it? if not intensified sky."[15]

For Romantic thinkers such as Schlegel, orgasm is our most authentic experience of communion. It is a unique instance of the coincidence of infinity with the instant: sexual fulfillment shows that darkness and opacity can be more transparent than the light of logic. Still, we cling to the illusion that we are distinct from nature, that animals and nature are materials for our use: a "standing reserve," to use Heidegger's term. During the past two centuries one of the main ethical objectives of Western poetic production has been to reveal this continuity through the capacity of the creative self to turn inward in search of its nature. By distancing itself from dominant scientific and technological tenets, poetic production discloses the prereflective solidarity between embodied consciousness, the world, and others, one that has also been described by phenomenology. Thus, poetic artifacts develop and engage a critical dimension: to demonstrate the fallacy of the *ego cogitans* as the basis of reality, and to question the objectification and commodification of nature and human.

Philia, erōs, and *agapē*

Without engaging in the complex philosophical discussion around the three different varieties of love designated by the Greek words *philia, erōs,* and *agapē,* it is worth summarizing some arguments about their differences and similarities. Generally speaking, both *erōs* and *philia* are forms of human love that perceive value and excellence in their object of desire, while *agapē* (as used in the Christian New Testament) is essentially God's unqualified love for his creatures, regardless of their virtues. *Erōs* is acquisitive, egocentric, and at times selfish, while *agapē* is a giving love that can even sacrifice itself for the sake of the beloved. *Erōs* responds to the value of its object, while *agapē* creates value in its object by loving it. *Erōs* is frankly sexual in origin, while the origin of *agapē* is not obvious and remains unexplained in theological texts. *Erōs* is ascending, a path toward the divine. *Agapē* is descending, God's route to humans.[16]

The early Christians used *agapē* to refer to a "love feast" associated with communion and the Lord's Supper. *Agapi,* meaning "brotherhood," "affectionate regard," or "high" esteem, was translated into the Latin Bible as *caritas* and *dilectio,* defining it more narrowly as the affection that is given unconditionally to all, regardless of character or appearance. Christians sought to imitate God's charity, which was distinct from the compassion of the Greeks and other cultures that originated in sensuous experience.

Despite theological pronouncements, *the three modalities of love are never unrelated in human experience.* Indeed, the Western categories are insufficient to grasp the nature and primacy of the "erotic phenomenon." In a recent book on the phenomenology of love, Jean-Luc Marion argues that even though we always speak about love and experience it often, Western culture has actually failed to understand it, polarizing it between *erōs* and *agapē,* brutish pleasure and abstract charity, pornography and sentimentality.[17] The Western philosophical tradition has generally interpreted love as deriving from self-consciousness, as an irrational variant of clear thought. Love is lowered to the rank of doubtful and irrational passion. Marion questions this view and attempts to recover the primacy of love as the gift of being human. He claims that love does not derive from the ego and demonstrates that the opposite is true, thereby reconnecting with the Socratic tradition.

The seemingly obvious distinction between *erōs* thriving on distance and *philia* thriving on communion is already questioned in Plato's *Lysis.* Socrates tries to define the word *philos,* which can mean both "loving" and "loved," both "friendly" and "dear." He tries to unravel the question of whether the desire to love or befriend someone is ever separable from its fulfillment. His interlocutors acknowledge that all desire is a longing for what properly belongs to the desirer but has been lost (although in this case no one says how).[18] Furthermore, the "irrational" moment of "falling in love," the feeling of being overcome by the furor of *erōs,* is phenomenologically related to the "blind" valorization of the beloved associated with *agapē.* In *Phaedrus* Plato advocates moving from *erōs* to a love for all people, similar to *caritas,* and this notion appears in many other treatises on the subject, from Boethius to Dante. While the vocabularies and theological premises may differ, the ethical direction is clear. In the words of Elaine Scarry, beauty is distributional: "the fact that something [or someone] is perceived as beautiful is bound up with an urge to protect it, or to act on its behalf, in a way that appears to be tied up with the perception of its lifelikeness."[19]

The philosopher José Ortega y Gasset and the poet Rainer Maria Rilke both insist that human love is not so much "acquisition" as a "gravitation" toward the other, a gift rather than expectation. While Ortega tried to differentiate love from sexual desire, Rilke always stressed the sexual origin of human love.[20] For Rilke, however, accomplished love is never mere possession; it is the respect of the beloved's "solitude" that entails a measure of "detachment."

Philia, as it appears in Aristotle's *Nicomachean Ethics,* is at its best the fullest expression of human love. Like *erōs, philia* accounts fully for the experience of perception pregnant with values, yet it understands it as a gift, with the view to acknowledge and contribute to the order of civil society. With the help of time, erotic love invites friendship; *philia* celebrates the communicative capacity of oral speech as the vehicle for assent and communion.

Indeed, *philia* partakes of *erōs* and *agapē,* and it is particularly significant in a world where human fabrication has taken precedence over cosmic order. For Aristotle, *philia* is the solidarity that keeps the *polis* together as a political entity. A person, according to Aristotle, is a *zōon politikon,* a being whose proper habitat is the *polis* and who seeks harmony and equilibrium through *philia. Philia* also presides over the truest form of justice: a friendly arbitration through discursive speech rather than an application of law. Like *erōs* it may originate with seduction, but it seeks ideal friendship to preserve the common good. *Philia* can thus be defined as "social sympathy"; without friends, notes Aristotle, no one would choose to live. *Philia* is more about loving than being loved. Nevertheless, *philia* should be abandoned if the relationship becomes harmful. A friend must be helpful, but *philia* implies reciprocity and thus has limitations. Like exponents of Eastern philosophies of compassion, Aristotle affirms the imperative of self-love. This is a principle of ethical and poetic action: the *logos* of love.

"*Philos* is another self, *allos autos.*"[21] As the love that joins friends and citizens, *philia* depends on a perception of the other's virtue. *Philia* is also the unconditional love for one's family members who "are in some way the same being subsisting in separate individuals."[22] *Philia* is a love that valorizes, and *also* cements the links between a couple after sexual fireworks have died down. It is significant that *philia,* unlike *erōs,* is never directed toward things, only toward other persons.[23] Aristotle recognizes three kinds of *philia:* for utility, for pleasure, and for likeness in virtue. Though the third and perfect kind is infrequent, it may be experienced in oral communication. Although it is often asymmetrical, as in family or institutional relations, *philia* seeks the good of the other. This is the basis of the *promise.* Our ability to utter and keep promises is the basis of social relations, perhaps even the origin of humanity. Rituals are collectively sanctioned promises, and the architectural program, particularly after the eighteenth century, is a promise made by the architect to a client or to society at large. In *Rhetoric,* Aristotle defines *philia* as "wishing for someone what you believe to be good things—wishing this not for your own sake but for his—and acting so far as you can to bring them about."[24]

II *Philia*, Compassion, and the Ethical Dimension of Architecture: Program

Opening conversation

If the main task of architecture is indeed, as [Sigfried] Giedion claims, interpretation, architecture must possess the power of speech. But it is not at all obvious that—and, if so, in what sense—architecture can be said to speak. . . . [If this is its main task] architecture first has to free itself from the aesthetic approach, which also means freeing itself from an understanding of the work as fundamentally just a decorated shed. . . . Our dwelling is always a dwelling with others. The problem of architecture is therefore inevitably also the problem of community, which is only the other side of the problem of the individual. The ethical function of architecture cannot finally be divorced from the political.

Karsten Harries, *The Ethical Function of Architecture*

In its original sense, poetics refers to a way of making (*poiēsis*) in which the result preserves continuity with the conditions of its origin. In other words, what characterizes a way of making as poetic is the situatedness of the results in the communicative space of culture. The phenomenon of situatedness stands in clear contrast to instrumental thinking and to the subjective experience of aesthetics. It represents deep respect for the given reality of the natural world, manifested in the rich articulation of typical situations.

Dalibor Vesely, *Architecture in the Age of Divided Representation*

Among the Haida Indians of the Pacific Northwest, the verb for "making poetry" is the same as the verb "to breathe."

Tom Robbins, *Another Roadside Attraction*

It is clear that an *ethical fairness* which requires a "symmetry of everyone's relation" will be greatly assisted by an *aesthetic fairness* that creates in all participants a state of delight in their own lateralness [or radical decentering].

Elaine Scarry, *On Beauty and Being Just*

Restoring the communicative role of architecture is a necessary step toward restoring its role as a topological and corporeal foundation of culture. . . . What the book is to literacy, architecture is to culture as a whole.

Dalibor Vesely, *Architecture in the Age of Divided Representation*

4   *Philia*, Ritual, and *Decorum*

There is an important difference between two kinds of actions, actions done by man and actions done by man in the belief that their efficacy is not human in any reducible sense, but proceeds from elsewhere. Only the second kind of action can be called [ritual].

Roger Grainger, *The Language of the Rite*

Origins

Human participation in political and religious institutions, and in the cultural and cosmic orders they represented, traditionally took place through rituals framed by the appropriate architecture. For individuals in traditional societies, such participation constituted a crucial aspect of existence. While buildings always housed the actions associated with private life, architecture was especially dedicated to the representation of significant human action, of meanings that involved the physical and spiritual well-being of society at large. Until the end of the ancien régime in the late eighteenth century, human solidarity was generally experienced in this manner. Whether political or religious, or combining both functions after the European Middle Ages, rituals allowed for recognition of the individual's place in society and in relation to the natural world. While some religious grounds were questioned during the Enlightenment and rituals often took new forms—in Freemasonry, for instance—the experience remained important for culture at large. Hannah Arendt and Richard Sennett have pointed out that during the eighteenth century the public realm in large cities became a self-conscious theatrical space, operating as the "space of appearance."[1] Once the hierarchical structure of society and its cosmic referents were finally questioned during the nineteenth century, the public realm as the space of significant action was mostly reduced to a network of social relations. Human actions, emancipated from a divine will, were believed to "make history" and were viewed as almost exclusively responsible for our destiny. Public space was associated with consumption and voyeurism, while privacy gained the upper hand and started to be seen as the foundation of "authentic" life and personal freedom. This late-modern transformation of Western culture had important consequences for architecture, problematizing its traditional role as the representation of significant action.

In the opening paragraphs of his second book, Vitruvius describes the origins of architecture as a clearing in the forest that *makes possible* language and culture.[2] The space of architecture is suggested by necessity, by the possibility of maintaining a fire initiated by lightning during a storm. In Vitruvius's story the space of architecture *coincides* with the space of culture. A primary technique emerges with culture; the domestication of fire brings men together. They recognize the others, begin to *speak,* and eventually *build.* The pointedness of this story cannot be overemphasized. The fire is not stolen from the gods. It is a gift, a heavenly spark generated by the wind, still perceived by Vitruvius as the breath of nature, an invisible force that lights up human desire in our hearts and is responsible for our health and well-being. Appropriated by the first humans, a clearing opens up: a place for dwelling. Architecture is poetic, yet coincidental with the origins of language and culture.

Vitruvius's clearing is the space of human communication, the place where the miracle of language "happens." There is an analogy between the space of language and the space of architecture, understood as the space of communion among those that speak. *Language and architecture bound human reality.* Vitruvius's awareness reveals the manner in which architecture, as an exoteric, political construction, is intrinsic to ritual action. Rites, bound up with promises, establish bonds. Such linking is the character of human culture, of domestication and domesticity (*domus* is the Latin word for home, and also for the heavenly vault), and according to the wise fox in Saint-Exupéry's *Little Prince,* also a condition for true human knowledge. Not surprisingly, in this light, Vitruvius's account seamlessly continues to describe the first human dwellings (primitive huts) as he could imagine them. Walking not prone but upright, looking upon the magnificence of the universe and the stars, humans used their hands to construct houses in imitation of nature. The "geometrical" nature of such constructions is implicit, and further elaborated in Vitruvius's retelling of Aristippus's shipwreck. The philosopher, washed up on the shore of Rhodes, noticed that geometric diagrams had been drawn on the sand and exclaimed: "Let's hope for the best, I see human footprints."[3] Contrary to later interpretations of architectural origins, Vitruvius is not interested in naming a typological origin, be it the private home or the funerary monument. His interest is to recognize the origin of architecture as the establishment of human dwelling.

Ortega y Gasset thought it was both insightful and somewhat funny that the "essence" of the European city, of the Greek *polis* and the Roman *urbs*, was not the accumulation of private houses that grow to become villages and then cities, such as might be inferred from a quantitative planning model, but rather a "hole," in analogy to a cannon.[4] The Greek agora is both the association of citizens and the space that holds them. The agora in Sparta was called the *choros,* recalling a deep analogy between the space of political participation (through oral conversation) and the space of ritual communion (through distant participation in the theater). According to Pausanias, the reason for this attribution was that in Sparta the *gymnopaidiai,* a festival in which naked boys danced in celebration of Apollo, took place in the agora.[5]

The Greek invention of democracy was only possible because of an emerging consciousness of space as a stable (geometrical) structure, capable of holding a limited number of citizens. Prior to Anaximander's work in the sixth century B.C.E., geometry did not exist in the sense that is familiar to us. Spatiality was not grasped independently of temporality; time (and other material qualities of the environment, such as weight) was often used for spatial measurement. Anaximander introduced the first stable spatial structure into lived experience with his notion of *archē,* understanding the source of all things in a primary, indefinite substance with qualities "other" than those of matter in the world of experience (fire, earth, air, or fire). He characterized this originative substance as *apeiron,* spatially indefinite (implying unlimited extent and duration). Not surprisingly, Anaximander was reported to have introduced the gnomon (one of the Vitruvian architectural objects) into Greece, and to have produced one of the earliest maps of the known world.[6]

The Platonic *chōra,* which was discussed in chapter 1, evolved from this consciousness. In his *Elements* (ca. late fourth–early third century B.C.E) Euclid uses the term *chorion,* referring to an area enclosed by the perimeter of a specific geometric figure. Contrary to many modern misunderstandings, this "Euclidean space" is an abstraction and has little to do with physical space; it is certainly not the same as modern Cartesian space. Soon after Plato, Aristotle gave renewed priority to the world of experience and thus denied the existence of Anaximander's originating substance. With this denial he also put into question the reality of space as an existing empty substance:[7] Aristotle's "chain of being" remained normative for philosophers until the end of the Middle Ages and beyond. Western architecture gained a partial awareness of the geometric structure of space only during the Renaissance, through a renewed interest in Euclid's work and the invention of *perspectiva artificialis*. In his *Physics*, discussing optical phenomena, Aristotle had struggled to understand the "intermediate" reality of geometry. He observed that the geometer worked with naturally occurring lines "but not as they occur in nature," while optics deals with mathematical lines "but as they occur in nature rather than as purely mathematical entities." Since nature (*physis*) ambiguously refers to both form and matter, it must be understood from two points of view.[8] This is the geometry that serves the mimetic intention of traditional architecture, bounding a human situation and thus establishing places for communication that recognize nature as the goal for the sake of which the rest exists.[9]

During the Middle Ages, as Hannah Arendt has suggested, *ecclesia* replaced the *polis;* it was the brotherhood of the Christian church as well as the stone building around the congregation where both discursive understanding and ritual communion took place.[10] Without entering into great detail, I wish to underscore that the discursive understanding of medieval architecture was never in terms of a "simultaneous" appreciation of space (such as we may imagine from a modern history book). Whenever architecture was described, the emphasis was on its accommodation of specific rituals, always in time. Such description is analogous to medieval representations, in which places and individual scenes are located within a frame in relation to a narrative structure and not subject to a unifying (perspectival) space. The places for ritual in a church or cathedral were determined not by geometric space but in view of a cyclical temporality that linked days, years, and religious events with the participation in rites involving personal salvation in distinct parts of the building. Furthermore, medieval building processes were not driven by a priori geometrical lineaments: they involved a careful negotiation of complex site issues and constructive problems using techniques that often entailed sophisticated geometrical operations and never merely assumed a preestablished typology.

There is scant reference in architectural treatises to the association between architecture and ritual. Writers often took for granted the question of appropriateness and associated it with other issues of signification. The framework for interpretation was explicit in the traditional practice of architecture, always a collaborative endeavor with multiple cultural connections. While architecture's ties to rituals are obvious in history, especially in the context of its specific cultural uses, historians operating under the assumptions of modern aesthetics have tended to describe monuments in stylistic terms, deliberately divorcing ritual function from so-called aesthetic attributes. More recently this approach has been questioned by proponents of social theories of space, which characterize monuments as products of anonymous cultural forces. Both groups have failed to grasp the fundamental thrust of architecture as a poetic representation of significant human action.

A general history of architectural space as the place of communication is beyond the scope of this book. Nevertheless, I would like to examine some examples close to the beginning of our tradition. A fascinating precedent in ancient and classical Greece is the *prytaneion*. This institution, usually located near or in a city's agora, was the conceptual center of the *polis* and often symbolic of it. For example, Athens was called the "hearth and *prytaneion* of Greece."[11] The *prytaneion* was a communal house whose most important purpose was to offer, through formal invitation, different kinds of ritual banquets for citizens and ambassadors. Besides nourishment, it provided a place for meeting and communication.

Illuminating analogies between this center of public life and the Greek private house point to the primary nature of architecture as *dwelling,* more basic than the categorizations of public/private, interior/exterior, masculine/feminine that operated in the preclassical organization of lived space. As in the private house, the second important function of the *prytaneion* was to maintain an eternal flame associated with Hestia. Hestia is the goddess of domesticity, femininity, the earth, the dark innards (the complex and vulnerable seat of consciousness), and stability. Images of this goddess are rare; she is sometimes associated with the presence of fire itself, or portrayed sitting on an *omphalos* (navel/phallus).[12] As Jean-Pierre Vernant has shown, she is always coupled with Hermes. The pairing of Hestia and Hermes, as noted in chapter 2, is a fascinating enigma that speaks to the deeply felt interweaving of time and place in ancient Greece.[13] Hermes was identified with the masculine values of communication and interpretation, mobility, changing states, openness, and contact with the outside world, the light, and the sky. He was everywhere, on street corners and important inner-city boundaries.[14] People spoke to him, wherever he was found, and he always breathed advice. While with Hestia one would relate in silent communion, with Hermes relationship was always through dialogue. The pair reveals how space and movement, interiority and exteriority, could never be dissociated: the dark space-time of ritual communion and the space-time of discursive communication were interwoven and interdependent. Hermes, a stone pillar with male head, genitals, and erect penis, was always at the house door, together with Apollo Aguieus, lord of the roads, and Hekate, mistress of crossroads.[15] The Greeks were particularly concerned with thresholds, with what came in from outside or went out from inside, forces and emotions personified as divinities and *daimones,* at a personal as well as a political level. The *prytaneion* was both the center and threshold of the *polis,* greeting guests and sanctioning the communal action of citizens.

Burning on the common hearth, the flame in the *prytaneion* signified the life of the *polis.* Originally taken from the pure light of the sun, it would be carried on their expeditions by colonizers, hoping to ignite the communal fire of their new foundations with the same spark. The private house was a woman's domain, characterized by dark innermost quarters (*muchos*), a word that can be used to designate a prophet's cave or a bodily cavity, analogous to the woman's genitals or *aidoia.*[16] The *prytaneion,* on the other hand, projected the blood links of the family onto the whole citizenry. It was the domain of the male citizens, coming together literally and metaphorically through the sharing of a meal and discursive memory.

Indeed, the third major function of the *prytaneion* was to provide a home for interesting memorabilia of past events in the city's history, artifacts that could be identified as having historical or allegorical significance for the community. This museum function was not truly archival (archives have been found in other buildings in Athens and elsewhere); rather, the collection deliberately served as a trigger for discursive memory and became a source of shared understanding. The *prytaneion* thus functioned as a memory theater for rhetoric, providing commonplaces that grounded the words and deeds of citizens. In analogy to the household, *prytaneia* also functioned as social welfare institutions, particularly for the care of the families of citizens that had given their lives for the *polis.* Finally, the institution served as a law court exclusively for homicide cases, that is, crimes against the brotherhood of the city. Not only were murderers condemned by a court in the *prytaneion,* there is also evidence that murderous objects (such as a tile that fell from a housetop and killed someone) could be found guilty and banished beyond the city limits.[17]

The *prytaneion* was an institution of crucial importance for Greek society. In it, male citizens found a purposeful life through participation in the larger whole that was the *polis,* discovering a sense of belonging to the political order, which was keyed to a cosmic order. In view of the institution's centrality, it is particularly significant that archaeologists and scholars have had a most difficult time determining a formal type for the building. With only the most general commonalities, such as the presence of a dining hall, a kitchen, and a room for Hestia's altar, buildings of vastly differing plan configurations have been identified as fulfilling the role. These have ranged from the circular *tholos* in Athens to roughly rectangular *prytaneia* in Delos and Lato, some with courtyards and subsidiary rooms and some without.[18] Perhaps this diversity derived from the particularities of the local cultures; these institutions responded more directly to political than to religious forces. The clarity of discursive understanding, a political *logos* stabilized through the many functions of the institution, was represented in a rather informal way. Nevertheless, it is clear that the building was a representation of significant action, apart from formal or stylistic considerations.

At the other end of the spectrum we find the formalized circular plan of the Greek classical theater, an institution evoked in a previous chapter. The theater is a clearly distinguishable type, present in many Greek cities and only barely transformed in its Roman incarnation. According to Vitruvius, the theater plan reflects the heavens; a division of the circumference into twelve parts guides its internal disposition. This highly formalized harmonic space became an important civic institution during Greece's classical period. The citizen attending a representation understood order through *katharsis,* in the dark recesses of his *splanchna,* the entrails perceived as the seat of consciousness. There he experienced the effect of a destabilizing frisson through the self-same organ that was also called *phrenes*—literally, the mind, capable of containing, together and undifferentiated, objects of consciousness such as emotion, practical ideas, and knowledge, yet capable as well of articulating discourse. *Phronēsis* denotes the practical wisdom that grounds, through rational argumentation, ethical actions. A few centuries later Vitruvius described the theater's objective characteristics as a harmonic object, ruled by geometry and mimetic of the cosmos. Though Vitruvius's focus is indeed the stable configuration of the plan, in his description the meaning of the building appears only to spectators involved in ritual, sitting quietly "with their spouses and children," with their pores open, as if in a trance.[19] For Vitruvius, the geometric configuration propitiates the "winds" (the breath of nature), and enhances the harmonic sound of the words and music of the performance, thus contributing to the spectators' psychosomatic health. In the case of the Greek theater, the central ritual was the tragedy, theorized by Aristotle in his *Poetics.*

Dalibor Vesely has argued that Aristotle's definition of the work of art in his *Poetics* applies equally to architecture: it is a definition of the lived situation and of the architecture that provides its place.[20] Classical tragedy, an incarnation of mythical themes through authorial voices, was described by Aristotle as a *mimēsis* of *praxis,* a representation of significant human action.[21] The tragedy, he adds, is a work involving plot, character, diction, thought, spectacle, and song. Not merely a text, it operates through erotic space and communicates in the realm of the poetic. Its main characteristic, however, is the plot: a story that can be articulated discursively. It is a representation of action because "life consists in action, and its end is a mode of action, not a quality." Furthermore, Aristotle insists that the role of the poet is to open up the future, "to relate [not] what has happened, but what may happen, what is possible according to the law of possibility or necessity."[22] Poetic fiction, often destabilizing the spectator by taking the form of plausible yet impossible plots, was *the* vehicle for the comprehension of ethical action.

As long as the poetic word could be reconciled with legitimate knowledge, ritual would provide the basis for social participation. Indeed, recent sociological studies of classical tragedy have emphasized the communitarian character of the Athenian scene, tangibly displayed in the spatial relationship between a factitious community (the citizens of the ten tribes, and some women, occupying specific wedge-shaped sectors of the amphitheater) and the arena of the dramatic action—a relationship which reproduces that between a real community and a forum of political action.[23] The convention that governed theatrical staging and the relationship between the scene and the public required "that the audience were the citizens, sitting round the marketplace to watch the royal family conducting its affairs."[24] The performances during the Dionysian festivals were hardly entertainment in the modern sense. Usually they were daylong marathons of three tragedies and one satyr play, ritual/political events celebrating the *polis* itself and the god Dionysos.

Through participation, in solidarity, individuals would understand their place in the world and grasp a sense of purpose at many levels, from the immediacy of politics to the larger questions of being and life—including the articulation of gender, space, and society.[25] Rituals, pagan and Christian, sacred and profane, were all the enactment of myths. And mythopoetic speech allowed for the reconciliation of opposites, an experience partaken by society through rituals. In framing such rituals, architecture reinforced its inherent capacity to communicate poetic and ethical insights through formal *mimēsis.*

Thus I have argued that architectural meanings are fundamentally temporal. The ethical and poetic dimensions of architecture can operate only in space-time: any "aesthetic" objectification robs architecture of its double potential. Today, in the mental space initially opened up by modern Cartesian science, the interpretation offered by modern architectural writers such as Aldo Rossi—capable of dissociating the "permanence" of a building, its presence and beauty, from its initial particular historical function usually obsolete after a few years—appears as a fact. But this realization is itself a product of our post-Enlightenment historicity. In other words, the quality of architecture as lasting and transcending the moment becomes overriding only after humanity starts believing that historical, self-generated change is real and definitive.

The original temporal dimension of architecture was crucial for its conception as a "master-craft"; the original Greek hierarchy of the arts (unlike the later "fine arts") had to do with their proximity to the universal good. Both poetry and communication are rooted (and refer back to) oral speech. Our experience of architecture has this quality of oral encounter as well. Orality demands participation rather than distance; it is situational rather than abstract. Architecture attains meaning as "speech," both as a poetic image and as ethical representation, and thereby enables the perpetuation of culture.

Architecture, in its diverse cultural embodiments over millennia, has actively participated in the human quest for spiritual health. Despite our justified suspicion about its historical associations with power and its modern tendency to become aestheticized, we would err gravely if we were to simply ignore architecture's potential capacity to give form and limits to existence and thus open up, through the *situations* it frames, opportunities for self-understanding *in experience*. How we may start to grasp this possibility is a crucial question for the discipline of architecture in a world polarized between the forces of globalization and a growing desire to preserve cultural distinctiveness. Rather than merely continue to promote a Western architecture driven by scientific instrumentality, in the guise of ideological, aesthetic, or openly technological products, we must explore the possible points of reconciliation between the insights of phenomenology, and its recognition of an embodied, multilayered consciousness, with a meditation on architecture as a linguistic, culturally specific artifact.[26]

From *decorum* to character

As the art which creates space [architecture] both shapes it and leaves it free. It not only embraces all the decorative aspects of the shaping of space, including ornament, but is itself decorative in nature. The nature of decoration consists in performing [a] two-sided mediation; namely to draw the attention of the viewer to itself, to satisfy his taste, and then to redirect it away from itself to the greater whole of the context of life which it accompanies.

Hans-George Gadamer, *Truth and Method* (trans. Garrett Barden and John Cumming)

While the primary objective of premodern architecture was to harmonize with a cosmic order, it also had an ethical mandate to seek a form that would appropriately represent its use. Vitruvius conceptualized such appropriateness as *decorum,* a category that he includes among the basic terms of architecture in book 1 of *Ten Books on Architecture.* Like many of the terms he used, it is ambiguous and loses much of its richness in modern translations. *Decorum* has been rendered as "décor" or "correctness." It refers both to nature and to culture, including the specific purpose of a building and its historical precedents. A "natural" decorum could express a harmony between the building's use and the site chosen, such as was found at the sanctuary of Aesclepius, god of medicine and healing. For Vitruvius natural *decorum* was fundamental for psychosomatic health, which requires a deep continuity between human works and the natural world. This was a central consideration in his theory, never independent of issues of architectural form or meaning.

In Vitruvius's text, *decorum* also refers to historical traditions of building. He states, for example, that Doric columns are more appropriate than Ionic or Corinthian for temples dedicated to masculine divinities. His reasoning was based on metaphorical allusions in stories about the origins of the various columns (which he recounts at length, and which would be retold by writers until the eighteenth century), as well as the accepted usage of an ornamental "vocabulary."[27] *Decorum* also dictates that heavenly divinities should be venerated in open-air shrines—a concept of appropriateness dictated by both use and custom. *Decorum* obviously alludes to the Aristotelian definition of the work of art as representation of significant action. Nevertheless, in the Vitruvian text, with its emphasis on proportionality and cosmic *mimēsis,* that definition remains mostly tacit. The Greek quality of *prepon,* meaning "that which stands out as good," was associated in the Western tradition with the regularity of architectural artifacts, ruled by numerical proportions and geometrical figures. Such artifacts certainly stood out in the context of a mutable, ever-changing mortal world.

It also bears remembering that the central purpose of Vitruvian theory was not to express a direct relationship to practice as a set of techniques (as do modern theoretical discourses), but rather to understand the significance of the discipline from the contemplation of the order of creation.[28] In this connection, the original meaning of *kosmos*, both "world order" and "ornament," is significant. Georges Gusdorf also speculates that the Indo-European root of the Greek *kosmos* denotes in the first instance a political and military order; *kosmos* designates not only the ordered cycles of the planets but also a system of norms and values apparent in the human domain.[29] Conversely, Gadamer reminds us that in their original meaning, the ornamental and the decorative were the beautiful as such. He believes that this ancient insight can be recovered and that it qualifies the meaning of contemporary architecture: ornament is not primarily something that may have an aesthetic import of its own. Rather, "ornament or decoration is determined by its relation to what it decorates, by what carries it."[30]

This notion of *decorum* was always present, yet generally taken for granted until the end of the seventeenth century; unlike proportionality, it was never a central factor in architectural theory. Claude Perrault's writings on architecture then shifted architectural meaning from a cosmic referent to a historical referent.[31] For Perrault, beauty was no longer based on a system of mimetic proportions. He and his more famous brother Charles viewed architecture as a language whose forms came from an inherited tradition but could well have been otherwise. The central aims of architectural theory then became cultural appropriateness and communication on the basis of a linguistic analogy. In the French context, writers discussed *caractère,* while the Italian disciples of Lodoli often spoke of *indole.*[32]

Following the transformation of the traditional public space of ritual into bourgeois social space, Enlightenment writers started focusing on architecture as the embodiment of *philia.* The new site of architecture was now inevitably the site of historical and technological action. Already sensing a loss of meaning in the public realm and its buildings, Enlightenment theories promoted participation by encouraging architecture to contribute to the development of a civilized society: buildings could embody and express a social contract grounded in historical conventions. While this stance put in question the notion of architecture as embodying a discursive truth of reality as expressed in the traditional *theōria,* it was still possible to reconcile theories of character with poetic expression. After the French Revolution marked the final dissolution of the old hierarchical order and rational positivism became dominant, ushering in the thorough identification of lived space with geometric space, the new theory of architecture would have to negotiate the pitfalls of functionalism and aestheticism.

Once human affairs were no longer governed by divine will (a position expressed clearly in Voltaire's lucid writing), the chain of being was definitely broken. The break would lead to bourgeois mobility and modern science and politics. Technology and democracy could seek the actualization of ideal models, often oblivious of historical precedent. Architecture would no longer depend on its capacity to connect our souls to a divine order. Writing during the first decade of the nineteenth century, Durand postulated instrumental reason as the only viable alternative. Rightly concerned with the aesthetization of architecture, he ended up denying architecture's traditional role as the representation of significant action. Instead, following the model of scientific prose and its one-to-one relationship to its signifiers, he claimed that as long as the planning problem was adequately solved, the building would *automatically* express its function, fulfilling its communicative role.[33] The historical, *fictional* character of architecture escaped him. Indeed, poetic architecture had always presumed an ethical dimension that could be expressed seamlessly in the language of theory. Nevertheless, the continuity between poetry and prose began to be questioned and broke down completely during the nineteenth century. Not surprisingly, when it looked for alternatives to Durand's functionalism, architecture generally sought to become a *clear* and *lasting* language that would survive into posterity (no longer an afterlife). In most cases its aim was to reflect the prevalent rationality (supposedly drawn from its history) or values associated with religious and national identity, contributing to humanity's self-understanding through identifiable styles generated by convention.

To shed light on this transformation and ultimately our own inheritance, I will make a short detour through the mysteries of language proper, I hope without straying too far from architecture.

5 Architecture at the Limits of Language

Opening conversation

Now listen: all the earth uses one tongue, and the same words. Watch: they journey from the east, arrive at a valley in the land of Sumer, settle there.

"We can bring ourselves together," they said, "like stone on stone, use brick for stone: bake it until hard." For mortar they heated bitumen.

"If we bring ourselves together," they said, "we can build a city and a tower, its top touching the sky—to arrive at fame. Without a name we're unbound, scattered over the face of the earth."

Yahweh came down to watch the city and tower the sons of man were bound to build. "They are one people, with the same tongue," said Yahweh. "They conceive this between them, and it leads up until no boundary exists to what they will touch. Between us, let's descend, baffle their tongue until each is scatterbrain to his friend." From there Yahweh scattered them over the whole face of the earth; the city came unbound.

That is why they named the place Bavel: their tongues were baffled there by Yahweh. Scattered by Yahweh from there, they arrived at the ends of the earth.

The Book of J (trans. David Rosenberg)

Impish to a high degree, Yahweh overthrows by mischief, the baffling or confusion of languages. The scatterbrains indeed will be scattered, will become men without a name, because they would reach beyond Yahweh's boundaries, as though they were commensurate with the incommensurate. Scattered, their city unbound, stone falling away from stone, "they arrived at the ends of the earth." All the world has become Babylon, permanently baffled.

Harold Bloom, commentary on *The Book of J*

The possibility of the city of man and a universal architecture depends on a shared language, yet it depends as much on our ability to build in silence. Yahweh was probably more fearful of silence.

Hun Gris, conversation of October 1985

From his vantage point at infinity, Yahweh may have known that from up high, grasping the horizon as both boundless and limiting, we may have understood earlier that there is nothing totally unfamiliar, that there is always the possibility of communication as long as we exist in the utter darkness of the sky, as long as we live in emptiness.

Frances C. Lonna, conversation of May 1990

The Tower was both an assault on Heaven and a vast Jacob's ladder allowing man to ascend towards his Creator. Rebellion and worship are inextricably mixed. Yahweh would have allowed the building of the tower on the condition that humans not climb it to the top. If humans could use their universal language without pursuing meaning as absolute clarity, to the forbidden edge, we might still be speaking and building in one undivided tongue.

Franz Kafka, "The Great Wall of China" (trans. Willa and Edwin Muir)

Contemporary culture is very skeptical of the social role of architecture. Disillusioned with modernity's utopian and ideological programs, clients and practitioners typically seek artifacts that provide efficient shelter and perhaps aesthetic titillation. Even renowned international architects, those with an identifiable style or "manner," are inclined to measure their success commercially, or by counting the number of tourists that stop to photograph their innovative buildings. Architects and critics tend to believe that architecture oversteps its boundaries when it reflects critically on society or attempts to shape it by proposing a vision for a common good.

A cursory look at historical origins, however, has demonstrated architecture's role in making a social order, providing a space for *philia*. Because architecture has been concerned with human existence, *politics* has been tightly woven into our discipline. For Aristotle, politics was nothing less than the human quest for equilibrium, a desire to be whole, a psychosomatic balance involving participation in civil society and its institutions, personal accountability, and reconciliation with our mortal condition. Modern politics after the French Revolution, driven by the noble ideals of equality, fraternity, and liberty but often ignorant of history, has tended to degenerate easily into tyranny and anarchy. This tendency has lead critical theory to regard with suspicion any attempts by individuals to reconstitute the space of *philia*. Nevertheless, it is equally important to recognize that the presence of this space is crucial for the survival of culture.

In Plato's *Euthyphro*, Socrates named the architect Daedalus as his ancestor.[1] Socrates was referring especially to the lifelike artifacts made by the architect (*xoana*, and eventually *daidala*), which had to be "tied down" to prevent them from escaping. The tectonic wisdom of Daedalus, his particular form of *poiēsis*, was to reveal fixity in becoming, the inherence of the ideal in reality. Socrates alludes to Daedalus's wisdom when he says that words spoken by a good philosopher should show stability and an experience of truth. But buildings are *not* identical to language, and an architect's traces (at all scales and in all media) are not identical to writing. They are not a script that encodes the intricate references in spoken words. Architecture operates instead at the *limits* of language: it establishes limits and opens up a space for linguistic forms of expression to take place.[2]

Language and architecture

The biblical story of Babel, quoted above in David Rosenberg's rendition, is an extraordinary account of the origins of human language and its association with human making. Languages and techniques lie at the origin of the human condition and constitute its central enigma. After Babel, when the mythical enterprise of universal speech was acknowledged to be beyond the reach of mortal humans, an incredible diversity of languages proliferated on the face of the earth. Indeed, according to George Steiner, between 4,000 and 5,000 different languages are in use at the present time, and many are rapidly disappearing.[3] Linguists estimate that around 2,000 languages have disappeared during the past few centuries. The number of existing languages reflects a broad diversity of "worlds," cultural outlooks, and frameworks of categories; in turn, it suggests the plurality of responses to fundamental human problems, including poetic dwelling and building. While many of these answers are still to be found on our compressed planet, the threat of linguistic and cultural extinction is as serious for humanity as the extinction of species is for our global ecology.

Endowed with language, humans have always wondered about the purpose of existence. Explicitly or implicitly, related questions have influenced what we say and make, including our ability to make promises (projects) and fulfill what we promise. Our responses, articulated in words, deeds, and artifacts, in prose and in poetry, have been infinitely diverse. As a whole, they constitute a rich cultural heritage that reveals a concern for meaning over and beyond the pragmatic and even cynical motivations often noted by modern observers. Steiner also suggests that scientistic and evolutionary models for explaining human culture on earth are always stumped by a simple question: Why are there so many languages, even in a small geographical area, given our basic mental and physical resemblance? If we are a product of either biological chance or material necessity, how can we explain the diversity of cultures and architecture? Can this diversity indeed be reduced to historical "errors," to an excess of mythology or imagination? Although modern technology seems to be on the verge of becoming a universal language for the human condition, its unquestionable mathematical premises, global economics, and pervasive communication network are alienating and obliterating other cultures around the globe.

Phenomenology has revealed common "referents" underlying languages, and a shared basis can also be found for the social enterprises we call art and architecture. Categorial intuition cannot be explained as an intellectual ability. Spontaneous in perception, it allows for the recognition of similarities, identities, and differences in the continuum of our experience.[4] Theories based on this premise have made "interpretation" and "translation" key terms in the humanities. As Steiner has shown, human communication is essentially translation, whether "inside" or "between" languages, or even in the form of interior "monologue."[5] To a mentality that seeks simple universals, this claim would seem paradoxical. Human communication does not depend on some perfectly intelligible common language. The absolute referent is obviously beyond reach (even for a mathematical language), but it can be approximated only through translation. Issues of truth, justice, and beauty, rooted in cultural diversity, can never be addressed through strategies of identity and homogenization. The poetic utterance is language-specific, and yet it is eminently translatable.

Translation can never be reduced to a system or mechanism; it is always circumstantial and case-specific. There is always a dimension of uncertainty attached to the task. By translating, we create significant words and deeds. As hermeneutic philosophers have shown, human understanding, our own self-understanding, depends on the presence of other humans. One's personal reality is inconceivable without a social dimension. Furthermore, self-understanding is diminished if the other is encountered either as a "mirror-image" that is fully transparent or as an alien being, believed to be opaque and inaccessible. To understand "myself as another," contact and communication must transcend the forms of "enframing" described by Heidegger in his late essays, such as "The Age of the World Picture."[6] Only by encountering the other through dialogue and translation can I understand myself and establish authentic communication with my contemporaries, with different cultures, and with other historical periods.[7]

Narrative interpretation and translation are crucial concepts for the theory and practice of architecture in a post-Enlightenment context. Even within our own culture, the capacity of artifacts to address our innermost questions and provide a sense of orientation and continuity depends on the act of "interpreting" something that is alien. At the same time we should recognize that even a thorough historical account cannot fully contextualize the works of the past (or those of other contemporaneous cultures), although we can still understand their meaning—as is particularly clear in artistic and poetic works. Despite deconstructive and critical suspicions, we must allow the legitimacy of such meanings. Couched in language yet transcending it, familiar yet always new, they contribute significantly to our self-understanding.

Architecture possesses this rich ambiguity. Like other seemingly stable artistic practices, architecture is actually an ontological mutant. Despite the recent objectification of architecture as buildings and "the environment," throughout history architecture has undergone continual change. It has been manifested in artifacts that are extremely varied, including temples, gnomons, ephemeral constructions, and gardens. Only after the beginning of the nineteenth century was it generally accepted that architecture refers exclusively to the conception of totally coherent "works" that come from the mind of a "creator," are mediated by autonomous representations, and are realized as buildings. Since the Renaissance discovery of the "dignity of man" and the demiurgic power of the personal imagination, the human act of creation has been a complex transaction. Emulating creative actions of nature that act "from within matter," as Marsilio Ficino put it, artistic creation has been a personal endeavor, but never an imposition. Ficino believed that although works of magic (including art) are initiated by humans, they are ultimately the doing of nature, like the miracle of life itself. During the Enlightenment architecture started to be understood as a category of autonomous works, both characterized by the genius of an author and pregnant with historical responsibility. The notion that this responsibility should end before the building is complete, leaving a precise set of architectural notations for engineers and laborers to execute, dates only from the nineteenth century.

This problematic inheritance has to be negotiated through a recollection of alternatives in our tradition. The continuity between architecture, cultures, and the natural world cannot be reestablished through naïve contextualism, through vague ecological interests, or by disavowing the poetic imagination. By grasping the nature of the poetic image we can start developing a critical view that distinguishes poetic works in erotic space from aesthetic objects that are merely products of fashion. The final moment of communion and catharsis in architecture's previous incarnations invites silence and communicates an *experience* of unity, which nevertheless cannot be paraphrased as a conceptual totality. However, this evanescent realization, shared in our own time by a relatively limited audience, cannot become a simple program for action. The diverse human cultures in our shrinking world demand otherwise. Architecture is inextricably linked to politics, and our world is already brutally and falsely unified through technological mediation. Thus Heidegger and Walter Benjamin advocated strategies of defamiliarization and disorientation in art that would reveal the fragility of any presumptions of "absolute truth" or universal totality. When we speak about architecture, we refer to significant buildings that frame diverse cultural situations and enable their inhabitants to participate in the order of things. This ability is, of course, another definition of the poetic, the confluence of truth and beauty. To attain the poetic while acknowledging the political nature of post-Enlightenment architecture and the primacy of ethics, we must affirm cultural differences. Cultural boundaries in architecture are obviously not rigid, especially in our era of telecommunications. As Kenneth Frampton has pointed out, this is perhaps the greatest challenge for modern architecture: to reconcile the universal and the local.[8] But cultural boundaries cannot be reduced simply to geography, nationality, ethnicity, or gender. Recent writings on the subject are limited by such assumptions. I contend that our best bet to understand this problem is to consider architectural diversity in relation to fluid linguistic differences, embracing the call for a critical rethinking of the categories of politics.[9]

Architecture, embodied in the *shattered* tower of Babel, has operated since time immemorial at the limits of language. It inhabits the margins and constitutes a limiting zone for cultures, representing and enabling human action in specific ways that have changed throughout history. Like the luminous bodies in the sky that suggest order and the presence of horizon, architecture is *ornamentum* of human action, always present, sometimes in focus and often becoming background. Its association with the crucial yet inarticulate poetic utterances of *mythos* was recognized in the early eighteenth century by Giambattista Vico, amid the triumphant, highly articulated speech of modern science and philosophy. Following Vico's *ricorso*, architecture could not be simply poetic expression. Acknowledging specific cultural constructs in ethics and politics requires articulate speech and historical interpretation. This discourse, however, is based not on mathematical rationality but on storytelling and the practical philosophy of Aristotle. To interpret texts or buildings from the past and from other cultures, translation may be appropriate when they seem particularly resonant with our contemporary questions.

To interpret a building fully requires a restoration of the intent of the architects and builders, as well as an understanding of its use by the culture. To interpret a text, a similar operation is needed to understand its language and ideas in relation to changing epistemological horizons. Recent architectural scholarship offers some brilliant examples of this sort of interpretation, schooled in phenomenology and hermeneutics, which had hitherto eluded more conventional architectural history.[10] *Interpretation* offers architecture a life beyond the time of its making and the place of its immediate experience. To understand and project the lessons of our human heritage, we need memory, and memory is built from linguistic interpretation. This basic operation enables the project to become an ethical promise, contributing to the evolution of humanity and not merely producing irrelevant novelties. All the while we must acknowledge that the full transformative power of architecture is an act that can be paraphrased poetically but is impossible to explain systematically. The next two chapters will discuss the role of *phronēsis* in mainstream architectural theory and its central importance in practice. In the concluding chapter I will elucidate the nature of "philosophical history" and the role of hermeneutics in contemporary practice.

Architecture as language

Most of the buildings that our societies manage to build are inherently conservative; building construction (and most architectural practice) is thus analogous to common language. The early nineteenth century conceived "style" for the first time as a syntactic system of formal combinations that had to be present as a condition for "expression." While today we may recognize that codification is ultimately futile, historians recognize the "syntactic" particularities of regional architectures, even within the large rubric of modernism and despite its quest to become a "tradition against itself." The rate of significant change in buildings depends on the temporal or cosmological premises of different cultures. Some changes may be totally imperceptible within the timescale of human life, while others (especially since the nineteenth century consecrated "progress" and the cult of the genius) are evident even within a single generation. Beyond the specific agendas of technology and politics, receptivity to metaphor may have been crucial to the longevity of certain formal "styles," such as "classical" and "Gothic" architectures. Nevertheless, every architecture act has a temporal situation, and no form is timeless.

All this notwithstanding, architecture must contribute to communicative space. It would not survive if it ignored the deep semantic conventions through which it can be understood. Contrary to naïve postmodern attempts to revive historical forms and apply them to contemporary situations, its aim is rather to grasp architectural modes of expression and responses to the enduring questions of humanity. We can understand historical art and architecture because we have learned to translate through time. Though humanity lacks a shared cosmology, our historicity is a gift that we have barely begun to appreciate. This is our capacity to recollect specific cultural traditions that may ground our work. In light of many failed colonial enterprises, including the most recent attempts at globalization, anthropologists and linguists have discovered the true "otherness" of foreign languages, which is due to their distinct frameworks of categories. The challenge it poses is actually an opportunity and should not deter us from the task of translation. Our future hinges on this possibility.

Compared to the remarkable diversity of human languages, architecture is less various because it is bound by universal gravity and deeply rooted in the a priori structure of the local world, the scale of "chorography." Yet, in a planetary context, architecture is also rich and multiple, and different architectural expressions have often appeared simultaneously in similar places. On the European continent, for example, we can distinguish between the forms of French, English, and Italian baroque buildings, while recognizing the same basic mentality, grounded in philosophy, theology, or science, that generated the work. Differences in material expression are perhaps like bread: similar or even identical recipes yield radically different results when baked by English or Italian hands.

Opening up the way for a hermeneutic understanding of human artifacts,[11] both Leibniz and Vico sought to reconcile a monadist position with a universalist position. Their work confronted a seemingly paradoxical aporia that had developed with the advent of modern science and its technological imperative. After Descartes and Galileo, the earthly space of humanity could be assumed to be identical with the geometric space of the immutable heavens, and therefore it followed that "the book of nature" was written in mathematical terms. *Physis* had previously been alive and understood through vitalistic analogies, but the assumptions of modern epistemology had to be "proved" through "experiments" replacing experience and contemplation. In the same spirit, works of art and philosophy, ranging from the baroque frescoes of Pozzo to the poetry of Góngora and the ethics of Spinoza, contributed to "demonstrate" this truth. While refuting Descartes's position, Vico retained from this epistemological shift an awareness of the limits of scientific rationality. Since geometry has its origin in the human mind, experiment is a human act, framing nature in its own terms. For Vico it followed that humans could never fully "know" a reality that they have not created (such as the natural world). Conversely, he concluded, humans "know only what they make."[12] This new concept, which would initially include all of "nature" and "culture," was given a twist by Vico, one that still resonates with our contemporary questions. According to him, all primitive men sought expression through "imaginative universals." Cast in diverse tongues and various modes of *poiēsis*, including artifacts and poetry, these universals rapidly acquired very different configurations. Though human artifacts addressed similar questions about the human condition that could be traced to common myths, they engendered different worldviews for different cultures.

Meditating on the common origins of human cultures, Vico recognized the fallacy of seeking a primal universal language based on the logic of mathematics. The high degree of diversity in the infinite particulars produced by cultures suggests that attempts to devise such a universal language are hopelessly reductive. It follows that attempts to produce a universal architecture from scientist models of form generation are also futile. On the other hand, poetry in both language and architecture *can* be translated. It is only by scrupulously re-creating *a* given architecture/world that new practices can build on older practices to produce coherent work amid our global world in crisis. Retracing the growth of our architectural consciousness can enable us to project new promises that account for the presence of the Other and frame a space for brotherly love.

6 The Language of *Philia* in Architectural Theory

. . . that heaven and earth and gods and men are held together by communion [*koinonia*] and friendship [*philia*], by orderliness [*kosmiotēs*], temperance [*sophrosynē*], and justice [*dikaiotēs*]. [Do not fail] to observe the great power of geometrical equality amongst gods and men: you hold that self-advantage is what one ought to practice, because you neglect geometry.

Plato, *Gorgias* 508a (trans. W. R. M. Lamb)

[Geometry facilitates] the apprehension of the idea of the good [and forces] the soul to turn its vision round to the region where dwells the most blessed part of reality, which it is imperative that it should behold.

Plato, *Republic* 526e (trans. Paul Shorey)

Vitruvian theory

Words connoting signification in architecture, such as "theory," "practice," "signifier," and "signified," all belong to the Western tradition. Today they are used indiscriminately when referring to other historical eras and cultures, suggesting to a contemporary reader that they are timeless concepts with constant meanings, while in fact they carry a rich set of connotations that have transformed over time. Fleshing out some of these differences within the history of Western architectural discourses will clarify the role of architecture as a communicative practice.

Vitruvius, the first known writer in the lineage of architectural theoreticians, clearly connects his discourse to the original Greek concept of *theōria* as reflective language. Though most direct references in his text mention only Epicurean and Stoic sources, this Greek genealogy is unquestionable.[1] "Theory" may be etymologically related to the contemplation of gods through a recognition of order in nature, particularly from the "star dance" of the heavenly bodies. Their regular motions provided a model for all human affairs, including the order of the state, the eternal return of time events, and the configuration of human artifacts such as music and architecture. *Theōria* is also related to the political role of the *theōros,* an envoy or ambassador of a city-state to other assemblies (*agorai*) in the Panhellenic confederation. He participated simply through his presence, being forbidden to speak and thus barred from effective political action.

Vitruvius is clear about the cross-disciplinary nature of theory as a ground of discourse and action.[2] In the Stoic tradition, nature was omnipresent, rational, and divine, and humanity was part of it. According to Vitruvius, architects, physicians, and others share the same theory: an understanding of the order of nature (*physis*) that provides the basis for particular disciplines and conversely can be learned from literature, history, law, astronomy, geometry, medicine, arithmetic, and music, the principal threads constituting architectural studies. In our terms, this is the order disclosed by philosophers (Vitruvius referred to "physiologists," alluding to the *logos* of *physis*) following the model of *Timaeus*. Nevertheless, he adds, a wounded or sick person would naturally call a physician and never resort to an architect. Each "profession" has a particular expertise that can only be partially articulated in words and stable concepts. *Theōria* is nevertheless crucial to ensure a meaningful architecture. It enables the architect to frame rituals appropriately and to reveal the order of the cosmos in our worldly lives. It is the necessary knowledge that guides *poiēsis* toward truth and goodness.

In his first few paragraphs Vitruvius writes about the importance of theory and practice. He relates practice (*fabrica*) to the hands and to the meditative making of the craftsman who gives form to materials. Like Aristotle, he recognizes that the hands are both inherently talented (or not) and trained by regular employment: the hands are "the tool which makes tools." *Technē* (technique) always emerges from *practical knowledge,* from experience; *it is never the application of theoretical knowledge.*[3] Theory (*ratiocinatio*), on the other hand, "is the ability to demonstrate and explain the productions of dexterity on the principles of proportion."[4]

After giving these definitions, Vitruvius characterizes architectural meaning in terms of a general relationship between words and things. Architecture, he declares, appears as a "pair": "In all matters, but particularly in architecture, there are two things: that which signifies and that which is signified. That which is signified is the thing proposed about which we speak; that which signifies is a demonstration unfolded through rational precepts [*rationibus doctrinarum*]."[5] The translation evokes modern semiology, but this association must be qualified. The issue is not that theory

"gives significance" to practice. Architecture embodies multiple meanings, and Vitruvius relates them to all orders of nature and civil society. But
ratio, in the sense of mathematical ratio or proportion, has special status.

Ratio underscores *theōria*, yet it is also the "signified" of architecture. The two terms of the pair are intertwined, making it impossible to conceive their relationship in terms of modern semiology. It must be stressed
that the concept of proportion is merely the clearest instance of analogy in
language; the basis of proportion is linguistic and its mode of conveying
knowledge is the metaphor. As Aristotle pointed out, metaphor is the central operation of human knowledge.[6] Through metaphor we can know nameless distant things by their resemblance to familiar local things.

According to Vitruvius, *ratio* is fundamental in all categories that a
work of architecture must possess to be of value (*taxis, eurythmia, sym-
metria*).[7] This commensurability of parts and whole, architecture's communicative and ethical dimension, is directly related to its capacity for
seduction (*venustas*), translated as beauty. Proportion is ultimately identified with harmony, a concept etymologically derived from a well-made
joint. The Greek *harmonia* referred to the basic operation of bringing together disparate parts into a meaningful assembly that characterized the
daidalon. Thus *ratio* is a precise analogical order that appears at all levels
of reality in the cosmos. Such an order, ruled by *mathēmata* (stable relationships), was expected to be embodied in the microcosm of architecture
to bridge the ontological distance between the mortal, sublunar world of
humans and the immortal realm of the heavenly divinities.

In Stoicism, mathematical truth was directly related to empirical
truth. Stoic doctrine claimed that the only things that truly exist are material bodies. This meant that even the soul and the divine must be corporeal, potentially excluding any mediating space such as the Platonic *chōra*.
It is possible (though it never has been proven) that Vitruvius took some
of his ideas from the mathematician Geminus, a Stoic philosopher from
the island of Rhodes who was a pupil of Posidonius and was the only
member of the Stoic school who was known for his interest in the mathematical heritage of the Greeks. Geminus, who lived around 50 B.C.E. and
whose mathematical work we know only through Proclus's fifth-century
C.E. Neoplatonic commentary on Euclid's *Elements,* made a clear distinction between two kinds of mathematics: a distinction that is a key to Vitruvius's own concept. One part of mathematics is concerned only with
intelligibles, while the other works "with perceptibles and in contact with
them."[8] It is worth following Proclus's account here in some detail. By "intelligibles," Geminus means objects "that the soul arouses by herself and

contemplates in separation of embodied forms"; they include arithmetic (dealing with quantity) and geometry (dealing with magnitude) (31). The mathematics of "perceptibles," on the other hand, includes six sciences: mechanics (including the making of "useful engines of war"), astronomy (including gnomonics, the art of making "shadow tracers" for orienting buildings and cities), optics (including catoptrics, concerned with angles of reflected light and represented images that will not be distorted when seen from a distance),[9] geodesy (mensuration in general), canonics (music as a division of the monochord: *kanon* in Greek), and calculation (for everyday counting) (31–33). Significantly, these sciences account for the "departments" of architecture stipulated by Vitruvius (buildings, machines, and gnomons or solar clocks) and for the broad range of topics in his *Ten Books,* including astronomy in book 9 and machines and military engines in book 10, which have sometimes appeared strange to modern scholars and architects.

In other words, architecture coalesces the mathematical disciplines that belong to the mortal world, and its meaning is *not* equivalent to the ideal. Aristotle had already interpreted forms (*eidea*) as something that the eye could see, and this view helped bridge the gap between intellectual speculations about the geometric order of creation in Plato's *Timaeus* and disciplines such as anatomy, physics, and architecture. The bridge opened the way to Stoic doctrine, in which the *eidos* became inseparable from matter. In Aristotle's *On the Parts of Animals* the anatomist looks beyond the repulsive stuff of the body to contemplate Nature's purposive design; this *theoretical* operation was identical to that of the diviner.[10]

The Greeks believed that human and animal entrails—our dark *splanchna,* the seat of consciousness—were made of the same fabric as the physical universe. *Splanchna* mirror the qualities of divinity in the universe. By cutting and dividing the entrails, the anatomist/sacrificer revealed the "folds" that enabled humans to understand the designs of the gods. Haruspicy (divination of entrails) assumed that such designs were literally written in the entrails of animals. In late antiquity the term *theos* also referred to a part of the entrails.[11] God was both in the dark, earthly entrails and incarnated in Plato's heavenly luminaries. As many scholars have pointed out, Vitruvius never openly acknowledged divination practices (such as the Etruscan rites) as the basis for selecting a site and establishing the foundation of cities. In many ways his text appears more rational, motivated by the political circumstances surrounding Augustus; yet, without acknowledging this Greek background, it is impossible to understand the motivations behind the long-standing analogy between the macrocosm and the architectural microcosm *mediated* by the human body. Architecture does not merely "picture" the cosmos, as might have been the case in the famous shield of Achilles, described in *Iliad* 18. *Mimēsis* at the root of architectural *poiēsis* is not a copy; it entails a continuity between architectural creation and the natural world that appears as the revelation of purpose for human action.

The relationship Vitruvius sets out in his *theōria* is *through* the body, developing an analogy between body and building that would remain unquestioned in Western architecture until the seventeenth century. Furthermore, according to the Greeks our *splanchna* were particularly vulnerable to external forces such as the winds. The weather and assorted *daimones* were responsible for our changing health. Not surprisingly, architectural meaning in the Vitruvian tradition was linked to the promotion of psychosomatic health in humanity. Indeed, after discussing the importance of theory for architects and physicians, the education of the architect, the "departments" of architecture, and the main terms of architectural order based on *ratio*, Vitruvius's book 1 culminates with the orientation of the *mundus*, the *templum* of architecture, and long passages about health and the orientation of the city in relation to the winds. In setting out the geometry and proportions of a building, the architect's role is not unlike that of the diviner, visualizing a purposeful order, luminous and mathematical, in the opaque, material body of the work.

Evoking the precision and permanence of the divine mathematical realm in the mortal, ever-changing world, architecture was the substance and space of dreams: the archetype of the Platonic *chōra*. In fact, both Pythagorean and later Neoplatonic mathematicians would insist that the soul produces the mathematical sciences by looking not to its infinite capacity for developing forms but rather introspectively "to the species within the compass of the Limit" (Proclus, *Commentary*, 30–31). The separation that Geminus posited between intelligible mathematics and perceptual mathematics was carried forward in the Neoplatonic reformulations of Proclus, who was influential in the Renaissance recovery of the classical tradition of architecture, with its renewed emphasis on mental images as generators. Proclus writes: "In its lowest applications [mathematics] projects all of mechanics, as well as optics and catoptrics and many other sciences bound up with the sensible things and operative in them, while as it moves upwards it attains unitary and immaterial insights that enable it to perfect its partial judgments and the knowledge gained through discursive thought, bringing its own genera and species into conformity with those higher realities and exhibiting in its own reasonings the truth about the gods and the science of being" (17). For Neoplatonism the knowledge of mathematics issued from the soul and was a gateway to all knowledge and blessedness.

Not surprisingly, Vitruvius regarded "optical correction" as a fundamental technical skill for the architect, and this imperative remained intact in architectural theories until the end of the seventeenth century.[12] Correction is often invoked in the *Ten Books,* generally associated with *sollertia,* the particular kind of "cunning intelligence" or "practical wisdom" that is necessary for architecture to display its wondrous seductive power (*thaumata*) and disclose order. More specifically, it involved the adjustment of dimensional relationships, such as intercolumnar distances that must appear regular while taking account of the light or shade behind them; the apparent size of ornament, sculpture, and inscriptions elevated from sight; and the countercurvature of a temple's stylobate to compensate for retinal distortion. It sought not an ideal exactness but an eloquent precision that would be evident to the embodied, synaesthetic consciousness of an observer or inhabitant. This fundamental understanding of architecture was not substantially modified by the introduction of Renaissance perspective, as has been suggested by numerous scholars. Despite Vitruvius's obvious ambition to construct a body of theory from disparate fragments, inherited from Hellenistic sources and Stoic philosophy, his theory was ultimately not a vehicle for innovation. It is therefore far-fetched to connect it to a political program, as if it were operating in a modern (historical) context. Instead, Vitruvius expected that various adjustments to specific building programs examined in his text would enable the architect (or patron) to reveal appropriate meanings, drawn from a tradition embedded in manifold linguistic horizons, ranging from *ratio* and the natural world to specific historical narratives associated with Hellenistic forms and to the habitual and practical language underscoring contemporary ways of building during the rise of the Roman Empire.

Despite the differences emerging in the philosophical heritage of Plato—particularly disputes concerning the nature of the soul in Neoplatonism and Christianity, which eventually affected and transformed the ontological status of "mathematical ideas"—*ratio* functioned as an *Ursprache* in all cosmologically based theories from Vitruvius to the end of the Renaissance. The primordial language of the heavenly star dance ruled over human destiny and was expressed in musical proportions. After the opening of Pandora's box in the classical tradition, human action sought orientation through a totally intelligible language. References were implemented in works that would not fit our own narrow equivalence between architecture and buildings. Vitruvius, still operating in the tradition of Daedalus, believed that architecture includes all artifacts that allow for temporal and spatial orientation, constructed from parts harmoniously joined and "well tuned."

The participatory modes of "reception" assumed by Vitruvius are totally unlike those that issued from modern aesthetics after the eighteenth century and that today are usually taken for granted. The nature of this participation is evoked in Vitruvius's description of the theater as a quasi-meditative space in which spectators sit quietly and take in nature's rhythmic breath to understand the order of things.[13] Vitruvius says that the order of the heavens must be brought to the plan of the theater. The artifact, governed by geometrical precision, stands out from the natural world. As an embodiment of order, architecture itself is a *kosmos,* yet it acknowledges the distance between the human and divine realms. Vitruvius argues that proportion is crucial in all buildings, but especially for temples; still, proportion always had to be *corrected* to acknowledge the specificity of the site (a place—*topos* or *locus*) and the "program," and such correction constituted the true talent of the architect.[14] In this way, constructed artifacts might appear to imitate the star dance of the heavens. It was assumed that participation in buildings would always involve some manner of ritual action to situate humans within the order of the world. Reception was never a disinterested, optical event.

The poetic image, imprinted in the participants' memory, was wondrous because it belonged to the realm of dreams. At the time (and generally until the nineteenth century) dreams were considered part of one's continuous temporal and spatial experience, yet they revealed their enigmatic qualities by invoking the mathematical: symmetry, eurhythmy, and harmony. To think of architecture as an objective "built work" with an autonomous presence deployed for a voyeuristic visitor, or as a sign with a singular meaning, would have been impossible in the Vitruvian tradition.

The sequel

As the classical tradition merged with Christianity during the European Middle Ages, many assumptions changed and the nature of rituals was radically transformed. Drawing on Jewish monotheism and accepting influences from Neoplatonism and Aristotelianism, Christianity's central notions of *mystery, revelation,* and *incarnation* transformed the perceived relation between humans and the divine. While the space of the church, *ecclesia,* replaced the Roman forum as the place of participation, the earthly city became secondary to its otherworldly counterpart. It could be argued that while architecture continued to perform a similar role as a frame of ritual, it was more radically subordinated to the religious rites.

Christian architecture tended to remain "unfinished," since the City of God on earth would come to fruition only at the end of time, after Christ's second coming. The apocalypse was often believed to be imminent because Christ had already ensured humanity's redemption through his crucifixion. Consequently, the "master masons" had no real control over time or space. God was believed to be the only true architect, fully and exclusively responsible for the orders of space and time. Human techniques, such as the masons' techniques for "raising" elevations from in situ plans, were merely his instrument. Medieval guilds, however, also articulated an ethics of service and a new concept of symbolic architecture.

A document from the late fourteenth century called geometry the first and most important of the seven liberal arts and argued that it was a science given by God to Cain and his descendants to build a place for human dwelling.[15] God had condemned Cain, the murderous son of Adam and Eve, to a life of toil. Agriculture and architecture became his destiny. This was not necessarily a punishment for his sin, but it does represent the inherent limitation of the human condition: making is always tainted, even when intended to be in the service of ritual. In the biblical story, God always favored Cain's brother Abel, the nomad shepherd whose way of life, as a caretaker of nature rather than as a tiller of land, represented an unconditional respect for the given order of things. The medieval masons had a different interpretation that followed Saint Augustine: Cain received geometry, the divine language that God had used in his own creation, and it would be used by masons to build structures—particularly the Gothic cathedrals—in praise of God. The precision of the form and the mystical light of the stained glass enabled participants to grasp a mystery, the presence of divine otherness.

The building operation was conducted with the aid of many sophisticated in situ geometrical procedures. The resultant lucid structure and the luminous Gothic interiors are reminiscent of the New Testament description of God as sheer light, never overcome by darkness (John 1.5). They were also meant to provide an anagogical ladder, following Neoplatonic sources, such as Dionysius the Areopagite's *Divine Names,* which were crucial in shaping the vision of Gothic architecture, especially for Abbot Suger of St. Denis. Ascending through the light yields an irreducible darkness: an understanding of the Christian truths as mystery and of God as "supraluminous darkness."[16] This is embodied in all Christian rituals and reinforced by the experience of the building. In the Middle Ages faith in both the divine will of God and his goodness was unshakable, so Babel could be interpreted as both a curse and a blessing, to be resolved at the end of time. The human quest to build the City of God on earth was guided by the certainty of *mathēmata* and yet mostly valorized as process, *in via*, rather than as a finished image or artifact. The cathedral was believed to be God's design, but it remains unfinished. It "signifies" the absolute Other that can be known only after death, yet is present in all human actions.

Such is the poetic nature of the Gothic cathedrals. These centers of medieval public life were also embodiments of discursive thought. Hugh of St. Victor, who influenced Abbot Suger in the first synthetic manifestation of Gothic in the abbey church of St. Denis, was responsible for an emphatic understanding of Christ as wisdom, medicine, and remedy for our sins. Hugh believed that this wisdom was embodied in the book, now to be read silently by his monks; it was organized like a memory structure through his innovation of alphabetic indexing.[17] The Gothic cathedral, as a *Biblia pauperum*, organized the Word (iconology) according to an equally clear structure, a shining *claritas* of the light of God. Mystery and intelligibility thus coincided in the experience of architecture as a space of existential orientation and social participation. Recalling Daedalus's manual skill as *sophia*, Hugh was the first philosopher in the Christian West to valorize the techniques of the builder (a mechanical art) as a true form of wisdom: a ritual that partakes of God's presence.[18]

During the Middle Ages Christian revelation was believed to be the literal word of God. The message contained in the scriptures was univocal and set the limits for all theological and philosophical discussions. God's word, often identified with light, continued to be associated with a primordial mathematical language throughout the Renaissance. The geometrical essence of divine light discussed by medieval optics remained at the root of Renaissance representation, especially *perspectiva artificialis*.[19] Nevertheless, since the fifteenth century, the correspondence between human actions and the will of God has not been taken for granted, as is evident in thinkers such as Marsilio Ficino, Giovanni Pico della Mirandola, and Niccolò Machiavelli. The wars of religion and the Reformation in the sixteenth century presented even more difficulties. Hugh of St. Victor's twelfth-century appreciation of *technē* as a form of wisdom leading to salvation had anticipated the promotion of architecture to the realm of the liberal arts in the Renaissance, but this new categorization was not understood consistently during the fifteenth century.

Architectural theory was pursued in works of humanist philology, such as Alberti's *De re aedificatoria;* in treatises with an Aristotelian emphasis, such as Francesco di Giorgio's manuscripts and commentaries on Vitruvius, which were based on Renaissance practice and military engineering; in narratives addressed to a "prince," such as Filarete's description of Sforzinda, which associated architecture with fiction and the making of a new city with political hegemony; and in narratives addressed to the lover of Wisdom (Poliphilo), which sought personal enlightenment through the Neoplatonic ascent of the soul with poetic images of architecture. Architecture was related to theurgic magic (and indeed to painting) by conveying *lineamenti* or geometrical figures to the mind's eye. Fra Luca Pacioli also associated architecture with alchemical practice, a craft guided by mystical geometry and believed to be capable of transmuting lowly substances such as sand and stone into glass and polished gems. These discursive practices cannot be reduced to a single, modern genre. We can identify humanistic and technical commentaries of Vitruvius and other classical sources, didactic dialogues in narrative form, erotic/philosophical novels, philosophical allegories, treatises on perspective, and geometrical manuals of Christian theology. The significance of architecture always lay beyond a specialist's control; yet architects, from Alberti to Palladio, remained convinced that *mathēmata* in proportions were important to ensure a mimetic correspondence between their architectural work and Nature, God's architecture. Proportions enabled architecture to convey the experience of unity beyond number.

During the sixteenth century the disciplinary boundaries of architectural theory became sharper. This new clarity is most explicit in the theoretical testament of Palladio, who was responsible for the diffusion of classical architecture throughout the world. Palladio's *Quattro libri* (Venice, 1570) marked the culmination of architectural theory as cosmology. He abandoned most philological concerns and instead sought a correspondence between a universal mathematical order and an experience of classical buildings that had been scrupulously observed and measured. Palladio's theory was *scientia* in the sense of the traditional liberal arts; it was not hypothetical. It always started from the presupposition that order is given to perception, whether in nature or in artifacts inherited from tradition. Unlike Copernicus's modern theory of heliocentricity, written from a godly perspective, Palladio's theory did not abandon Aristotle's original quest to "save the phenomena." Whereas modern scientific theories would substitute experience for experimentation, positing the truth of hypotheses structured from an "eccentric" viewpoint, the ground of Palladio's theory was an understanding of the world not dissimilar to that described by Aristotle and assumed by Vitruvius.

Palladio's primary objective was "proportionality." His text demonstrates proportionality at work both in ancient models (which he freely reconstructs from his observations) and in his own architectural works. It is probable that he took the notion from the mathematician Silvio Belli, his friend, and from Daniele Barbaro, his patron. It refers to a relationship of proportions among whole (natural) numbers in three-dimensional space. Whereas earlier Renaissance theories of proportion, such as Alberti's, had presumed proportionality to be predominantly a planar (or painterly) dimensional relationship for the mind's eye, Palladio extended this notion to the built volume, perceived (and constructed) as a sequence of rooms sharing a common dimension.

Palladio's text, coupled with an emerging systematization of the tools of architectural representation (plans, elevations, and sections), presents architecture as geometric space (a three-dimensional "modern" entity), modeled on the structure of the Platonic universe. This reading has led to many fallacious comparisons between Palladio's "compositional techniques" and modern architecture.[20] The issues at stake in Palladio's theory and practice are far more complex.

Palladio's practice, his architectural *technē*, was not an application of theoretical knowledge but a special form of practical knowledge that is specific, grounded, and driven by an ability to produce. In other words, techniques are subordinated to *praxis,* itself grounded in practical philosophy, in *phronēsis.* His approach is clear to anyone who examines his diverse production, in both urban and rural sites: for example, the commission to "renovate" the Basilica in Vicenza. This was obviously an important building for the governance of the city, but its medieval form had been occupied by many different uses, ranging from the imparting of justice to the pleasures of the flesh. Palladio's design adopted a prudent attitude that acknowledged the meanings embedded in the historic fabric. The ideal Basilica is formally regular, a carefully proportioned rectangular plan represented without a context in his *Quattro libri,* whereas the real Basilica is a more complex reconciliation with the older structure. It is easy for a visitor to assume that the ideal plan has actually been built. The ideal pervades the real but does not override its richness and complexity. There are hardly any right angles in the built work, yet we perceive the orthogonality and "perfect order" of the architecture. For Palladio the earthly world of human affairs was still distinct from the ideal world of geometric space represented by theory.

During the same period, philosophers of the occult such as Cornelius Agrippa and Jacob Böhme recognized the difficulties posed by fragmenting human expression and distancing it from the original divine word. Agrippa, best known for his *De occulta philosophia* (1533), believed that a lost harmony could be recovered through magical operations. He was interested in the use of kabbalistic combinations to search for the name of God, and thought that other languages would later return to this fount of being. Interestingly, he regarded translation as a necessity, indeed as the very destiny of Cain, who had experienced man's exile from the *harmonia mundi.*

Architects soon became concerned with similar questions.[21] For architecture to reflect the true harmony of the world, it had to synthesize the classical and Christian traditions, and thus formulations such as Philibert de L'Orme's "divine proportion" were proposed. De L'Orme, the first original writer on architecture in the French Renaissance,[22] stated that these proportions must come from biblical passages about buildings rather than exclusively from the classical tradition. However, he believed that the two orders were united by their perception of *mathēmata,* and thus architecture could retain its significance as a transcription of the *harmonia mundi.*

The Jesuit Juan Bautista Villalpando had similar concerns in his late-sixteenth-century reconstruction of the Temple of Solomon, based on Ezekiel's description in the Old Testament.[23] Villalpando was aware of differences between the classical and Judeo-Christian traditions of architecture and sought to reconcile these languages in his model of "God's architecture." He attempted to show how the primal architecture of the temple included a composite order of columns that was later separated into the familiar Doric, Ionic, and Corinthian orders by the Greeks and the Romans. Other new orders could also be permitted if they were derived from this primal order. In other words, the historical diversity of architecture, especially architectural innovations in the Christian world, was always seen as aligned with God's architecture, however distorted or oblique these developments may have appeared.[24]

Jacob Böhme, a shoemaker and Christian gnostic who wrote in the early seventeenth century, thought of human languages as erratic and limited, unable to express the word of God. This view is consistent with the suspicion of *logos* in much earlier forms of gnosticism.[25] Yet Böhme advocated an instinctual language that all humans could learn without teachers, a language of nature and natural man. He believed that God's "grammar" echoes through nature; all we have to do is listen. Böhme associated this "sensualistic speech" with the "unmaking" of Babel at Pentecost: the fire, usually associated with the Holy Ghost, that enlightens the disciples of Christ so they can preach the Gospel to all peoples of the world.

While the connection between an *Ursprache* and nature had been present in earlier architectural theory, the new emphasis on the sensual aspects of Böhme's language relates to the major transformations in seventeenth-century treatises on architecture.[25] It is well known that baroque architects were much more self-consciously innovative than their Renaissance counterparts. Fueled by the principles and theological assumptions of the new science, they believed that the architectural microcosm not only had to reflect the *eidos* of a visible universe but also had to be constructed by the architect through geometric projections and combinations (as God had made the cosmos). The architect's rational imagination was believed to be kindred to God's, a belief that originated in medieval scholastic debates against Aristotle and was probably first articulated for architecture in Neoplatonic Renaissance texts such as the *Hypnerotomachia Poliphili.* This geometric construction would enable architecture to communicate through the senses the fullness and sensuous richness of nature, and therefore its true order.

During the European seventeenth century, the plurality of languages was accepted as a fact. Many intellectuals were motivated by the idea that the origin of this diversity could be found, and perhaps by the belief that the diversity could be reconciled into unity. According to Michel Foucault, the project to define an absolute but occult language for the divination of truth mutated into the project to define an absolute and completely transparent language.[27] This language, which would eventually crystallize in Diderot's *Encyclopédie,* no longer connected sign and signified across the opaque boundary of the world. Instead, it aimed at completely abolishing the world's opacity. The quest for a universal language was associated with the interest in geometry as a "universal science" that underlies all human endeavors, particularly the new science of Galileo and Descartes. Athanasius Kircher, the Jesuit polymath and prolific author, believed that Egyptian hieroglyphs held a key to this effort, and he sought to trace the origins of all written scripts to this form of "pictographic" writing. He devoted entire books to biblical buildings such as the Tower of Babel and Noah's Ark, interpreting passages from the Old Testament and making lavish graphic "reconstructions" of these buildings. His interpretations responded to the Judeo-Christian myths and reflected the geometric order of the new mechanistic universe.

Toward the end of the seventeenth century, Claude and Charles Perrault's writings on architecture indicate a significant shift away from the cosmological ground of earlier practices. Their contribution is complex and difficult to summarize, as they follow in the wake of Descartes as truly modern thinkers. While playing an important role in the court of Louis XIV and France's "Golden Age," they clearly questioned the fundamental premise that architecture can reconstruct the order of the cosmos.[28] In doing so, they raised questions about architecture's meaning, its connection to the institutions of civil society and to history, and its legitimacy as both artistic vision and social practice. Their position was considered highly polemical by most of their contemporary colleagues, including François Blondel at the newly founded Académie Royale d'Architecture. It is highly significant that most French eighteenth-century writers on architecture felt obliged to address Claude Perrault's position, and arguing different points they ended up taking sides against him. Indeed, the questions raised by the Perrault brothers reveal the normality of previous *praxis,* at once capable of creating a seductive and truthful architecture and contributing to culture's communicative space.

The Perrault brothers believed that architecture, like human language and civil law, changes over time and is constituted by human conventions. However, their belief that architectural meaning is based on "custom" rather than "nature" did not make it any less important. Like the French language itself, architecture could and should be open to further refinement and "progress."

After Claude Perrault translated, scrupulously annotated, and published an edition of Vitruvius's *Ten Books* in 1673, he decided to write a second book to dispute some of the most cherished assumptions of traditional theory. In the preface to his *Ordonnance,* he dismissed the analogy between architectural and musical harmony because the two phenomena are different. He also questioned the validity of optical corrections to reconcile architectural theory and the reality of buildings, as well as the absolute certainty that architecture is an *analogon* of the cosmos. He agrees that architecture should be guided by an efficient proportional system but does not believe that such an approach can embody universal meaning. The system he devises rationally in the *Ordonnance* was arguably based on an average of past examples. He emphasizes that the proportional rules guiding Roman and Renaissance architectural practice had no higher significance. They were produced by rational thought, as architects and writers struggled to prescribe clear and simple rules that might be followed in practice. Failures by past theoreticians had led to irregular systems. Discrepancies between theory and built works had been justified by invoking "optical correction," which Perrault considered either an excuse or a delu-

sion. In its Cartesian incarnation, the inherently mobile, multilayered embodied soul of Neoplatonism became the static, pointlike pineal gland in
the brain. This was the site of vision for Perrault, which he believed was a
priori perspectival. Therefore, the only purpose of mathematical rules in
architecture was to facilitate practice and to standardize measurements so
that the ideal design of the architect could be externalized systematically
into built form.

Within this new "tradition," now perceived as an ornamental syntax,
the task of the architect was to make works increasingly refined, expressive,
and magnificent to reflect the glory and accomplishments of contemporary
France. Claude Perrault's famous east wing of the Louvre, one of his very
few built works, embodies this intention precisely. Its polemical message,
conveyed through the use of paired freestanding columns with larger-
than-usual intercolumnar distances, was understood clearly by his contemporaries, who thought that such innovation was problematic since it
questioned the authority of the ancients and would lead to unrestrained
license. Claude's brother, the more famous writer Charles Perrault, suggested that the use of classical orders is merely a historical contingency,
since other cultures make buildings in very different ways.[29]

Could architecture as a form of knowledge, as an embodiment of
value, make sense once it was no longer understood as a microcosm of a
divine order? Architecture started to fall into history at the same time that
nature and history were identified as distinct and autonomous. Johann
Bernhard Fischer von Erlach was the first writer to try to base practice exclusively on a compilation of "monuments" from the past. In his *Entwürff*
(1721) he prepared lavish, idiosyncratic illustrations from heterogeneous
sources such as medals, prints, and traveler's accounts, including not
only Western but also Near Eastern and Far Eastern examples.[30] Although
Fischer believed that all architectural differences might be reconciled in
present practice, his book indicates a significant change in orientation.
Like Perrault, he looked for signs of good architecture only in visible attributes, such as the richness of materials, the grandeur of buildings, and
the precision of execution. In fact, the holistic "significance" of architecture as a frame for ritual was being reduced to separate aspects, aesthetics
being only one among them. A building could be composed of discrete
fragments from the past that were combined in a novel manner to create
an intelligible order. In his own practice Fischer combined a Greco-Roman
temple front, towers, a central dome, and Roman triumphal columns in his
design for the dynastic Karlskirche in Vienna. This suggested an imperial
genealogy appropriate to the patron, the Holy Roman Emperor Charles VI,

and historical roots in the Temple of Solomon in Jerusalem, but it avoided direct cosmological analogies.

Those who took the time to read Perrault's preface, rather than simply regarding his book as one more treatise on the classical orders, found his position very controversial. Mathematical proportions traditionally stood for a universal language, enabling architecture to express unity as a symbol of the divine monad. Perrault's interpretation of proportions as a case of "arbitrary beauty" was considered untenable and contradictory by many of his contemporaries and successors. François Blondel declared that this instrumental understanding of proportions denied the existence of real principles for architecture and risked robbing architecture of its ultimate meaning.[31] Architects became self-conscious about the historical (and potentially relative) nature of architectural values. Often they could simultaneously assert a belief in progress and in the perfection of their own time, while associating progress with a recovery of natural origins. But the cultural climate was indeed changing. During the Enlightenment many architects took up the challenge of understanding architecture as *a* language rather than *the* language. *Expression* then became a priority, along with a need to signify human society rather than the divine cosmos. Even for conservative architects, the ability of architecture to express a true order was mediated by this consciousness. Not surprisingly, in architectural theory the questions addressed by *decorum* in the Vitruvian tradition took precedence over other issues of order. Yet *decorum* was itself reduced and assimilated to the concept of *character*.

Indeed, eighteenth-century architecture found its grounding in its internal history and sought to represent a political order increasingly dissociated from the divine. Its character was understood in theoretical texts as a hermeneutic endeavor. Architecture was expected to be formally appropriate and correspond with the order of society. The task was first mimetic, placing emphasis on architecture's capacity to contribute to a social space that represented institutional hierarchies and the client's status in society. Later in the century, once the traditional political structures of the ancien régime were radically questioned, the hermeneutic task of the architect could become openly productive. Thus Claude-Nicolas Ledoux conceived an architecture to embody new poetic visions of a socially responsible political order. Based on a linguistic analogy, character involved aspects of prose and poetry. Early character theory was mostly concerned with typologies and physiognomy, while later *architecture parlante* emphasized its capacity to convey emotions and harmonious poetic effects. In this

manner architecture saw itself as contributing to the order of a polity—
one no longer grounded in transcendental forces.

The many theories of character and expression that were developed
during the eighteenth century tried to conceive the significance of architecture in different terms. Their central concerns were to express the use
for which a building was destined and to convey the status of the building
as if it were a social entity, a "mask" for its client. A major advocate of this
ambition was Jacques-François Blondel (not related to François), the most
important teacher of architects in Paris around 1750 and a prolific writer
of treatises and discourses on architecture between 1737 and 1777. In his
eclectic *Cours d'architecture,* published in nine volumes between 1771
and 1777, Blondel appears also as a staunch defender of the classical tradition. Arguing against Claude Perrault, J.-F. Blondel stated that beauty
is immutable and that architects, with an open spirit and a keen sense
of observation, should be able to extrapolate it "from the productions of
the fine arts and the infinite variety of Nature."[32] Although he could not
abandon some traditional premises, Blondel was enthusiastic about architecture's association with the power of expression in other arts. The classical orders, for example, were related to musical modes and became a
plastic means to express different intensities, according to the traditional
associations of the orders (Doric is virile, Corinthian is delicate). Excellent
buildings, he claimed, possessed "a mute poetry, a sweet, interesting, firm,
or vigorous style, in a word, a certain *melody* that could be tender, moving, strong, or terrible." Just as a piece of music would use harmony to
communicate its character, evoking various states of nature and conveying
sweet and vivid passions, so proportion was a means of architectural expression. When used appropriately, proportion could present the spectator
with terrifying or seductive buildings, expressive of their purpose: "the
Temple of Vengeance or that of Love."[33]

Departing from traditional assumptions of Renaissance theory,
Blondel emphasized that "we cannot ignore customary conventions [*la bienséance*]; they lead to truth, since they naturally keep the artist away from
the temptation of abuse, pointing him toward the rightful place of the sublime, the grand, the simple, and the elegant."[34] The transmission of conventions, crucial for an ethical practice, had now become rooted in history
and everyday language. It focused on oral or written speech, closer to
phronēsis, and no longer on mathematical language. This shift was present in most eighteenth-century theories, and the importance of language
as narrative, and eventually fiction, grew throughout the century. Blondel

sought an absolute congruence between the *distribution* of a building in plan, its ornamentation, and its use or destination. Such congruence was particularly important in the design of houses, which should represent the ranks of the owners in this highly stratified, theatrical society. In eighteenth-century France, individuals were literally defined by their rank, which was represented through dress, wigs, and cosmetics. Similarly, architecture's *character* expressed the owner's status. As traditional ritual space slowly gave way to the "social" space of the modern city, this characterization of architecture enabled the built environment to maintain its legibility. Blondel believed that architecture should be intelligible: "A building should announce what it is at first sight."[35] The city, now literally a stage for public life, was constituted by buildings that represented the men and women who lived in them, opening a space of communication for the construction of nonautocratic cultures.

Blondel was hardly alone in thinking about these issues. Around midcentury, Charles-Etienne Briseux wrote a book about "essential beauty" in art and architecture, using Newton's discovery of "universal harmony" and Jean-Philippe Rameau's theories of music to make an argument similar to Blondel's.[36] Briseux also argued against Perrault, yet he outlined an instrumental theory to modulate expression in architecture, emulating Rameau's compositional theory to express sentiment in tonal music. Indeed, the association of architecture and the fine arts became commonplace during the eighteenth century.

This link indicates a different concept of architecture than the premises that had operated since Vitruvius. While not totally immanent, the significance of architecture became increasingly internalized as a problem of "composition" that could be resolved through an objectified building. The temporal *situation* framed and represented by architecture receded in favor of a concept of architecture as an "aesthetic object" that should be "read" out of time. This transformation offered great difficulties but also new possibilities for modern architecture. The tendency developed after 1800 into an architecture of autonomous "artistic works." They were often reduced to places for voyeuristic tourism that were more suited to offering objective "pictures" than to enabling participatory experience (a reduction that even today is the usual fate of avant-garde design). They also led to monuments that provided a literal framework for discursive writing, as in the famous Temple Décadaire by Durand and the façades of Labrouste's Bibliothèque Ste.-Geneviève (more recently the typical aim of corporate and institutional buildings).

In the midst of this problematic transformation, some late-eighteenth-century French architects such as Nicolas Le Camus de Mézières and Ledoux sought alternatives and tried to reintroduce a temporal dimension to architectural meaning through *nonlinear* narrative structures, anticipating surrealist techniques and cinematographic montage. Inevitably operating as historical, self-conscious creators, they nevertheless engaged interpretation to produce poetic and eloquent architecture, transcending mere self-expression and revealing cultural continuity. Others during the early eighteenth century, particularly Jean-Laurent Legeay and Giovanni Battista Piranesi, and later Jean-Jacques Lequeu, had merged architecture and painting to escape the tyranny of a space out of time, as embodied in systematic perspectival representations.[37] All these architects seemed particularly aware of the power of light to qualify space, over and beyond its geometric description. Etienne-Louis Boullée pushed this to the extreme through his innovative poetic language of forms that sought to invoke our intuitive senses rather than using what he identified as a scientific prose, the classical tradition. Architectural expression was characterized by Boullée as *architecture parlante*. A significant architecture had to "speak" in order to engage the inhabitant in effective participation. If the architect "wrote," he must write "poetry." Unlike written prose, poetry demands to be "heard" by the reader in a "thick presence"; it "temporalizes" space and "spatializes" time. While acknowledging (as did Perrault) that architecture is a language rather than an *analogon* of the cosmos, the architect would be in a position to "make a second nature" (*mettre la nature en oeuvre*) from the depths of his creative self that might "speak" to all.[38] This idea of creation, more fully developed by Romantic philosophers such as Schelling and Novalis, superseded the eighteenth-century paradigm for the fine arts (architecture as a re-presentation of Nature), which had run its course.

Not surprisingly, the very nature of theoretical writing about architecture was also questioned. New concepts of transmission and education radicalized or totally rejected the premise of theory as applied science. This polemic would in turn shape the problematic *praxis* of architecture during the nineteenth and twentieth centuries, with its mixed cultural reception. Late-eighteenth-century authors such as Boullée, Ledoux, and Jean-Louis Viel de Saint-Maux declared the need for a new architectural discourse that could transcend the limited "scientific" articulations of Vitruvian theory. Thus, they thought, the intentions of a novel, poetic architecture could be better expressed. Personal expression became a condition for this poetic possibility: a retrieval of the universal *in* the creative soul of the architect.

The work of Viel de Saint-Maux will be the focus of a more detailed analysis in the following chapter.

On the other side of the equation, Durand declared that it was futile to understand architecture as an art form, which he could grasp only as a concern for "aesthetics." He postulated instead a model that would become dominant during the next two centuries: a totally positivistic architectural theory in which the value of architecture could be discerned from its utility and efficiency, and not from an "illusory" expressive capacity. The architect, emphasized Durand, had to be *unconcerned* with meaning. Architecture, through its "mechanism of composition," could function outside of language, outside interpretation. Thus, the work became a singular *sign* of its purpose—a simple, unambiguous cipher of technological value. Durand's teachings helped significantly to institutionalize architectural education as a school program in the Parisian Ecole Polytechnique.[39]

Out of the same juncture, continuing and further radicalizing many late- eighteenth-century positions, our own modernity and postmodernity would emerge. Functionalism in later architectural theory and practice inherited, transformed, and perverted the eighteenth-century interest in an architecture for a human brotherhood. Despite its now obvious limitations, to merely reject functionalism and substitute an aesthetic interest for it, as often occurred in the second half of the twentieth century, is insufficient. The transformations evident during the eighteenth century have to find their proper expression in the twenty-first century, but they cannot be disregarded. Given their roots in modern epistemology, they constitute the inescapable condition of a truly significant and ethical architecture. In the next chapter I will exchange my panoramic lens for a close-up lens to examine the complex work of two lesser-known architectural writers straddling the eighteenth and the nineteenth centuries.

7 A Tale of Two Brothers: Jean-Louis and Charles-François Viel

In an article published in 1966, the French historian Jean-Marie Pérouse de Montclos demonstrated beyond any doubt the distinct identities of Jean-Louis Viel de Saint-Maux (born ca. 1736), "architecte, peintre et avocat au parlement de Paris," and Charles-François Viel (1745–1819), "architecte de l'Hôpital général."[1] Both were authors of important theoretical works, published in Paris during the late eighteenth and early nineteenth centuries. Nothing certain is known about Jean-Louis's civil status, and Charles-François's biographies are very limited.[2] Scholars typically had attributed to the latter a book authored by Jean-Louis, the *Lettres sur l'architecture* (1787), a devastating critique of Vitruvian theory that resonates deeply with the objectives of Boullée's "revolutionary" *architecture parlante*.[3] Pérouse de Montclos rightly set out to correct the improper attribution. Indeed, Charles-François and Jean-Louis seem to have had very different ideas about architecture and very different writing styles. Jean-Louis probably was never a practicing architect. His text is often visionary, biting, and ironic, while Charles-François's much more extensive theoretical testament is didactic yet grounded in practice, resentful of innovation, and often boring. Pérouse de Montclos characterizes Charles-François's writings as reactionary, and his architecture as mediocre. While this judgment may be partly justified, Pérouse de Montclos seems to miss the profound implications of the multiple layers of his critique. Furthermore, Charles-François dedicated the compilation of his writings (in three extensive volumes) to his architect brother, "loyal companion of [his] studies in art, sharing [his] first drawing lessons, and zealous collaborator in the execution of many [of his] public buildings."[4] It is not impossible that Jean-Louis was involved in one of the most interesting projects attributed to Charles-François, the Monument consacré à l'histoire naturelle (1776). Pérouse de Montelos cites a notarized document from March 6, 1784, that jointly names Jean-Louis Viel, "peintre," and Charles-François Viel, "architecte."

This curious detective story has other ramifications that I will not pursue. Jean-Louis, a member of two Freemasonic lodges,[5] apparently was a rather strange character who spent time pretending to be a mason in order to understand the abuses of *toiseurs,* the inspectors who measured buildings after their execution to determine the correct payment for workers.[6] Charles-François, on the other hand, held a bureaucratic position and was frankly upset with the chaotic political changes he had seen after the French Revolution; his conservatism obviously was reflected in his architectural theory. My interest here, however, is rather to re-create the intellectual legacy of the Viel brothers, in which *philia* and *erōs* became polemical. The aim is to discern the importance and real possibilities of the crossing—a missing gene, perhaps—which can be imagined as a missed potentiality emerging from the same cultural context in early modernity.

The poetic architecture of Jean-Louis Viel

The artist seems capable of stealing from the Eternal the creative power which, to our eyes, expresses the miracles of Nature[;] . . . in his noble delirium he can paint even space.

Jean-Louis Viel de Saint-Maux, *Observations philosophiques sur l'usage d'exposer les ouvrages de peinture et de sculpture* (attributed to Charles-François Viel after 1820)

Both Jean-Louis Viel de Saint-Maux and Charles-François Viel believed that most architecture by their contemporaries was decadent, and they wrote their respective works as a candid response to a perceived crisis of meaning in the practice and teaching of architecture. As I have suggested, the "problem" of expression for a "historical" architecture based on human convention rather than divine Nature had been present in eighteenth-century theory since Claude Perrault, but it threatened the legitimacy of the discipline during the final decades of that century. As the ancien régime became weaker and the French economy went from crisis to crisis, classical architecture appeared oppressive to the masses, and "prosaic" or "inauthentic" to theoreticians. Classical architecture, which had represented a social hierarchy by divine right, finally started to crumble along with its intrinsic concepts of theory and practice. Although Carlo Lodoli and his disciples had earlier raised similar questions in the Veneto, it was not until the 1780s that new modes of theorizing appeared in France, with novel uses of language and different forms of architectural expression.

Jean-Louis published his first two letters on architecture in 1779 and 1780.[7] The compilation of his *Lettres* appeared in 1784, three years after

Boullée's famous design for Newton's cenotaph. His project to discuss the "symbolic genius" embodied in the great monuments of antiquity resonates with Boullée's theoretical position. Jean-Louis wanted to "paint space," while Boullée's Cenotaph for Newton emphasizes the emptiness of space signifying the omnipresence and eternity of a deistic god.[8] Like Boullée, Jean-Louis thought that ordinary writing on architecture did not teach young architects to produce eloquent works that evoke "this enthusiasm that takes over and transforms the soul of the spectator."[9] Consequently, he avoids proportions and prescription; using an epistolary form, he builds his arguments through sharp criticism, irony, and a hermeneutic reconstruction of architectural origins.

Jean-Louis criticized his contemporaries for their inability to speak properly or to articulate the cultural importance of architecture instead of reducing it to a pragmatic provision of shelter.[10] To him, it was absurd to blindly follow rules of Vitruvius that were reduced to rational measurements and proportions. As he demonstrates in his fourth letter, the classical orders originated in sacrificial altars and symbols of fecundity, but the rules employed by architects fail to convey this original meaning. Thus, dismissing most of the writings of his contemporaries and predecessors as ridiculous and trivial, he instead sought a theory of architectural origins in the sacred and symbolic "cults of fertility" that were associated with agrarian cultures. Despite the limitations of his imaginary reconstruction, this was no reactionary flight from reason: Jean-Louis criticized all "superstitions" in traditional architectural treatises.[11] He associated agriculture with the beginning of civilization, the capacity of humans to compensate for a "lack" in the natural world. This awareness was indicated by the cultivation of food and by rituals of sacrifice that sought to reconcile humans and nature. Architecture provided a place for sacrifice through the primal act of setting a stone upright to mark a sacred place, the presence of divinity, and the site of an altar. Comparing the architectures of primitive agrarian societies around the world, very much in the spirit of comparative religion and anthropology, he claimed that monuments were like liturgical fragments, *poems* elevated to celebrate fecundity.[12] Jean-Louis saw the vertical stone, consecrated to the divinities of the earth and the sun, as the prototype for columns. These "daughters of agriculture," eventually ornamented with hieroglyphs and associated with the "natural history" of writing, presided over social organizations after nomadic life was replaced by civilized settlements. Thus, monumental architecture was not derived from the primitive hut, an account that he deemed "pure fantasy." The first temples were circular, and their starry vaults illustrated a theogony and a cosmogony. According to Jean-Louis these temples represented the revolution of the sky as understood by Newtonian science: a motion that came from the same creative forces earlier venerated in nature cults and that in his own time was still associated with divine Nature.

Architecture for Jean-Louis embodied attributes of a Freemasonic divinity, both rational and poetic. According to Dupuis (an obvious influence on Jean-Louis's thinking), this "god" is "destined to express the idea of a universal force, eternally active, which impresses motion to all of nature, following the laws of a constant and admirable harmony, pervading all matter and being its principle of animation."[13] The concept of this god accounted for the diversity of primitive nature cults and became the only appropriate object of "religion" for the Enlightenment. Dupuis had argued that all primitive peoples would have admired this force that moves the world as a basis for their multiple divinities. Later, "metaphysical" religions merely "invented" a "creator," an imaginary abstraction apart from the world. Dupuis thought that we must contemplate nature with admiration, without changing it for the self-interest of humans.[14] Human virtue, he thought, should be cultivated without intermediaries (i.e., priests) between God and man. While standing against poetic fiction and religion, Dupuis argued for an aesthetic participation with the order of creation. He posited scientific (Newtonian) reason as the only universal, yet questioned the old belief that nature is made "for us" (*propter nos*), thereby short-circuiting the fundamental intention of technology and promoting a sense of awe and respect for nature.

Unlike Vico, who earlier in the eighteenth century had gone "through" reason to recover the necessity of myth and the poetic utterance, Dupuis was adamant in his rationality, which could not lead to a full recovery of *poiēsis*. Nevertheless, Dupuis's meditation resonates with contemporary ethical and ecological concerns. His insight was generally ignored by nineteenth-century positive reason and was no longer entertained in architectural theory by either Durand or Charles-François Viel.

Jean-Louis Viel admired ancient temples for their capacity to "sing the marvels of Creation, the perpetual miracle of fecundity, the wonders of statics and the laws of motion, etc."[15] He advocated an architecture that is the "figure" of the universe, a geometrical figure that underlies the initiation rituals of Freemasonry, maps the world and the cosmos, and plots the motions of the sun and the stars. Its realization is best exemplified by Boullée's famous Cenotaph for Newton, a poetic representation of the Newtonian void that is also God's *plenum*, in which opposites such as night and day, light and space, are reconciled. This desire was evident also in the work of many of Boullée's contemporaries, such as the texts and projects by Ledoux,[16] as well as Vaudoyer's project for a House for a Cosmopolitan Dweller (1785), but achieving it would soon be considered impossible. Yet, despite the growing skepticism about the capacity of architecture (and science) to paint a rational, transcendental nature, Jean-Louis insisted that the essence of architecture is poetic: it should speak of our need to reconcile our mortality with a more-than-human cosmos and transcend the ephemerality of historical time to sustain the vitality of culture.

The ironic tone of his writing suggests not a mythic understanding of origins that can simply be retrieved but a historical understanding of origins in which the past is distinct from the present. He recognized that in a mythic context there was no sense of individual genius or personal invention, a condition "absolutely different" from his present circumstances. Perhaps with greater clarity than any of his contemporaries, Jean-Louis stated the central issue for architecture: If architecture is to matter, it must convey the unity of knowledge; it must configure the human world so that it makes sense.[17] He says that architecture originated with nations, and had nothing to do with private dwellings.[18] This meaning was not reducible to aesthetic pleasure, nor was it based on conventional preferences proposed by eighteenth-century theoreticians.[19] Architecture offered a place where humans could recognize their humanity through action: a fusion of mortal humus and immortal spirit.

Indeed, Jean-Louis understood how difficult it had become for architects to provide this "place." A few years later, Durand would become disenchanted with the struggle to express meaning in architecture and would declare the search futile. Flowing with the dominant forces of postrevolutionary culture and its new political orders, Durand drafted his successful theory, stating succinctly that the objective of architecture is public and private utility, and that if the architect follows the rules of economy and convenience, meaning would follow. The discipline would be justified by its own processes. Because human action could no longer be based on a suprahuman order, both Durand and Jean-Louis turned to history to justify their respective positions. Durand regarded history as a progressive series of functional building types that merely "proved" his rational argument; Jean-Louis, on the other hand, still regarded history as a story about a natural origin that had become "corrupted," but he considered human artifacts to be poetic projections of a complex, embodied consciousness.

Jean-Louis conceived architecture as a "speaking poem" that is written for posterity to convey a *symbolic* rather than a *literal* meaning. He was critical of earlier eighteenth-century theories of character, which assumed that architecture must rely on *convenance* for its meaning. This stance owed much to the works of the Protestant pastor, Freemason, and linguist Antoine Court de Gébelin (1725–1784).[20] Court's lifelong project was to study the primitive world through its artifacts, with language as his primary model: "We paint our ideas through words and render this painting stable through writing." By following the rules of grammar, writing "makes speech into marble, transporting it to the end of the world."[21] Believing that words are not arbitrary, despite the diversity of languages, he sought to reveal a "natural history of speech" as the basis of human knowledge, and thereby to challenge the authority of arbitrary conventions as the foundation of civic institutions.[22] Court believed that all modern languages derived from a single origin, along with other human faculties such as sight and walking. Although language was God-given, Court could not imagine it as an "arbitrary result" of divine power. Instead, it came from an interplay of elements in nature: man, his mind, the physiology of speech, and the objects he must "paint."[23] Despite being "natural," it was qualitatively different from animal cries: human speech enables humanity to accumulate and share knowledge, to make history and project a future. In short, Court's theory of language was already very different from the theologically inspired *clavis universalis* of the seventeenth century. He viewed language not as invented directly by God but as mediated through nature. In typical Enlightenment fashion (but unlike Vico, whose quest was explicitly cultural), Court sought a natural origin of civil societies: a "universal grammar issuing from the need to be clearly understood."[24] But this could only be inferred from existing languages; it could not be objectified into a universal language. He believed that civilized languages did not result from random transformations or the arbitrary capriciousness of each nation. Commonalities among languages, and internally between natural objects and their names, could be grasped only through mimesis or metaphor: "all objects are named through imitation or comparison."[25]

Court viewed writing as analogous to speech. He understood it as a form of painting that originated in hieroglyphs and eventually was transformed into a common alphabet that became more differentiated over time. Thus, even the letters of the alphabet referred to "pictures" of objects. This reference was metaphoric or metonymic rather than literal, however, "uniting the intellectual with the physical senses."[26] Even though primitive artifacts may seem diverse and disparate, "all is born from our needs." The space of language is the space of desire, the desire for the common good ("le désir du bonheur commun").[27] In an engraving at the back of the book, Mercury/Hermes is conducted by Cupid/Eros while he teaches humans how to speak and write. This juxtaposition suggests a link between humanity and everything that is made: our current arts, laws, and customs started from basic needs in antiquity and have been perfected by subsequent needs. All arts that respond to necessity, such as language and agriculture, "maintain today all that they had been."[28]

Although Court still emphasized "reason" and a functional understanding of myths, he declared that "fables are truth," mythology is a respectable discourse, and primitive man is not stupid or despicable.[29] With the clear mind of a comparative linguist and not a hermetic philosopher, he proclaimed a primordial monotheism as the basis for all established religions. It encompassed the sun, the moon, and the zodiac with a divinity symbolized by a shimmering fire, not unlike Vico's "Jove."

Jean-Louis Viel's understanding of language and nature drew from Court and Dupuis to substantiate his call for an expressive modern architecture that would recover its origins through a hieroglyphic writing that is both intelligible and poetic. Court believed that languages could and should be refined to recover "the energy of primitive speech." Myths would thus be a resource for understanding antiquity and perfecting the arts. As "a sublime, noble, and significant imitation of nature," they could illuminate the relationship among human needs, the works of men, and public happiness.[30] Therefore, the language of architecture should abandon its stifling classicism and write a new form of poetry that is both culturally specific and universal.

The political architecture of Charles-François Viel

Charles-François Viel also understood architecture as writing but as bound *within* the Greco-Roman tradition. Except for his project for a Monument Consacré à l'Histoire Naturelle (1776), which used all the orders and showed considerable programmatic invention, his practice was very conservative. He used a simplified and humble version of neoclassicism, predominantly with Doric columns or pilasters, simple perforations for windows, and internal volumes recalling stripped-down Roman imperial architecture. Interestingly, however, Charles-François Viel was the first architectural theoretician to identify *style* as the central issue in architectural expression.[31] In itself this is highly significant. Despite many later misconceptions in art history, architectural significance was never based on the coherence of style or formal syntax prior to the nineteenth century.

According to Charles-François, the mastery of style is a precondition for an architecture that communicates its character and significance. By analogy to literature, architecture is an arrangement of words (architectural lines) and phrases (architectural orders) "to render diction pure and elegant, at times sweet and suggestive (*insinuante*), strong, persuasive, and always noble, even in its simplicity."[32] Style depends on the place and the nation for which one builds, just as literature depends on language and custom. An architect without style is like a writer without grammar.

Court de Gébelin had argued for the existence of a universal grammar that is immutable and underlies the many different languages that express the "mutable genius" of individual nations. Grammar provides rules "to paint ideas in the clearest, most energetic, and fastest way."[33] By analogy, Charles-François believed that architectural style relies on the choice of elements, their disposition, and their resulting purity in the building. Works with an appropriate character and correct syntax therefore convey "a happy harmony" to their inhabitants.[34]

Unlike Durand, Charles-François regarded architectural expression as a primary problem. However, he rejected radical departures from tradition in the works of contemporaries such as Boullée and Ledoux. Architectural order had to be rooted in a collective, historical understanding associated with the political realm. Charles-François identified architectural decadence with political chaos, and he was bitterly critical of the "deranged imaginations" of his contemporaries and immediate predecessors. He admired the political dimension of architecture in Perrault's theory and practice, while refusing to accept that architecture could be reduced to a relativistic expression of customs. He often stated that the main cause of artistic decadence was *the immoderate desire for novelty*. He opened the first volume of his *Principes* with a statement about the influence of the sciences and fine arts on the health of the body politic. Even though the arts and sciences may have fathered vice, he argued, they are needed to stop crime. Defending architecture in postrevolutionary France, he agreed with Rousseau that "the same causes that have corrupted nations are often useful to prevent a greater corruption" ("Discours Préliminaire"). He thought that the most beautiful discoveries came from the flourishing republics of antiquity and that modern republics should follow the ancients in both politics and architecture.

"Purity of style" is difficult to attain. According to Charles-François, it "means that the whole of the *ordonnance* partakes from the spirit of the most beautiful buildings in antiquity" (*Principes*, 98). Seeming to argue for syntactic consistency and "visible" harmony (not unlike Laugier in his

Observations of 1770),[35] he exhorts the architect to adopt "happy" transitions and reject small, annoying members that would spoil the clarity of style in a building. Opposing the Greco-Gothic ideal of the Enlightenment, Charles-François was disgusted by "monstrous" combinations of classical and Gothic elements: for example, at St. Eustache in Paris (77). His notion of "visible coherence" would become a normative understanding of style during the nineteenth century.

Charles-François includes concerns previously associated with character under the rubric of style. Much as of Boffrand had done, he argues that just as a poet should not use the form of a fable or an idyll to describe a military exploit, so the architect should use an appropriate style for each project. He also suggests that mathematical relationships provided a universal grammar within a given tradition, recalling earlier eighteenth-century texts that associated the orders with musical modes. Style (here connected etymologically to *stylus,* or column) is associated with the three classical orders, the Doric, Ionic, and Corinthian, by the proportions of their diameter to their height, respectively 1:8, 1:9, and 1:10. However, applying a style involved judicious changes to proportions within the orders, according to the intended character of the building. The Doric, for instance, can be elongated and "grow" (as a child does) from 1:6 to 1:8. All the orders may be adjusted in this manner, but his preference is for the Doric because it is the most ancient and is the origin of the other two (chaps. 22–24). Gone, of course, is the long-standing debate between proponents of Greek and Roman architecture. For Charles-François, the age of Augustus merely brought the orders to perfection, since they are all essentially the same (151). Doric is usually sufficient, as its proportions can be modulated to convey an appropriate character for any building. The result is an architecture of simple trabeated relations and plain orifices, regulated by proportions that are ultimately fixed by natural law.

Charles-François's notion of syntax as a basis for architectural expression is even clearer in the following chapters on profiles and moldings, and on how these differ from "contingent ornament" (152; see chaps. 25–27). Profiles are a combination of simpler moldings, with proportions that are determined by the member for which they are adapted and by the expression of the whole *ordonnance.* A knowledge of moldings is essential in architecture; without them, constructions would be mute masonry bodies without taste or character (152). Following a long-standing tradition in practice rarely mentioned in theoretical texts, Charles-François stated that the invention of moldings (and templates) relied on the imagination and genius of the architect, who is responsible for "the divisions of lines and their relationships," the "elementary science" of architecture (152). He understood architectural writing as a geometrical skill for articulating a coherent whole, from the molding to the profile, the order, and the building. He even declared an admiration for Piranesi's valorization of ornament, but was worried about his "effervescent imagination" (158).

Taking up a well-rehearsed notion from Montesquieu and from the eighteenth-century theories of Briseux and Le Camus, Charles-François reflected on how harmonious proportions and arrangements "coincide with our organization" (158) and the innate capacity of our eyes to grasp detail. Despite his critique of "revolutionary architecture," he echoed Boullée's desire for eloquence:

Eloquence derives from nature its most cherished secrets to convince and engage our hearts. Architecture also derives from the same sources its own means to captivate our eyes, and although nature doesn't provide architecture with fixed models to imitate, it does offer, by its harmony, the just correspondence of parts that compose it, and certain rules that reveal a precision of relationships . . . from which architecture derives its magnificence, its elegance, its correctness, and expression. (157)

He viewed architecture's expressive power as achieved not by imitating nature directly but by consciously using style (a form of writing) as a mediation to convey meaning through persuasion. Charles-François's suspicion of novelty precluded his mentioning "poetic intention," but he did identify rhetoric as a crucial factor in the political context of architecture. Architecture had to communicate "clearly," but not merely by following the dictates of science or instrumental theories. Aristotle recognized rhetoric as a fundamental discipline enabling the expression of truth in both ethics and poetics, and thus as crucial for politics and art. Charles-François believed that architecture, like rhetoric, must identify commonplaces to further the communicative space of culture.

For Charles-François, ultimately nothing in architectural practice can be prescribed or tabulated. There are only a few invariable rules: "Invention is a conception of masses whose varied forms are subject to dimensions expressed by straight or circular lines, simple or in combination" (241). From these combinations of lines emerge plans and elevations that should be composed clearly with symmetrical forms and solid proportions. Examples are always better than precepts. The rules are consistently drawn from historical precedents, always referring the architect back to experience and embodied perception rather than to textual or scientific knowledge. Proportions are a "universal language" that can be grasped only through specific historical examples. Indeed, Charles-François still embraced proportion and eurhythmy as the two fundamental principles of architecture. These premises even led him to criticize Perrault's use of paired columns in the east façade of the Louvre because he (like François Blondel) thought that they contradicted the authority of the ancients (51–52). He repeated the traditional view that nature was the origin of the basic elements of architecture and added that it was also the source of the principles of construction (198). However, he observed that because architecture has no direct models in the natural world, it demands a different strategy than that of the experimental natural sciences (26).[36]

Charles-François Viel wrote many short works on technical topics during his career. He thought that their mathematical demonstrations would help a reader to understand principles but could not instruct an architect on the specific proportions or forms of a project.[37] Though he advocated careful applications of geometry in stonecutting and algebra in structural testing, he believed that these geometrical exercises did not provide absolute results. True stability (*firmitas*) could be attained only by establishing correct proportions among points of support, foundations, and supported masses. These dimensional relations had to be derived from a correct distribution of solids and voids, which was based on the traditional classical orders: an "admirable correspondence" used by great masters of the past (*Principes*, 200).

Charles-François was obsessed with this theme and developed it in several essays, eventually published independently during the first decade of the nineteenth century. In *De l'impuissance des mathématiques pour assurer la solidité des bâtimens* (1805), he examined the limitations of geometrical hypotheses to ensure the stability and durability of buildings. The problem had been recognized in the early eighteenth century but it was not a crucial question in architectural practice until the successful development of applied sciences in construction in Charles-François's lifetime. While acknowledging that mathematics is useful for solving mental and ideal problems, he did not think that it is infallible when applied to physical quantities with attributes that are indeterminate and infinitely diverse.[38] His own attempt to establish rules for designing sound buildings is set out in *De la solidité des bâtimens, puissé dans les proportions des ordres d'architecture* (1806). He devoted over thirty pages of that work to describing how his understanding could be applied in specific examples. His rules, however, did not provide a table of dimensions or a formula. He declared with some sarcasm that he preferred to leave the production of such "harmful" books to others and would not contribute to "undigested and arguable compilations" that simplify great matters.[39] Although his method provided some rules, he still advised architects to study the classical orders and building procedures in contemporary and historical examples.[40]

Charles-François often cited Quatremère de Quincy in claiming that all aspects of an art are intimately related, calling this "the fundamental theorem from which derive all the truths that constitute the art of building."[41] This concept challenged specialization and specialized teaching. He believed that architecture could be perfected only by imitating the great buildings of the past, which were universally accepted because they embodied all the rules at once. Architecture is "self-sufficient" because its best works incorporate all principles of the art of building; therefore, it doesn't follow rules but makes them. Drawing on many examples, including the well-publicized failures of Soufflot's Pantheon, he tried to prove that abstract principles of statics produced results that were never in accordance with reality.[42] He rejected the popular notion that "to be an architect one should necessarily first be a geometrician." He also believed that knowledge and study are not sufficient for architecture: "one [is] born an architect," with a delicate and sensitive spirit that can discover the mysteries of construction by observing exemplary structures.[43]

Charles-François explicitly rejected the reduction of theory to a specialized technological instrument. In his *Dissertations,* he wrote that the modern science of construction was so confused that professors were teaching not fundamental architectural principles but only the theory and practice of techniques such as masonry, stonecutting, and carpentry.[44] Because the new school-centered education in France was based on such theories, his criticism of these new institutions was scathing. Charles-François was concerned that aspiring architects were not being taught the true principles of architecture. He regarded treatises on descriptive geometry as misrepresentations of architectural meaning. Young architects who had been trained in this method never fulfilled the hopes that the public had placed in them; he pronounced them to be incompetent in both design and construction.[45] In *Des anciennes études d'architecture* (1807) Charles-François defended the traditional methods of architectural education, particularly apprenticeship and the lessons at the Académie Royale d'Architecture, and attacked the new methods adopted by the Ecole Polytechnique that avoided the true "principles of composition" and allowed architects to modify the proportions of the orders. He was also critical of functionalism: if the various options for a functional plan resulted in equally beautiful compositions, it would be impossible to distinguish a good building from a bad one.[46] Exasperated by the contradictions in the new theories, he exclaimed, "What a delirium of perfection has taken hold of this physicomathematical faction, composed of different sects, some accepting and other refusing the existence of universal principles in architectural design, all devoted exclusively to the exact sciences!"[47] With remarkable insight Charles-François recognized that architecture belonged neither with the applied sciences nor in the realm of aesthetics. Architecture could not be taught according to the models of either engineering or painting. The result in both cases would be an unacceptable reduction of architectural values, as architecture's dimension as a communicative practice with deep cultural roots was ignored. Architectural meaning was based in history and had always transcended techniques. Thus he dreamed of a new *école spéciale d'architecture* that would provide a solid education in the humanities (*lettres*) as a ground for the future architect.[48]

Convinced that students were learning only geometry and drawing, Charles-François thought that "the study of architecture was being reduced to the elaboration of projects," although "the beauty of architecture depends on its conception."[49] Drawing is simply a means to express thoughts, but it can become an obstacle in producing good work. In *Principes* he speculated on why there are so few masterpieces in architecture, compared to other arts. He noted that architects, unlike painters and sculptors, did not learn their métier by actually making buildings (chap. 42). He viewed drawings as a hindrance because they cannot determine many attributes of a building or ensure its perfection. Even full-scale models are limited. Regardless of their age and talent, architects always encounter a "fluctuation" during construction; their quest for expression always follows an uncertain road (238–239). Even good buildings, he argued, would be better if the architect could correct the work as it is being executed. Interestingly, his critique shows that architectural practice already assumed that drawing is a tool for planning and prediction: a conclusive picture of a future building rather than an instrument for divination.

Charles-François thought that the emphasis on drawing and the misleading connection between architecture and painting (evident in the works of eighteenth-century architects such as Legeay, Boullée, Ledoux, and De Wailly) led young architects to abuse their imaginations, to ignore the principles of their art, and to design without good taste. Consequently, they could produce only terrible exercises, often simple images that could not be built.[50] Charles-François rejected Durand's notion that efficiency is the main objective of architecture. He could not accept the immense buildings that his contemporaries took only a few weeks to design. The conception of an important building had to take a long time; it required a vast, fruitful imagination and an eminently sensible mind. Speed in the process of design, prompted by the grid of Durand's mechanism of composition, created the illusion that architecture is an easy discipline and that rendering drawings is its sole difficulty. In fact, the talent of an architect could be measured only in the execution of buildings.[51] Charles-François thought that the best practical education for a student would involve the careful inspection of buildings while accompanied by a master, as detailed observations and reflections were recorded in a journal. After seven years of this training, the apprentice could start to build.

Charles-François also criticized the comprehensive projects—using working drawings and specifications to forecast the entire sequence and cost of construction—that were recommended by Jean Rondelet as a key to successful building. Today these aspects of a project are associated with engineering and finance, but for Charles-François they had the same limitations as predictive drawing and design. Emphasizing working drawings and cost estimates, he thought, would hinder the artist's genius by altering his initial ideas and causing him to lose sight of perfection.[52] He stressed that estimates had only a didactic value; using them was not more economical, because they failed to generate better buildings. The process of building could not be reduced to planning, and building construction could not be learned through books that collected typical details. Contemporary architects should rather imitate their ancient predecessors, who never endangered their structures by using dubious building systems or accepting miserable economic requirements.[53]

Charles-François sought an architecture of durability and stability in a world that had just experienced violent revolutionary change. Chaos had resulted from humanity's newly discovered "historicity," as the vector of progress destabilized the present and threatened to undermine the ground of humanity. As a contemporary engineer, Rondelet argued in his *Art de bâtir* for a progressive history of architecture in which the most significant forms were generated by structural ingenuity. He praised Gothic and French eighteenth-century builders, but denigrated the Egyptian pyramids as almost stupid and the Greeks' use of stone lintels as incompetent.[54] In opposition, Charles-François had already ridiculed Rondelet's view that most architects in the past had followed "no rules or principles" and that "where there should be less mass there was more" and vice versa.[55] In his opinion, the eighteenth century was no more enlightened than previous ones, because calculations did not necessarily lead to superior judgment. He thought that masterpieces from the past were obvious, but the Gothic "species" failed because the public could not perceive how its structural forces are transmitted. For Charles-François, the best architecture communicates clearly.

The "true principles" that nature teaches architecture are durability and stability, and these values are crucial for modern institutions that must transcend historical change. Although his argument may seem either traditional or banal, it was made with a scientific knowledge of structural behavior and a full understanding of architecture's historical role in the "construction" of civil society (*Principes*, 250). Durability therefore expresses value and acquires symbolic status. Even if buildings ultimately must die, it is the architect's responsibility to produce long-lasting, "immortal" buildings.[56] They can help reconstitute a tradition at a time when living traditions have begun to vanish. In mountains, for example, the architect may discover "the mystery" of forces and resistance in equilibrium, "the geometry of the pyramids that have lasted for 4,000 centuries" [*sic*]. Although buildings generated by the new "geometricians" have a stereotomic virtuosity that captures the attention of observers, they soon leave people restless (208).

Unlike Jean-Louis Viel, Charles-François believed that the origin of architecture is ultimately unknowable (94). It probably coincided with the birth of societies and displayed a primitive simplicity. As architecture became more complex it required precepts and rules to produce "more commodious and durable buildings." Theory should provide rules that are stated in words rather than numbers, based on experiences gathered from books, trips, or meditation. It must rely on history, and it is useful mostly for students and clients (especially the new, uneducated *citoyens*). Practice determines the real ability of the architect, who acquires it only by studying examples and by executing and supervising the construction of buildings. It is *only* through historical examples that we can understand the "universal grammar." In fact, he associates his teaching of rules through precedent with Buffon's *histoire naturelle*: "contemplating often the same objects durable impressions are formed, which are linked in our minds by fixed and invariable relationships."[57] He thereby also indicates an analogy with the study of classics in literature.

In examining the Western tradition, Charles-François argued for a continuous line of development: a "European" architectural language in which every "species" (*espèce*)—that is, Gothic, Renaissance, Italian, and modern French—derives ultimately from the same Greek roots and develops from its predecessor. Some, such as the Italian Renaissance works of Palladio and Vignola or Les Invalides in Paris, correctly adapt the Greek style to modern needs, while others, such as the "angular architecture" of Borromini and Guarini and the French rococo, corrupt the principles by making capricious and arbitrary changes. Gothic, for instance, was not a distinct "invention" with autonomous principles but a result of decadence due to circumstance, the absence of historical models, and the decline of political structures (*Principes*, 70).[58] The diversity of customs and opinions, argued Charles-François, had terrible consequences, even in ancient times. The desire for novelty is "an internal enemy," even during times of political stability (43).

His argument against inordinate freedom, coupled with his concern that excessive competition had led to recent architectural decadence, sounds reactionary at first. Charles-François repeated this virulent critique in many of his works, most notably in his best-known essay, *Décadence de l'architecture à la fin du dix-huitième siècle* (1800), where he assailed two popular late-eighteenth-century architects. Without naming them, he characterized one (possibly Soufflot) by the extension of his ruinous enterprises, and the other (possibly Ledoux or Boullée) by the great number of his excessively imaginative designs.[59] For Charles-François, construction could not be reduced to mathematical formulas, or architecture to the art of drawing.[60] It was not sufficient to possess imagination or to study the theory of construction; only the traditional complementary pairing of words and deeds could lead to an expressive and politically responsible architecture.[61]

Charles-François did not simply advocate a conservative view but instead sought "progress" within a tradition that was neither nationalistic nor egalitarian. His criticism in *Décadence* was addressed primarily to "fashionable architects" who seek principles from diverse nations rather than from their own tradition, which is based on "Greek masterpieces." His rational bias did not permit him to acknowledge "truths" in mythical expressions, so he dismissed the "capricious productions of barbarians" that his brother so much admired.[62] He was also critical of the new "historical" books (possibly referring to compilations by Durand and Legrand) that assembled buildings from diverse cultures and had thus contributed to architecture's decline. Viel obviously comprehended both the danger and the potential opened up by architectural history. He rejected the possibility that "real beauty" could emerge from a mélange of different architecture or that each *espèce* of architecture could have its own relative beauty.[63] In our search for true taste, he insists, we must be "persuaded" (*persuadé*) that the taste one follows is the best. For him, this was the Western "language," with its Greek principles. Without this persuasion, one cannot correct ideas and one's path will be vague and uncertain. For us, the Greeks are preeminent *because* they are ancient and because they originated our language; our architecture at least has the potential to become more perfect. Charles-François's syntactic *architecture parlante* is structurally similar to the poetry about words of the literary avant-garde.

Yet it is also keenly aware of its responsibility as a political gesture, based on historical interpretation.[64]

Charles-François's contributions are difficult to assess. Unlike most of his contemporaries, he understood that architecture could not be reduced to specialized knowledge. Although it is not "the most important among human disciplines," it is certainly part of "high knowledge" and must be engaged with other disciplines (*Principes*, 20). He deplored the chaotic situation that followed the revolutionary struggle, and even cited political convulsions as a reason for the disorienting obsession for architectural novelty.[65] His attitudes appear to be conservative, rejecting innovations that now seem to anticipate the modern movement, but he clearly recognized the relationship between architectural and political orders, in the broad sense of humanity's search for equilibrium and public participation. He believed that architecture had to function primarily as a space for social communication. Without this relationship to society, there was little hope for a coherent architecture (or a coherent culture), regardless of the architect's talents. His views on the revolution as a cause of architectural decadence probably condemned him to oblivion, yet they are tempered by a confidence that architecture could indeed be *otherwise;* as a result, he had an almost postmodern, weak faith in progress.[66]

Principes was intended as a reception theory—an address to the new bourgeois *citoyen* who had to be educated to read traditional architecture properly, despite its association with the values of the ancien régime. Given Charles-François's political understanding of architecture, his aim to educate the user is significant: both the architect and the amateur should know the rules by both *sentiment* and *théorie*, while the *praxis* of the architect could be obtained only through "immersion" in architectural culture (*Principes*, 19). The *vrai beau* must rely on historical principles because the imitation of nature in architecture is not as direct as in painting or sculpture. A dry enumeration of a few precepts, however, is mostly useful for the public and for beginners. The practitioner learns through examples, observations, and comparisons, and must engage the history that has now become really accessible" (29–30). He advises the young architect and student to read not just Vitruvius and Palladio but also books on antiquities such as those by Le Roy, Desgodetz, and Stuart and Revelt ([*sic*]; chap. 8). Only with this experience can imagination ("a feeling that creates") and taste ("a feeling that judges") become manifest in architectural productions that exhibit "ingenuity" and "convenience" (27).

Viel was promoting *praxis* as history, a discourse founded on experience and a predominantly oral basis, rooted in practice and driven by questions arising from action in a particular place, for a particular client and cultural context (50). This is a historical reason, unlike the reason of science, technology, or mythology. Its lessons cannot be reduced to precepts. Indeed, Charles-François often repeated his argument about the connection between words and action that implicitly questioned the emerging technological models around him.

Interweavings

If you write deplorable twaddle using Surrealist techniques, it will still be deplorable twaddle. No Excuses. If you belong to the species of individuals who do not know the meaning of words, it is more than probable that the practice of Surrealism will simply serve to highlight this gross ignorance.

Louis Aragon, *Treatise on Style* (trans. Alyson Waters); cited by Dalibor Veseley, *Architecture in the Age of Divided Representation*

The notion of a progressive history of "works" became dominant in nineteenth-century architectural discourse. It assumed that architectural language was expressed rationally through building styles, as a form of elegant yet "scientific" prose. Once a style (or a deliberate combination of styles) had been chosen rationally to communicate a programmatic issue, a national identity, or even a voyeuristic plot, all that remained was an exercise in "composition."

The framework established at the Ecole Polytechnique and described in Durand's two books became the basis for most modern programs of architectural education in Europe and North America.[67] Many of the pedagogical assumptions in Durand's theory were also internalized almost immediately at the Ecole des Beaux-Arts. Despite the fierce dispute over "architecture as art" versus "architecture as engineering" during the nineteenth century, both camps took for granted the most crucial presuppositions. This unproductive debate has continued into our own time as a narrow and distorted understanding of history and rationality, has led to the discipline's polarization into functionalist and formalist positions.

Charles-François Viel was the first to identify the "question" of style as a basic grammar to ground creativity. The architect had to write well and had to know the meaning of words. Unlike his contemporaries, however, he also recognized that style could not be generated a priori by a simple act of will and reduced to the creative impulse; it depended on the nation and the place. The appropriate style could be discovered only through historical reason and active making. He tried to imagine a different alternative that did not reduce architecture to applied science, mindful of the dangers involved in the aestheticizing of architecture to manifest personal fantasies, which he believed were often meaningless and socially irrelevant. At his most conservative, he deplored personal creativity and maintained that ancient examples are almost impossible to surpass.[68] His understanding of theory as a discourse that engages the past synthetically, through the great buildings of the European tradition, was obviously a construction. Nevertheless, as a limited form of hermeneutics, it questioned the notion that architecture is a "progressive" discipline driven by mathematical reason as are the exact sciences. To Charles-François, the meaning of past works was based on their historical endurance, a phenomenological significance that transcends time. If the great historical models provide the rules and contemporary practice imitates them, architecture would be generated though a *mimēsis* of history. A crucial issue is the precise significance of "imitation." As Nietzsche would explain a few decades after Charles-François, history can offer a point of departure for significant human creation in the absence of cosmology, but it can also be a terrible obstacle that makes us feel like latecomers, always operating in the shadows of giants. If an imitation is merely a copy or a transcription, the result inevitably will be conservative; if it is a translation, however, we may expect true innovation: a work that appears new and unexpected, yet ultimately familiar—a work that lasts.

Reading the Viel brothers as complementary rather than merely polemical offers a point of departure for imagining a possible architecture at the end of progress, beyond conventional notions of ethics and aesthetics. Although Jean-Louis still championed a Newtonian poetics and believed in poetry as science, he fully understood the need to engage criticism in constructing a productive history that could demonstrate the truth in *mythos* and the affinity between truth and beauty. Charles-François, on the other hand, also understood the importance of criticism. Arguing that poetry demands science, he criticized his contemporaries for having segregated the art of drawing from the science of composition and construction. Science, for Charles-François, is "historical reason," a practical reason that could not be seamlessly merged with mathematical logic and that a poetic architecture demanded in order to be ethical.

On many issues the two brothers held widely differing positions. Jean-Louis offered a devastating critique of the Western classical tradition, which for Charles-François was the self-evident language based on a Greek grammar. Charles-François reduced the Greek grammar to a minimal expression of simple lines, tectonics, and proportions, almost reminiscent of the buildings in Giorgio De Chirico's metaphysical paintings or of Aldo Rossi's theoretical projects. Jean-Louis's understanding of architecture as language related it to the realm of cultural universals, expressing universal rituals through simple geometry. Jean-Louis provided a lucid exposition of the theoretical premises behind the innovative architecture of the revolution, which Charles-François interpreted as an obsession for novelty based on a delusion about origins. In this web of differences and affinities we find crucial contemporary questions, arguments against mainstream developments, and potential options for an architecture built upon love, accountable to both *erōs* and *philia*.

If architecture is a form of writing, it must be either poetry or eloquent prose. The Viel brothers conceived the architect/author as a responsible individual endowed with historical perspective. Architecture can be neither instrumental production nor mythical creation. For them, technological and cultural automatism is out of the question. Whether it relies on an introspective search for the inherent limits of embodied reason and the structures of consciousness, ultimately opening up an understanding of *mythos,* or on an exoteric grounding in historical reason, architecture is articulated as spiritual growth. Discourse is understood as action, as both men reject the new technological understanding of theory (as applied science) and practice (as technology), as well as the naïve desire for their fusion or perfect match.[68] The architect must be wise, capable of understanding the cultural significance of his work, rather than a technical specialist in the arts or the sciences. Opposing reductive notational systems, from Durand to the new fashions of "diagram architecture," the Viel brothers fashioned an understanding of architecture as writing that was open to *translation.* Whether architecture is paired with hieroglyph or style, poetics or politics, the issue is rhetoric, and the problem is finding appropriate expression for effective social participation. While their emphases on reason and poetry differ, and in some respects they point in opposing directions, the Viel brothers seek an architecture founded on cultural universals, both eloquent and truly intersubjective. Between them, they suggest the possibility of an architecture that is both a poetic utterance and an ordering device for our social existence.

Charles-François rejected Durand's technological theory, while Jean-Louis bitterly criticized the useless aesthetic discussions around eighteenth-century neoclassicism. Each in his own way was mindful of the dangers involved in the aesthetization of architecture and its manifestation in self-gratifying fantasies that allowed no effective social participation. If architecture was an art, that was because beauty was socially relevant and involved human situations, because its order was a manifestation of truth.

8 Poetry and Meaning from within *a* (Western) Architectural Tradition

Opening conversation

A tear can be shed [in the face of beauty] on several occasions. Assuming that beauty is the distribution of light in the fashion most congenial to one's retina, a tear is the acknowledgement of the retina's, as well as the tear's, failure to retain beauty. On the whole, love comes with the speed of light; separation with that of sound [language]. It is the deterioration of the greater speed to the lesser that moistens one's eye. Because one is finite, a departure from [a place of beauty] always feels final; leaving it behind is leaving it forever. . . . For the eye identifies itself not with the body it belongs to but with the object of its attention. . . . A tear is the anticipation of the eye's future.

Joseph Brodsky, *Watermark*

Crying is the rooting of vision in the ground of our needs: the need for openness; the need for contact; the need for wholeness.

David M. Levin, *The Opening of Vision*

There is . . . no problem of the *alter ego* because it is not I who sees, not he who sees; because an anonymous visibility inhabits both of us, a vision in general, in virtue of that primordial property that belongs to the flesh, of being here and now and of radiating everywhere and forever.

Maurice Merleau-Ponty, *The Visible and the Invisible* (trans. Alphonso Lingis)

Architecture from within

A real tradition is not the relic of a past that is irretrievably gone; it is a living force that animates and informs the present. In this sense the paradox which banteringly maintains that everything which is not tradition is plagiarism is true. . . . Far from implying the repetition of what has been, tradition presupposes the reality of that which endures. It appears as an heirloom, a heritage that one receives on condition of making it bear fruit before passing it on to one's descendants.

Igor Stravinsky, *Poetics of Music in the Form of Six Lessons* (trans. Arthur Knodel and Ingolf Dahl)

Contrary to first impressions, the rupture of living traditions [in the modern pe-
riod] does not signify a loss or devalorizing of the past. It is even probable that only
after this rupture took place the past could reveal itself as such, acquiring a weight
and influence hitherto unknown. The loss of tradition means rather that the past
has lost its transmissibility and that unless one finds a way to recover a relationship with it, it may simply become an object of accumulation.
Giorgio Agamben, *The Man without Content* (trans. Georgia Albert)

With the dominance of Newtonian epistemology, during the eighteenth
century God's language was still associated with mathematics: the language of the unquestionable "laws" of Nature, such as "universal gravitation." As they extrapolated Newton's insight into the human sciences,
artists and theoreticians (such as Rameau in music, Batteux in the fine arts,
and Briseux and Laugier in architectural theory) believed they could deci-
pher this mathematical language and use it to establish the ultimate
ground of their respective disciplines.[1] Theories of expression in architecture sought the "cultural" origin of architectural forms, but still relied on
proportion as the means to establish their analogies with Nature.

However, during the same century, and often in works by the same
writers, the linguistic analogy gradually became more important. Despite
the self-evidence of mathematical reason demonstrated in experiments and
technical products, Giambattista Vico questioned the legitimacy of mathematical logic as both the original and ultimate ground for a universal language. Vico's insight into myth as the original mode of human expression
led him to a very different understanding of language: he believed that a
universal language must be *poetic* rather than rational or mathematical. In
a nondialectical way, he affirmed both the specificity of individual cultures
and the reality of imaginative universals. This insight is invaluable for us,
and it may have been conveyed to architects for the first time through the
teachings of his intellectual friend, the Venetian Carlo Lodoli.[2] Vico's understanding of history as neither exclusively linear nor cyclical is crucial
for a postmodern theory of interpretation that recognizes the fallacies of
progress and Western logocentrism, while avoiding relativism and drawing from our multiple traditions to construct an ethical *praxis*.[3]

After architecture slowly fell into history, sometime between the
Entwürff of Fischer von Erlach (1721) and Durand's *Parallèle* (1801), we
encountered the challenge to think about architecture from within—to examine its potential significance from within one constructed order, our
own Western culture, with its deep spiritual and epistemological roots in
antiquity. In *Human, All Too Human* (1878), Friedrich Nietzsche lucidly
expressed the limitations and challenges of artistic production in his own

time and for centuries to come. On the one hand, our new historical vantage point enables us to appreciate art as never before, "when the magic of death seems to play around it." He predicted that the artist might "soon be regarded as a glorious relic," yet "the best in us has perhaps been inherited from the sensibilities of earlier ages to which we hardly any longer have any access by direct paths; the sun has already set, but the sky of our life still glows with its light, even though we no longer see it."[4]

Nietzsche eventually saw the capacity for poetic expression as the essential attribute of the new *Übermann* who could face the abyss serenely. His own philosophy sought to unveil new truths and itself became poetic play. He recognized that the stakes are high and the problem is highly complex, owing to the changes undergone by society after the French Revolution. He writes: "Artists nowadays often go wrong when they labor to make their works produce a sensual effect; for their spectators or auditors are no longer in possession of a full sensuality and the effect which, quite contrary to his intention, the artist's work produces upon them is a feeling of 'saintliness' closely related to boredom." The case is not hopeless, however. Nietzsche suggests that the sensuality of the spectator commences where the artist's ceases, and so they may encounter one another "at one point at the most."[5]

Reflecting on architecture and the problems that arise when it is perceived as aesthetic "work," Nietzsche points out that in general, we no longer understand architecture, "at least by no means in the same way as we understand music. We have grown out of the symbolism of lines and figures, just as we have weaned ourselves from the sound effects of rhetoric." This "cultural milk" is no longer something we imbibe. "Everything in a Greek or Christian building originally signified something, and indeed something of a higher order of things: this feeling of inexhaustible significance lay about the building like a magical veil. Beauty [in its aesthetic sense, as *pulchritudo*] entered this system only incidentally, without essentially encroaching upon the fundamental sense of the uncanny and exalted, of consecration by magic and the proximity of the divine; at most *beauty* mitigated the *dread*—but this dread was everywhere the presupposition."[6] Nietzsche clearly detected the basic problem that we still face in the reception of architecture: for his contemporaries, the beauty of a building was like a superficial mask with nothing behind it—mere contingent ornament.

Amid the diversity of world architectures, the incomprehensibility of rituals, the seeming irrelevance of theoretical speculations, and the useless pursuit of either the beautiful or the sublime, Durand's early-nineteenth-century dream of a logical and functional theory spread quickly. The dream, doubling as a nightmare, was soon expressed as an equation. Despite Gottfried Semper's insightful critique of architecture as a fine art and his sophisticated understanding of its origins in the realm of craftsmanship, he conceived architecture as a "problem" to be solved through the language of algorithms. Paradoxically, as Merleau-Ponty has pointed out, *the algorithm is a revolution against given languages.* Regardless of their sophistication, instrumental theories of architecture that respond to human life through quantitative or conceptual variables invariably bypass real cultural issues in favor of pragmatic solutions or organic analogies, thereby denying architecture its potential relevance to the human condition.

We may be certain of architecture's significance, but what we can say about its meanings (like what we can say about death) indicates that they remain out of reach. Architecture seems to reside in another realm, and this is evident in all of its embodiments: from notations to constructions of all sorts, including *machinae,* gardens, and buildings. This quality has led poststructuralist critics such as Mark Wigley to assert the homogeneity of "architecture" with its "representations." Its logical consistency makes this popular argument, derived from Derrida's notion of *écriture,* challenging; but, as George Steiner has pointed out, proving that a critical piece of writing about Rilke is homogeneous with Rilke's own writing does an injustice to our experience of the poetic. Participating in a poetic moment is transformative; conventional temporality collapses and, to paraphrase Octavio Paz, the incandescent moment of coincidence between life and death is made evident. While both may be embodied in written words, poetry (not necessarily verse) is qualitatively distinct from prose. In poetic works, regardless of their specific medium, the primary orality and embodiment of our prereflective engagement with the world are made evident: our full consciousness is addressed, not only our faculty for discursive reason. We meet the work halfway, and we "know" with that organ we cannot name, between the heart and the stomach. Truth appears as a spark, an ephemeral sound, a silence, never permanent, always an evanescent encounter. The poetic word is multivocal and thus eminently *translatable.* Of course, an audience must be willing to listen.

To deny the capacity of poetic works such as Andrei Tarkovsky's *Nostalghia* and Gaudí's Casa Battló to engage and transform, it would be necessary to agree with Descartes that sensory experience is a delusion, or to agree with poststructuralism that the work is merely a cultural construction; both positions deny a prereflective ground for human consciousness. Arguing the philosophical case for phenomenology would be inappropriate here, but it is important to note the debate between poststructuralism and phenomenology that has continued in recent years, with many critics demonstrating the importance of Merleau-Ponty's late philosophy as opposed to the assumptions of Derrida.[9] Specific encounters with works of art are never identical, even for the same person, but they enable humans to commune with a sense of truth, however ephemeral—Heidegger's *alētheia*—in a postcosmological world.

Both the poststructuralist critique and the response from existential phenomenology were anticipated by cultural transformations during the Enlightenment. Since the eighteenth century the "absolute" signifier has been one step removed, as in Newton's metaphysics.[8] God is present but distant, unaffected by the relative motions of bodies and human actions; eventually he is banished to the realm of personal belief. This condition is totally different from the medieval understanding of God as a *mystery*, an Other, yet continuous with the *logos*. During the eighteenth century, history became a progressive change generated by humans, a present distinct from the past and oriented toward the future. Architecture sought to communicate emotions through sheer visibility, without presuming a connection to the invisible. The linguistic analogy, with its complexities and contradictions, thus became the single option for modern architecture. According to Steiner, all linguistic discourses involve *both* the concrete and abstract poles of reality. For architecture, it is significant that the Platonic *chōra* is also the place of the "mystery of language," to use Merleau-Ponty's words, which is its simultaneous transformation in contrary directions.[9] Plato had recognized in *Timaeus* that the appearance and designation of cultural space enabled words to refer at once to the singular and to the universal. This quality points to the unique capacity of architecture to signify order and its reluctance to be reduced to a univocal sign.

Much debate has focused on the concept of extralinguistic thought. Merleau-Ponty pursued the prereflective ground of consciousness by studying very young babies. Humanity has often noted experiences that can be felt but are "too deep for words." Indeed, music and architecture seem to accommodate forms of thought or "energized significance" (to use Steiner's words again) that operate in modes that are highly abstract but also physical. Despite convincing studies about the linguistic nature of the human imagination,[10] architects usually believe that their "inspiration" is somewhat (if not totally) extralinguistic. The hybrid nature of language—its material/immaterial, abstract/concrete, physical/mental duality—is a central given of consciousness, and we must accept its inherent challenge to simple logic.[11] While language "constructs" different concepts of space and time in different cultures, a preunderstanding of space-time also has an impact on language. The constructivist argument is therefore circular, and the prodigality of languages remains the central mystery of our humanity.

Language is our human capacity to make promises. Anthropologists have suggested that a relationship exists between human evolution and the future tense in language. Primates never store tools for future use. Despite the concept of entropy in science, which declares the inevitability of decay, the future is needed to preserve our humanity. Today, at the "end of modernity," we may question the notion of endless progress and the belief in a single universal utopia, but our acts and deeds, particularly as architects, presume the ethical imperative of creating a better future for others. Our "projects" are enduring promises that are written in the future tense. Architecture, like a poem, is then received out of time, enabling us to discern the past of the present and the future of the present. In the *Poetics*, Aristotle left us an insightful meditation on the relation between "history" and "poetry": History recounts real facts from the past, whereas poetry (fiction or drama) opens up the future by transcending the first order of reference to reality; it therefore is more "philosophical" than history. In other words, fiction reveals what is essential for humans in recognition of our mortality and transcendence, and thus opens up potential realities for culture.

The relation between fiction and architecture is a large subject. Architects became aware of the affinity between fiction and architectural programs during the late eighteenth century, and a few pursued the idea during the next two centuries. The need for emplotment is still a hotly debated issue, and its form is not obvious. In oral poetry such as epic poems, the plot was never linear.[12] Linear plots became hegemonic in Western literature only with the nineteenth-century inception of the Romantic novel and the linear presentation of history. Nevertheless, it is important to recognize the affinity of architecture with *poetic language*. Poetic languages, including music and architecture, enable humanity to overcome its immediate presence and experience a time out of time that is free from both linear temporality and the dreaded return of the same.

Architecture as poetic writing

Words are not signs. Jacques Derrida has made the point that "there is no linguistic sign before writing" (*Of Grammatology*, 1976, p. 14). But neither is there a linguistic "sign" after writing if the oral reference of the written text is adverted to. Though it releases unheard-of potentials of the word, a textual, visual representation of a word is not a real word, but a "secondary modeling system." Thought is

nested in speech, not in texts, all of which have their meanings through reference of the visible symbol to the [ephemeral, nonobjectified, transitory] world of sound.
Walter J. Ong, *Orality and Literacy*

When Vitruvius named the forms of expression proper to architecture, he explicitly associated these commensurate "arrangements" with the Greek concept of *idea*.[13] The word "idea" (*eidos*, form) is visually based and recurs etymologically in the Latin *videre*, to see. Therefore, Platonic ideas are voiceless and isolated (like images) rather than interactive (like speech). *Ichnographia* (the modern plan), *orthographia* (the elevation), and the more ambiguous *scenographia* contain notions of inscription, trace, and writing.

The importance of writing in the long-term historic transformations of human consciousness has been evoked in the previous discussion of *erōs*, particularly in the invention of alphabetic writing in the Semitic tradition, brought to fruition in Greek classical culture. Unlike pictographic scripts, alphabetic writing "freezes" speech and inscribes it in the "visual" world.[14] It suggests that reading occurs in the participatory space of *erōs*. Plato's well-known ambivalence toward writing is significant, especially since he inaugurated the tradition of systematic philosophy in the West. Plato's work is a rejection of the old oral culture, the interactive world of the poets who were banished from his Republic, yet his thought is presented in dialogues that explore baffling issues through oral speech in which Socrates typically confuses his interlocutors. This dialogical form of writing continued throughout Western philosophy, with illustrious examples provided by Galileo, Bruno, and Charles Perrault. Plato understood that written language could obliterate memory, and he has Socrates say in the *Phaedrus* that writing is inhuman because it pretends to establish outside the mind what can be only in the mind.[15]

What, then, is the nature of the traces made by the architect, which include drawings, specifications, models, and constructions at all scales and in diverse media? The temptation to compare them to writing (script) took hold during the early nineteenth century, and the comparison has become very fashionable during the past few decades in the wake of post-structuralism and its extrapolations into architectural theory. Ancient iconic writing systems that employ pictographic, ideographic, or rebus-like characters rely on our participation in the natural life-world. David Abram, among others, has noted the capacity of the Greek alphabet to reduce language's frame of reference to the strictly human sphere,[16] and thus to permit a potential self-referentiality in language and a post-Enlightenment division between the human (historical) realm and the more-than-human (natural) realm.

Pictograms, ideograms, notched sticks and rows of pebbles are essentially "mute"—the original sense of *mythos,* according to Vico. The "symbols" that humans had inscribed for millennia, before the first cuneiform script was invented around 3500 B.C.E., could "speak" only through a re-creative dialogue that, throughout most of our history, involved ritual action. This transformative communication was always a unique encounter that evoked the experience of *erōs,* reconciling life with the awareness of death. These re-creations were never reductions of speech-thought. Like the producer of the oral literature of "Homer," their real author, the bard, was anonymous. Every telling of the story was original and depended on poetic re-creation by a participating audience.

Associating architectural artifacts with ideograms and pictographs, rather than with discursive script, is consistent with the common belief that architecture, like music, communicates emotions rather than discursive thought. In our early "postliterate" culture, this analogy may suggest new responses to the fallacies of the early modern dichotomy between "nature" and "culture." Postmodern philosophy has shown the limitations of future-oriented progress and of human action as the sole agent of change.[17] The demystification of technology does not generate a new "mythology," but it enables the contemplation of human purpose and spiritual evolution in a different light. Indeed, the potential of architecture in the postmodern world is best revealed by an analogy with poetic speech. The disclosure of architectural order takes place in the real lived time of human existence, in the thickness of the vivid present. Despite the modern tendency to identify meaning with the expression of unambiguous "signs," we need not imagine architecture as an objectified script. On the contrary, since our preconceptual, embodied experience is the ground of all (linguistic) reality, meanings will always overflow that which is embedded in the objective, decontextualized thingness of buildings or artifacts.

When architects in the past few decades stated that architecture *is* writing, they were merely articulating a premise that had existed since the time of Vitruvius (and Plato). Yet despite the invention of alphabetical indexing and the use of the alphabet to write vernacular (spoken) languages in the High Middle Ages, and despite the celebrated invention of printing in the Renaissance, orality retained its primacy in Western culture well into the eighteenth century.[18] In spite of the changing models of reality that appeared with modern science and philosophy in the seventeenth century and transformed architecture's relation to the cosmos and history, the discipline continued to function symbolically: in the traditional sense of Plato's *symbolon,* it allowed for authentic *participation* through an erotic encounter with cathartic potential for a *sense* of orientation.

In his seminal essay "Signs in Rotation," Octavio Paz sketched the possibilities for a "critical poetry" that fully acknowledges the transformations suffered by Western culture (and eventually world civilization) since the nineteenth century. He notes that Mallarmé proclaimed the end of traditional poetry, of the sort that revealed, like a medieval cathedral or a baroque palace, "the world and the transworld as a totality."[19] His poetic expression is made possible not by rejecting but by fully engaging the reduction of language to univocal signs that characterizes the technological world. His reflections are extremely relevant for architecture. Paz argues that technology is the reality that is left after the unified *kosmós* has disappeared. The universe and the self are no longer whole. Traditional techniques functioned as bridges between human and nature, but technology comes between us and the more-than-human world; "it closes every prospect of view: beyond its geometries of iron, glass, or aluminum there is exactly nothing, except the unknown, the region of the formless that is not yet transformed by man" (245). Technology is not an image, because "its aim is not to represent or reproduce reality." It is also not a vision, because it conceives the world not as shape but merely as resources that are more or less malleable by the human will. Thus, concludes Paz, technology is not a language in the conventional sense, "a system of permanent meanings grounded on a vision of the world." Instead, it is a "repertoire of signs that possess temporal and variable meanings: a universal vocabulary of activity, applied to the transformation of reality" (242).

The architecture of modernity must employ an analogous repertoire of signs. This is the core of our tradition, a tradition with deep historical roots whose main vocation since the early nineteenth century has been revolutionary: to fight against itself. To recover the "otherness" that characterizes the poetic image, the architect has to "write" amid dispersed fragments. "The poem," asks Paz rhetorically, "is it not that vibrant space on which a few signs are projected like an ideogram that might be the purveyor of meanings? Space, projection, ideogram: these three words allude to an operation that consists in unfolding a place[,] . . . fragments that regroup and seek to form a figure, a nucleus of meanings" (249).

In this new millennium, as writing is being transformed by computer technology, images are pervasive, and literacy seems to be on the wane, we may develop a new capacity to understand architecture as a form of spatio-temporal poetry. Perhaps the same revolution in information technology that characterizes our global village may open up horizons for architecture to communicate a more universal mode of embodied knowledge, recalling Paz's notion of critical poetry. Doing so would require different modes of architectural *praxis* and education that might bring together a deep understanding of the cultural origins of modern architecture with a local understanding of values rooted in regions and diverse cultural (linguistic) horizons. Elsewhere I have emphasized that the making of architecture is an issue of translation (rather than transcription) between poetic forms (drawings, models, and buildings, for instance).[20] Each translation demands a thoughtful rewriting rather than an automatic transcription of a supposedly unambiguous "sign" into its referent. This view does not nostalgically invoke a concept of practice as a craft. The challenge is to couple the awareness of translation with a critical acceptance of processes involved in modern practice that by definition demand precise stipulation for construction. The hope would be to operate within those margins while transforming tools of precision into ironic poetic instruments.

Architecture as critical poem

A critical poem: if I am not mistaken, the union of these two contradictory words [by Mallarmé] means: that poem that contains its own negation and that makes of that negation the point of departure for the song, equally distant from affirmation and negation.
Octavio Paz, "Signs in Rotation" (trans. Ruth L. C. Simms)

The fact is that words say nothing, if I may put it that way. . . . There are no words for the deepest experience. The more I try to explain myself, the less I understand myself. Of course, not everything is unsayable in words, only the living truth.
Eugène Ionesco (diary; quoted in George Steiner, *After Babel*)

Ultimately, no form of human discourse can be absolutely private. This is, of course, the central paradox of twentieth-century art and of linguistic philosophies such as Wittgenstein's. Yet *ethical* projects depend for their significance on public participation. For the architect, this implies the *engagement* of a tacit common ground, a physical and cultural context, which in our times of globalization is often indistinct and made visible only by the act of creation itself. Thus the poetic architecture of Alvar Aalto, Sigurd Lewerentz, and Luis Barragán can at once be profoundly modern and embody cultural values of Finland, Sweden, and Mexico, respectively (never merely re-presenting a nation-state). Obviously, no architect can be sure of a work's significance as it appears for others through time, but we are not absolved of responsibility on that account. The production of artifacts for consumption by passive observers (or even awestruck visitors!) does not contribute to the perpetuation of cultures and the growth of human potential.

Ionesco's suspicion that language does not enable us to convey our transformative experiences has characterized the production of art and literature in the Western tradition for the past 150 years. Schönberg repeats in *Moses und Aron:* "O Wort, du Wort das mir fehlt." The work of art challenges our expectations and confronts us with the abyss; it defamiliarizes the world and seems to evoke silence. Yet those spaces in our inner experience into which we are suddenly thrust by significant works are never silent; instead, they are loud with commonplaces.[21]

This concept of the deficient word has demanded radically different strategies for making. Poetry and art that no longer took for granted an external reality generated a different "reference." Octavio Paz and George Steiner have shown how the classical "pact" between the word and the world broke down abruptly after 1850.[22] Established language became the enemy, and all significant poetry moved against the current of normal speech and narrative, which was modeled on scientific prose. In poetic language, Paz notes, "the marriage of the word and the universe is consummated in an unusual way, which is neither word nor silence but a sign that seeks its meaning" ("Signs in Rotation," 254).

This transformation was echoed in architecture. Prior to the nineteenth century, architecture (and its theoretical discourse) was embedded in a linguistic order associated with *scientia* and metaphysics. Despite what may now seem like elitist connotations, architecture was always "understood" during the eighteenth century, because it constituted an effective place for social interaction. After it was transformed into a discipline subservient to engineering at the Ecole Polytechnique, and despite its nineteenth-century "reconsecration" as a fine art, architects concerned with meaning have considered standard language a prison rather than a fertile point of departure. So-called Romantic architects adopted polemic positions against the Ecole des Beaux-Arts by questioning the scientific prose of theory (used to describe the intended program) and the established "speech" of buildings (the formal conventions of "styles"). Practice had to become critical; the architect in search of *poiēsis* relied on inner certitude rather than collective assumptions. Neither the prosaic language of theory nor a rational style in practice could help the architect fulfill a project's poetic and ethical promise.

Arthur Rimbaud, in his *Lettres du voyant* (1871), beautifully expressed the task at hand: "To find a way to speak; of the rest, each word being an idea, the time of a universal language will come!"[23] The stakes are high. Empty silence often follows our experience of new works housed in museums, and displays of formal acrobatics in architecture often appear nonsensical. To express a living truth must be the aim of human making. Works such as Joyce's *Finnegans Wake* and Libeskind's Jewish Museum manage to speak through the prison of language. Sometimes the results seem extreme; yet, as Steiner and Agamben have pointed out, the frontier zone is a constant in language. Languages are always being acquired, even within one's mother tongue; hence the "nonlinguistic" (*le dehors du langage*) is always present. This is the overriding point: elision, paraphrase, private connotations, and personal habits of speech are basic components of normal speech and must be accepted as a (paradoxical) *condition* of meaning. The "radical" modernist position is thus a matter of intention and emphasis. The correspondence between words and things has been weak ever since Babel. In its search for meaning, modernism merely emphasizes this weakness rather than affirming a strong connection based on a metaphysical or theological imperative. In any event, the mystery of language and the world of human institutions are more fundamental than this intentional change. Poetic forms such as architecture seek participation by speaking not about the speaker but about the "world," by expressing not technological control or political domination but true wonder and the supreme mystery of humankind.

The difficulty of such a task should not be underestimated, however. Contemporary mental pathologies notwithstanding, modern man and woman remain determined to exclude whatever cannot be articulated through logical reason. Architectural education is generally oriented toward the narrow pragmatic interests of professional corporations and has largely excluded the poetic. A student receives a minimal cultural grounding in the profession; most architectural courses convey technical information and decontextualized methods for solving problems, rather than raising and engaging real questions. Despite our avowed interest in history, most architects since the nineteenth century have failed to understand the historical scope of the discipline, and thus have remained unaware of the alternatives that existed when the dominant modernist paradigms took shape. The history of architecture (or rather history of buildings, since the publication of the "Grand Durand") has been taught mainly as a sequence of styles or functional types, and more recently as a product of anonymous social forces. Even postgraduate architectural history programs tend to be myopic in their scope, concentrating on a narrow section of the modern tradition. Neither a fine art nor an applied science, architecture has only recently begun to realize its true potential, mainly through a hermeneutic approach that can engage the intricacies of its historical reality. Yet teaching and practice continue to be polarized between those two false alternatives: fine art and applied science. The introduction of computers into architecture during the past two decades has helped reduce architectural discourse to issues of instrumentality. The most popular discussions presume the importance of this so-called paradigm shift and focus on the potential and limitations of this instrument, aiding the perpetuation of the dichotomy. Thus theoretical discourse tends to remain caught up in instrumental issues of form (innovation) and production (efficiency), while the humanistic dimension of architecture is further jeopardized and educational programs become increasingly vocational.

Charles-François Viel identified style as *the* problem of architectural expression, projecting the linguistic analogy into a new realm and identifying architecture with politics. With this "syntax of form," new confusions emerged. Most architects pursued style to communicate a particular "referent," such as the rationality of structure (Viollet-le-Duc), the ideology of religion (ecclesiology), nationalism (English Gothic), or, more recently, personal and corporate propaganda. This new concept of architecture was aligned with other important changes in the technological West, today embodied by the United States of America. As Tim Mitchell has demonstrated, drawing on insights by Heidegger and Foucault, the colonizing power of the West was based on its capacity to reduce the world to a picture, and to reduce the word and the building to univocal signs. This capacity developed only after the French Revolution, when epistemological and political changes permitted a full "democratic subjectivity."[24] The methods of representation developed at the Ecole Polytechnique in postrevolutionary France were instrumental for the success of industrialization, and became entrenched in modern architectural practice, first in Europe and now globally.[25] The educational programs of the Ecole were exclusively applied science, unconcerned with questions of philosophy or theology. The language used in this teaching was the prose of a positive reason.

The programs of the Ecole Polytechnique soon became the basis for modern architectural education in the Western world. The institution itself, with its military background, was exported by France to its colonies, either directly or adapted in ways that promoted colonization.[26] This new text-based education was often resisted in the colonies. Printing, for instance, was rejected in Egypt and the Middle East (with its predominantly oral Arabic culture) as late as the mid-nineteenth century.[27] However, during the past two centuries various written languages (such as Turkish) have adopted the Latin alphabet to systematize communication. Similarly, the Western system of technical drawing, now implicit in computer software that reduces lived space to a geometrical entity, has also been taken up around the world to design buildings, machines, and cities. The postcolonial desire for an architecture responsive to regional differences and cultural roots is ill-served by the presumed neutrality of this tool.

"Prose writing" became the guiding *analogon* for architectural production and reception globally. Architects' documents, including drawings, construction details, specifications, and cost estimates, were legitimate only if they could "picture" and "predict" artifacts clearly and efficiently. Buildings, on the other hand, were expected to express direct and unambiguous messages dictated by ideology or technology, messages that ultimately receded into the background as the buildings supported material life. Like consumer products, they were unable to save and preserve regional or cultural specificity. Once truth is assumed to be "behind" a picture, the embodied wisdom of local cultural practices is undermined. Then traditional truths may seem unattainable or irrelevant.

So far we have recognized both the poetic potential of architecture and the enormous difficulties in building a more compassionate, poetic world. In a technological world, increasingly synonymous with the global village, many are skeptical that architecture has any meaning at all, other than providing shelter. This skepticism is hardly surprising, since for technology truth obtains legitimacy by association with the achievements of applied science, which ultimately issue from a mathematical language: the one thing that seems to stand for all, regardless of local languages or cultures. Today's world is driven almost exclusively by efficiency of means. Efficiency stands as the absolute value in all orders of life, since it can be demonstrated through mathematical argumentation. For technology, specialization is the only viable solution to the proliferation of information—a position that disregards the need for historical knowledge to enable our ethical capacity to respond to our actions, in view of a total life experience, here and now. Thus the means can claim to be unaffected by the social consequence of its ends. Within this framework, architecture may appear to be nothing other than efficient and at best aesthetically interesting building for a distracted world civilization that would rather live on the computer screen.

Yet, while our reason may be capable of dismissing the quality of the built environment as central to our spiritual well-being, our dreams and our actions are always set in some place, and our understanding (of others and ourselves) could simply not *be* without significant places. The ideal would be a world of poetic objects that embody the memory and future of nations, both culturally specific and *translatable* by the others' corporeal imagination. As in poetry, the very notion of "project" in architecture presumes a semantic innovation. While formal invention has been facilitated by digital tools, genuine innovation requires a wide-ranging hermeneutic of the discipline (a historical understanding of form, program, and intentionality) that provides the architect with an appropriate language to verbalize a position. Architecture is a political act. It is never value-free, a mere question of fine building or seductive detailing. The architect requires a broad cultural foundation to be able to generate an ethical response.

9 The Ethical Image in Architecture

Opening conversation

Baal does not command, he babbles.
Babel is its power place, energetic
babeloscope—site of the collapsed tower(s).
Bricks, earth turned stone, metal and concrete,
bearing joy and terror,
befouled by successive generations of
brainless pornographers.

BREATH, song of streams and
brooks and birds and butterflies
braces for unending struggle at
Bab-ili.
Baboonery surrounds the gate of Gods,
bacchantic libations of *logos*
brutalizing all sacred summits,
biting tongues of Pentecostal fire licking
beams of light notwithstanding.

Bachelors *en babouches* philosophize:
Bosch's *Garden,*
Botticelli's *Birth,* and
Bellini's *Angels:* the experience of melting, all
brainless delusions, they claim, like the
bright light of darkness and our visceral dream flight,
bitter-sweet,
beckoning the sky inside.
Beatifically grinning they affirm negating:
"Babies don't actually smile, and the
barking of dogs in mourning is not anything like crying,
poetry untranslatable."

From Frances C. Lonna, *Architectural Alphabet*

The essentialist . . . and the social constructionist . . . have no need to quarrel [about beauty]. For either our responses to beauty remained unaltered over the centuries or [they] are culturally shaped. . . . If they are subject to our willful alteration[,] . . . surely what we should wish is a world where the vulnerability of the beholder is equal to or greater than the vulnerability of the person beheld, a world where the pleasure-filled tumult of staring is a prelude to acts that will add to the beauty already in the world—acts like making a poem, or a philosophic dialogue, or a divine comedy; or acts like repairing an injury or social injustice. Either beauty already requires that we do these things (the essentialist view) or we are at liberty to make of beauty the best that can be made—a beauty that will require that we do these things.

Elaine Scarry, *On Beauty and Being Just*

Meaningful architecture depends on recognition and participation, while acknowledging that the two fragments of the knucklebone will never fit perfectly, like the space between an intended meaning and what we say or write.

  Meaningful architecture depends on a realization that visible form and language refer to something other, recognized only when the dominant sense of vision is mediated by the body's primary tactile and synaesthetic understanding.

Frances C. Lonna, diary, 1998

Hermeneutics and ethical intentions

These meditations have shown that the reality of architecture is infinitely complex, both shifting with history and culture and also remaining the same, analogous to the human condition that demands that we continually address the same basic questions as we seek to come to terms with mortality and the possibility of cultural transcendence: the ultimate horizon of human desire. Architecture cannot be reduced to a historical collection of buildings, whose main significance may be to offer superfluous pleasure through disinterested contemplation, or to a technical solution to pragmatic necessities. A more careful appraisal of our architectural tradition suggests a different way to understand architecture's cultural relevance at the paradoxical crossing of ethics and erotics, operating in the realm of what Vico has called "imaginative universals." We have discovered a discipline that over the centuries has offered poetic orientation to humanity through widely different incarnations and modes of production. At once poetic and critical, the work of architecture provokes its interlocutors' imagination, destructuring the mechanisms that merely fulfill pragmatic needs. Through the poetic image, at once destabilizing and productive, architecture opens up a space of desire in which fiction is interwoven with human actions; it entices the inhabitant/participant to reach out to know and engage desire without being destroyed, transcending rather than hiding our mortal condition.

In view of the possibilities and difficulties emerging from this study, it is clear that the architect is neither a mystical creator (operating outside of language) nor a productive engineer (operating through mathematical language). He or she must necessarily engage the linguistic dimension of *a* culture. The main concern of architectural discourse is *ethical,* seeking to find appropriate language that may frame a project in view of the common good, a language always specific to each task at hand. The practice that emerges from such a theory can never be an instrumental application or a totalizing operation, one that might be universally applied as personal style or method. It may be better grasped as a verb rather than through its heterogeneous products; it is a process with inherent value. The presence of a well-grounded *praxis,* the trajectory of an architect's words and deeds over time that embody a responsible practical philosophy, is far more crucial than the aesthetic or functional qualities of a particular work.

We have seen that the responsibilities of architecture go far beyond the efficient production of commodities and cannot be legislated. Forcing structures to meet minimum requirements of building or ethics codes will not bring about this deeper responsibility. Like literature and film, architecture finds its ethical *praxis* in its poetic and critical ability to address the questions that truly matter for our humanity in culturally specific terms, revealing the enigmas behind everyday events and objects. While technology by nature homogenizes diversity, architectural *praxis* involves much more than technical means and scientific operations—it concerns values articulated through the stories that ground acts and deeds in a particular culture. The enduring quality of architecture is essential for the perpetuation of cultures. Values, as they emerge in the life-world, are best preserved by institutions and by embodiment in the physical constructions that make them possible. These diverse practices, like the dying languages of many traditional cultures, are endangered species that must be preserved.

The argument for an architecture that can be at once beautiful and just, modern and culturally specific, locally significant and universally eloquent, seductive and respectful, is difficult to make in our present techno-political climate. The claim I have made that this architecture has existed historically, and especially that it exists in modernity, is often viewed with cynicism. The archetypal modern values emerging from the French Revolution have been distorted. The present excesses of empty computer-generated formalism, with its roots in liberal capitalism ("liberty"), and the far more insidious moral disasters that humanity witnessed during the last century in the name of health and beauty—associated particularly with fascism ("fraternity") but also with communism ("equality")—have made us justifiably skeptical. Throughout human history architecture has often provided authentic dwelling, enabling individuals to recognize their place in a purposeful natural and cultural context. At times, however, and especially during the modern period, buildings have contributed to tragedy. The aesthetic programs underlying Nazi Germany are a case in point. Rather than being underscored by the imagination, the Nazi programs were born from a rationalized mythology, transformed into the dogma of nationalism. Think as well of the way two very tall yet typical skyscrapers, secular products of a triumphant technology, were read as ideological signs by Muslim fundamentalists on September 11, 2001. The shocking event of their destruction transformed two largely conventional buildings into symbols and had a nefarious effect on our world civilization. For all these reasons and despite the loss of poetic enchantment in the world as it opens itself to nihilism, all we can do is continue to weaken the strong values inherited from the ideological positions of fundamentalism, organized religion, and technology, expecting that in the gaps a new, genuine spirituality may emerge. It would be truly unethical to pretend that there exists a unique and absolute set of values to be represented in architecture, articulated in one mythology, dogmatic religion, rational ideology, or technology. The most authentic modern architecture opens itself to the abyss and is meaningful precisely by not functioning as a sign; like poetry it operates *against* prosaic or scientific language. To attain the goal of weakening the strong values that remain embedded in our cultures, architectural *praxis* must consider every problem individually in its context, and the design responses should be specific. We may still expect the resulting well-adjusted "fragments" to induce wonder, yet the critical dimension must never be absent. Heeding the advice of Nietzsche and Heidegger, the architect must avoid the planner's dream of total solutions and be prepared to wait patiently for the rustle of the angels' wings that may be passing by.

Martin Heidegger has shown that humanity faces a serious danger because we live our lives in a world of objects that conceal our finite horizon and impede our access to and understanding of the more-than-human world, leading us to treat nature as no more than resources to be exploited. For us on the other side of modernity, to read the landscape like an Australian aborigine or to live at one with nature as did our mythical ancestors are not real options. If something has been lost through modernity, such as our cultural understanding of the *genius loci,* something has been gained as well. The highly artificial culture within the technological world is now capable, through its historical self-consciousness, of embracing the previously contradictory aporias of cyclical and linear time (reconciling cosmic time with historical time) and thus may recognize for itself the same mysterious origins once discovered and released through the earliest products of *technē-poiēsis*. Through historical recollection and future orientation, we can cultivate not only our capacity for stewardship and responsibility but also our poetic potential as makers to disclose and celebrate the original mystery as it appears in the primary structure of our embodiment: the meaningfulness of a *given* world that refuses to be reduced to universal categories.

The use of language has obvious limitations. Words and deeds can never fully coincide. Once a work inhabits the public realm it is beyond the architect's control. An expressed intention can never fully predict the work's meaning, and others decide its destiny and its final significance. But this circumstance is to be celebrated rather than deplored, since a strict word-deed consistency indicates a scientistic point of view. As George Steiner has suggested, the "opaqueness" of language characterizes human existence. Human language is unlike the words of gods for whom "to name is to make." The possession of symbolic, multivocal languages, analogous to diverse modes of gesturing, making, and constructing, is among our most precious gifts.

These observations indicate that despite potential slippages and logical "inconsistencies," our best bet as creators is to recognize and embrace the inherent phenomenological continuity between thinking and making, between our words in our particular language and our deeds. Architects are accountable for their intentions, which are what they truly control. Despite the predominant opinion that often dismisses good intentions in view of "real" deeds, well-grounded intentions are crucial and rare in the modern world. Beyond what an individual is capable of articulating at the surface of consciousness or through one particular product, intentions imply a whole style of thinking and action that takes into account a past life and thick network of connections with a culture. Intentional thinking is the ethical foundation of *praxis*, in the term's full Aristotelian sense. Prior to the early eighteenth century, architectural *praxis* took its orientation from *phronēsis*, a practical philosophy with its roots in everyday life that nevertheless was reconciled at different moments with the articulations of reality in mythology, theology, philosophy, or science. In modernity, this orientation must come from historical interpretation.

History enables alien artifacts to tell us their stories through a hermeneutic process. This is a history for the future, one meant to enhance

our vitality and creativity rather than one that may immobilize us through
useless data, unattainable models, or an immoderate respect for the old for
its own sake. The architecture and the words (mostly in form of texts) that
have articulated the *praxis* of other times and places must be engaged in
light of relevant prejudgments issuing from our contemporary questions,
yet also in the context of the language (and culture) of their makers, re-
specting the questions they originally addressed. Thus the process of interpretation, appropriating that which is acknowledged as truly distant,
should make it possible to render their voices in our own specific time and
politics, rather than assuming a universal language at work or a progressive teleology. Needless to say, this hermeneutic understanding is equally
applicable to our synchronic engagement with other cultures.

Hermeneutics involves the interpretation of architectural intentions,
reading the works of other times and places in relation to the epistemological contexts in which they were produced. To engage in a productive
dialogue and a fusion of horizons, the aim is to read between the lines and
with courtesy. The world of the work, and the world in front of the work,
must be allowed to appear, in an act acknowledging the human pursuit
of meaning over and above other motivations. Nevertheless, this reading
must also be critical, seeking to understand how these architectural works
and texts may respond to the questions of our present humanity. A critical
hermeneutics rejects the historical flattening and homogenization of deconstruction and proposes the valorization of experiential content, the
mystery that is human purpose, and the presence of spirituality. It always
seeks to account for what matters and can change our life.

Within this framework of understanding, ethics appears not through
norms or generalities but through stories that focus on specific works and
individuals. In recent critical theory and in the field of cultural studies, the
self is understood as a dangerous inflated ego invented by the eighteenth
century and has received a bad name. Feminist and social critiques tend
to render art and design as the result of more or less anonymous, more or
less insidious forces. The unmasking of ego-centered interpretations is of
course healthy. Following up this diagnosis with a desire to renounce our
personal imagination is very dangerous, however. The imagination is not
an evil, distorting device that can be replaced by an objective consensual
framework. I have already alluded to Richard Kearney's concept of the
imagination's primary ethical function. Compassion and love are impossible without it. The imagination is as crucial to ethics as it is for the labors
of Eros. The embodied author with specific cultural roots is also capable
of poetic speech, of making beyond the confines of a narrow style, ideol-

ogy, or nationality. My claim is that individuals in history, through their personal reformulation of basic human questions, have contributed imaginative, poetic responses to our universal call for dwelling—answers from which we can learn and develop an ability to act here and now.

A crucial part of architecture's linguistic dimension is the program. It is important to emphasize that the architectural program is a promise. The program is never neutral, a simple list of requirements given by a client or an institution that absolves the architect of responsibility. Agreeing to design a prison, a museum, or a hospital is a complex decision that may have grave consequences. If the architect accepts the commission, he or she must be convinced that the institution itself contributes to the common good. It may be possible to transform a given program through dialogue with the client or by means of political maneuvering, and to enhance a sense of fairness through beauty for the indwellers. It may also seem inconceivable to put away individuals whose moral worth may be superior to that of their jailers, to aestheticize or decontextualize human artifacts as some museums have done in the past two centuries, or to contribute to the pathologies of society by merely framing technological processes rather than proposing an environment for healing. Programmatic decisions commit the architect and should not be taken lightly. Every institution poses particular questions that cannot be answered by note. It does not suffice to make a facility efficient and pleasant. The program is a fundamental part of the project, since it is obviously a proposal for lives to be lived. The program is indeed the most articulate holder of ethical intentionality, entailing a vision of a life driven by the "common good." Its final formulation (or even the decision to carry out the project or not) is an ethical responsibility of the architect. This is so in spite of the often-argued fact that a few years later his or her building may be converted into a different function. In other words, architecture is neither "autonomous" nor a mere social practice.

The textual form of the program is not neutral either. Choosing to express it as an "objective" set of parts with specifications of size is obviously one more false attempt to hiding its true nature. A narrative fiction expressing qualities of poetic inhabitation with regard to a specific culture and its values is indispensable, particularly given the demise of ritual as the epitome of significant human action. I have described how early-eighteenth-century practice reflected the hierarchies of society through architectural character. Later in that century Claude-Nicolas Ledoux felt the need to "invent" a program for urban institutions that might be more conducive to poetic life.[1] This has been an issue ever since, and grasping its importance has been crucial for significant architecture during the last two centuries, particularly to avoid the pitfalls of postmodern parody (formalism) in its diverse incarnations.

Architectural theory as *phronēsis* involves personal and social issues that are reciprocal; the meaning of architecture reflects on the meaning of the architect's life. We may recall here Boullée's existential despair at the roots of his theorizing, when he declared how unbearable it was to imagine that architecture might have no true foundations, no cultural raison d'être. Driven by ethical intentions, theory as *phronēsis* breaks free from instrumental concerns and discloses *technē-poiēsis* or practice as an open-ended *process—as* a fully embodied, personal engagement with making.

For an architecture that seeks its meaning beyond the scientific understanding of ethics and aesthetics, design is neither problem solving nor mere formal innovation. The discovery of architectural order necessitates the same sort of critical destructuring that is familiar to other arts, engaging dimensions of consciousness usually stifled by technical education. Yet for architecture this is not an intuitive operation or unreflective action, but rather the continuation of a practical philosophy and a meditative practice. It is making with an awareness of expectations and in a collaborative mode whenever appropriate. Indeed, it is possible to develop an awareness to the wonders that we can reveal to ourselves and others through making. History demonstrates that this awareness is translatable and that architects have learned much from multiple artistic endeavors. Although the media of architectural design are no longer constrained to traditional drawing and model making, engaging vision and tactility is especially important. This activity shares its nature with Dionysian free play (in the sense invoked by Nietzsche and Gadamer), seeking to reveal the coincidence of chance and necessity in human creation. Gilles Deleuze expresses this very well when he states that play, as affirmation, is reserved for thought and art, where victories are for those that know how to play, how to affirm and ramify chance rather than dividing it in order to dominate or win.[2] This characteristic is what enables art to disturb the reality and economy of the world. Our imagination effectively constructs the world, an embodied imagination that must be recollected in our era of binary space. This process requires patience and open-endedness. Every moment of a plastic search is liable to turn up poetic disclosures through inward vision and externalized work, disclosures that may eventually be translated into different dimensions. Playing with materials and modalities of representation, deliberately disturbing the presumed linearity of planning in a design task, the architect may be in a better position to represent human action and lived space, avoiding the tools that reduce such lived space to a mere geometric entity. Thus a work of architecture may engage the primary geometry of human bodily orientation as the base line of a significant melody aimed at revealing the enigma of depth, the dimension of space as "the widest open of all mouths."[3]

On endless desire

Copulating in love: one is unanimously and unitarily two.
Copulating without love: one is alone and three.
Malcolm de Chazal, *Sens-Plastique* (trans. Irving Weiss)

A train stops at the station at night at 6:00 p.m. and lets off two passengers, a man and a woman. They do not know one another. She listens to the water falling on the earth. He sees the flames flowing upward into the sky. They both feel the silence. . . .

After leaving the court halls and rooms, the man and the woman enter the central Outdoor Court. Placed within this court are four elements. One is a clock in the shape of a thirty-foot high metronome. The pendulum has a flat circular metal disk suspended from an elongated iron rod. The clock is in operation only from 6:00 a.m. to 6:00 p.m. Tangent to this clock is an inverted metronome-shaped void descending into the ground. This void is filled with water; a sphere floats at the center at the surface. This works as a clock from 6:00 p.m. to 6:00 a.m. . . .

The man goes down through the apex and enters a large underground room. The north wall of the room bears the word VICTIMS in all languages. He attempts to read them all but fails. . . .

The woman waits above ground. They meet and face south; one goes to the left, and the other goes to the right. . . .

She crosses back over the water channel and climbs through the Cemetery of the Children and the Cemetery of the Mothers of the Children. The man on the east side begins his walk and climbs through the Cemetery of the Fathers. The structures for the children and their mothers are made of gray stone and black granite. The structures for the fathers are made of pewterlike metal. In fact, the Cemetery of the Fathers looks like waves, the high waves of a sea of water still stopped. The mother's structures look like a lament. . . .

At the same time they enter the U-shaped structures and look at the internal walls facing each other. On one wall are the photographs of the missing and the disappeared; on the opposite wall are the photographs of those responsible. . . .

A long while later they board the returning train and sit in the same compartment. As the train moves away from the station, she looks out the train window and thinks she sees a gray panther running parallel to the tracks. He looks out the window and does not believe anything at all.

John Hejduk, excerpts from the program for *VICTIMS II,* in *Pewter Wings, Golden Horns, Stone Veils*

Technology has taken the edge off the world of experience. The physical environment adapts almost perfectly to our needs, regardless of the snow-storm raging outdoors. Or we may take a pill to get rid of our headache, alter our consciousness, and ultimately become unconscious. This condition varies in intensity around the world but seems to be progressively taking hold. The living body has been disappearing from the Western collective consciousness ever since Descartes first considered it as an obstacle to true knowledge and conceived it as a mechanism apart from the logical brain.[4] In the wake of the industrial revolution the world has become increasingly domesticated. All sorts of technological systems and devices make it possible for us to live comfortably in the jungle, in the desert, in the arctic regions, or on the ocean floors. We challenge or ignore the pull of gravity, the most basic expression of desire of our earthly existence. Hiding our mortality, seeking pleasure, and avoiding pain may now appear as a somewhat normal trajectory for the human species. Radicalizing Cartesian "reality," Jean Baudrillard can even imagine human existence, beyond death and sexual fulfillment, as a perpetual state of aimless seduction "liberating" human nature from its quest for meaning and signaling the end of history.[5] Yet our consumer economy depends on framing and exploiting the desire for possession and consumption. The acquisition of goods and services, even when they are ridiculously superfluous, becomes humanity's most serious quest, fueled by the belief that it will bring fulfillment and happiness. Our built environment supports and promotes this quest by expressing ambiguous meanings, disguised by the pretended neutrality of the technology that produces it and thus becoming a crucial actor in our psychosomatic pathologies and political crises.

These misunderstandings of *erōs* produce great disorientation. The desire to consume demands an abdication of the personal imagination. National states and corporations displace the personal imagination with the help of publicity agencies. A global village is constructed, one where there is barely room for authentic desire and humans wait for a future that never arrives. Baudrillard's nightmarish fiction of earthly paradise is hardly an alternative. Critically opposed to this state of affairs, the poetic imagination seeks to act. Through the imagination, particularly as embedded in art, film, architecture, and storytelling, the difference between what is present and what is not is made clear, connected by the presence of the imagining self: this is the ethical gift of artistic practices.

Buddhist teachers often speak about the ruses of "desire/attachment." Desire associated with possession is a most destructive feeling. Wisdom entails the unmasking of such deceptions and an understanding of the ulti-mately ephemeral nature of all things human. This is not to deny the real-ity of desire itself, which is a characteristic of human embodiment, but to realize that attachment to desire brings unhappiness. The aim is to disclose that beyond desire, our minds (not our bodies) are already capable of com-munion with a universal mind. Thus we can smile: life may be a comedy.

The Western interest in *erōs,* as the open yet bounded space of desire and the unfulfilled Christian longing for God, is more tragic. Emphasizing embodiment, consciousness perceives this space as bittersweet, and in this space humanity finds the meaning of existence. This experience also re-veals that fulfillment is not happiness and that desire aims at something *other*—but smiling is not the outcome. The result instead is something like Michelangelo's *pathos:* If life is good, then death must also be good, the *coincidentia oppositorum* that characterizes all poetic work, and that in the absence of God can be resolved only as a desire for Desire.

Perhaps not surprisingly, it is in the fertile Western cultural land-scape that technology first took hold. And yet, when technology manages to *actualize* the ideal, humans expect happiness from fulfillment. The true space of desire vanishes, denied through the virtual acquisition of heaven on earth, and is replaced by its bastard, the space of consumption, end-lessly projected onto a utopian future.

This contemporary human dilemma can be approached from two main perspectives. The Eastern insight into the possibility of release from attachment to desire resonates with Heidegger's concept of *Gelassenheit.* Fully grasping our ephemeral mortal condition reveals the futility of at-tachment. Heidegger believed that "releasement" would help transcend the instrumental "will to power," ensuring a different, more compassion-ate relationship with the world and with others. Releasement is also echoed in Gianni Vattimo's call for "weakening" strong values in order to construct a more ethical future, free of all sorts of ideological extremes. This is a positive attitude to take when confronting the material and po-litical realities of our technological world.

As *makers* bound by history, however, we must especially engage the second alternative and recall the bittersweet space of experience to recon-cile ethics and poetics. Thus an appropriate architecture for the present world, beyond the utopias of progress and universal civilization, may seek the embodiment of compassion and seduction through beautiful form and responsible program. Grounded in their specific linguistic and cultural horizons, such practices are capable of producing meaningful work, both revealing and transcending their local cultural and historical conditions. Despite the dangers of solipsism that are inherent to modern creation (lacking a cosmology, a unified living tradition, or a set of rituals to orient our lives), the very possibility of creativity's playful deployment depends on architects' willingness to engage their personal imagination in a quest for beauty, coupled with an unflinching commitment to learn from history and thus continually sharpen their self-understanding.

Notes

Introduction: Architecture and Human Desire

1.   Plato, *Symposium* 186a–b, in *Selected Dialogues of Plato,* trans. Benjamin Jowett, rev. Hayden Pelliccia (New York: Modern Library, 2001).

2.   This story was told by Juhani Pallasmaa in an exhibition on animal architecture that he curated for the Finnish Museum of Architecture.

3.   Jean-Luc Marion, *Le phénomène érotique* (Paris: Bernard Grasset, 2003), 9–23.

4.   See the classic text (1913) by Jane Harrison, *Ancient Art and Ritual* (reprint, London: Moonraker Press, 1978), and my own "Chora: The Space of Architectural Representation," in *Chora: Intervals in the Philosophy of Architecture,* vol. 1 (Montreal: McGill-Queen's University Press, 1994), 1–34.

5.   See Alberto Pérez-Gómez, "The Myth of Daedalus," *AA Files* 10 (1985): 49–52, and Indra McEwen, *Socrates' Ancestor: An Essay on Architectural Beginnings* (Cambridge, MA: MIT Press, 1993).

1   Eros and Creation

1.   See Jean-Pierre Vernant, "One . . . Two . . . Three: Eros," in *Before Sexuality: The Construction of Erotic Experience in the Ancient Greek World,* ed. David M. Halprin, John J. Winkler, and Froma Zeitlin (Princeton, NJ: Princeton University Press, 1990), 465–478.

2.   Hesiod, *Theogony* 116–117, 120. Here I am following mostly Vernant's rendering in English in "One . . . Two . . . Three: Eros," with some modulation from a Spanish edition, *Teogonía,* trans. José Manuel Villalaz (Mexico City: Porrúa, 1978).

3.   In this passage, and elsewhere in this book, I owe a great debt to Anne Carson for her remarkable insights into the Platonic theories of love, as detailed in *Eros the Bittersweet: An Essay* (Princeton, NJ: Princeton University Press, 1986).

4.   Carson, *Eros,* 155.

5.   Clement of Alexandria, *Stromata* 1.21; cited in I. P. Couliano, *Out of This World: Otherworldly Journeys from Gilgamesh to Albert Einstein* (Boston: Shambhala, 1991), 127.

6.   Couliano, *Out of This World,* 129.

7.   Plato, *Symposium* 202d–e, in *Selected Dialogues of Plato,* trans. Benjamin Jowett, rev. Hayden Pelliccia (New York: Modern Library, 2001); all references to Plato in the chapter are to this edition, hereafter cited parenthetically in the text.

8.   Ioan P. Couliano, *Eros and Magic in the Renaissance,* trans. Margaret Cook (Chicago: University of Chicago Press, 1987), 21.

9.   Ibid., 20.

10.   For the connotations of *agapē,* see the interlude before part II in this volume.

11.   Couliano, *Eros and Magic,* 87.

12.   Marsilio Ficino, *The Book of Life,* trans. Charles Boer (Dallas: Spring Publications, 1980), 151.

13.   Ibid., 157.

14.   Ibid., 158.

15.   Paracelsus, *Selected Writings,* ed. Jolande Jacobi, trans. Norbert Guterman, Bollingen 28 (Princeton, NJ: Princeton University Press, 1988), 15.

16.   Ibid., 32–33.

17.   *Erōs, philia,* and *agapē,* the three Greek words for love, are traditionally associated with Plato, Aristotle, and St. Paul, respectively, and have been the topic of many books and articles. See Alan Soble, ed., *Eros, Agape, and Philia: Readings in the Philosophy of Love* (New York: Paragon House, 1989), for an excellent collection of essays and excerpts from primary sources.

18.   See particularly "A General Account of Bonding," in Giordano Bruno, *Cause, Principle and Unity and Essays on Magic,* trans. and ed. Robert de Lucca and Richard J. Blackwell (Cambridge: Cambridge University Press, 1998), 143.

19.   Couliano, *Eros and Magic,* 88.

20.   This comparison should always be qualified. For Machiavelli human freedom in political acts is dependent on the successful seduction of "Fortuna" and ultimately acknowledges a superior divine order.

21.   Couliano, *Eros and Magic,* 93.

22.   Ibid., 98.

23.   Ibid., 101. Unlike Couliano in his otherwise remarkable book, I don't find any modern cynicism in Bruno's insightful observation about the universality of "bonding."

24.   According to Hans Blumenberg, this discussion originates in the second half of the thirteenth century. Christian theology postulated the omnipotence of God and

led to a radical questioning of the Aristotelian world. Therefore God's creation indeed may be different from what appears to our vision. See *The Genesis of the Copernican World,* trans. Robert M. Wallace (Cambridge, MA: MIT Press, 1987), 135.

25.   Nicholas Copernicus, *De revolutionibus;* quoted by Fernand Hallyn, *The Poetic Structure of the World: Copernicus and Kepler,* trans. Donald M. Leslie (New York: Zone Books, 1993), 54.

26.   This gap explains the inherent metaphoric (symbolic) power of mathematics in Renaissance art and architecture. The gap is the space of the metaphor in which identity and difference coincide.

27.   This emphasis on instrumental knowledge is particularly clear in the proposals of Caramuel de Lobkowitz for an "oblique architecture" that I have examined elsewhere, together with the remarkable modernity of Girard Desargues's theoretical work, bent on producing a useful instrumental theory based on the first thorough formulation of projective geometry in the history of the West. See my *Architecture and the Crisis of Modern Science* (1983; reprint, Cambridge, MA: MIT Press, 1992), 97–104, and Alberto Pérez-Gómez and Louise Pelletier, *Architectural Representation and the Perspective Hinge* (Cambridge, MA: MIT Press, 1997), 125. The possibility of finding new poetic images through these combinatorial methods inaugurated what even today is understood as a relatively new paradigm in design, an architecture generated through algorithms and CAD-related computer software.

28.   Guarino Guarini, *Architettura civile* (Turin, 1737; reprint, Milan: Il Polifilo, 1968), 10.

29.   See Amos Funkenstein, *Theology and the Scientific Imagination from the Middle Ages to the Seventeenth Century* (Princeton, NJ: Princeton University Press, 1986), 3–9.

30.   Nicolas Malebranche, *Entretiens sur la métaphysique* (Paris, 1688), 12.

31.   This demystification is evident in the works of the brothers Claude and Charles Perrault. See my *Architecture and the Crisis of Modern Science,* 25–26.

32.   See, for example, Bathasar Bekker's, *The Enchanted World* (1693). Bekker discredits magic and sorcery. He describes the replacement of supernatural revelation by a "miraculous" nature in which there is no place for angels or demons.

33.   Denis Diderot, *Encyclopédie* 3, vol. 7 of *Oeuvres complètes* (Paris: Hermann, 1976), 35.

34.   *Encyclopédie; ou Dictionnaire raisonné des sciences, des arts et des métiers . . . publié par M. Diderot,* 17 vols. (Paris, 1751–1780; reprint, New York: Pergamon Press, 1969), 7:81.

35.   Ibid., 7:582.

36.   Giambattista Vico, *The New Science,* abridged trans. of the 3rd ed. (1744) by Thomas Goddard Bergin and Max Harold Fisch (1970; reprint, Ithaca, NY: Cornell University Press, 1979), 75.

37.   Friedrich Nietzsche, *Philosophy in the Tragic Age of the Greeks,* trans. Marianne Cowen (Chicago: Gateway, 1962), cited in Mihai I. Spariosu, *Dionysus Reborn: Play and the Aesthetic Dimension in Modern Philosophical and Scientific Discourse* (Ithaca, NY: Cornell University Press, 1989), 74.

38.   Ibid., 75.

39.   See Hans-Georg Gadamer, *The Relevance of the Beautiful and Other Essays,* trans. Nicolas Walker, ed. Robert Bernasconi (Cambridge: Cambridge University Press, 1986). Gadamer's insightful understanding of play is discussed in chapter 4.

40.   Friedrich Nietzsche, *The Will to Power,* trans. Walter Kaufmann and R. J. Hollingdale, ed. Walter Kaufmann (New York: Vintage, 1968), frag. 800, p. 421.

41.   Ibid., frag. 821, p. 434.

42.   See George Steiner, *Real Presences* (Chicago: University of Chicago Press, 1989); Elaine Scarry, *On Beauty and Being Just* (Princeton, NJ: Princeton University Press, 1999).

43.   Octavio Paz, *The Bow and the Lyre (El arco y la lira): The Poem, the Poetic Revelation, Poetry and History,* trans. Ruth L. C. Simms (Austin: University of Texas Press, 1991), 140.

44.   Nietzsche, *Will to Power,* frag. 809, p. 428.

45.   Scarry, *On Beauty,* 3.

2   Eros and Limits

1.   See Jean-Pierre Vernant, "One . . . Two . . . Three: Eros," in *Before Sexuality: The Construction of Erotic Experience in the Ancient Greek World,* ed. David M. Halprin, John J. Winkler, and Froma Zeitlin (Princeton, NJ: Princeton University Press, 1990), 467.

2.   Anne Carson, *Eros the Bittersweet: An Essay* (Princeton, NJ: Princeton University Press, 1986), 10.

3.   Ibid.

4.   Ibid., 16.

5.   Ibid.

6.   Ibid., 21.

7.   Ibid., 26.

8.   This realization turns into pathological frustration for late-industrial societies. It suffices to compare the smiling faces of Tibetan nomads on the high plateaus of the Himalayas with the dark countenance of our affluent middle classes promenading on busy shopping streets and malls.

9.   See, for example, Walter Ong, *Orality and Literacy: The Technologizing of the Word* (London: Methuen, 1982); David Abram, *The Spell of the Sensuous: Perception and Language in a More-Than-Human World* (New York: Pantheon, 1996); and Carson, *Eros*, 41.

10.   Abram, *Spell of the Sensuous*, 93.

11.   Kevin Robb, "Poetic Sources of the Greek Alphabet: Rhythm and Abecedarium from Phoenician to Greek," in *Communication Arts in the Ancient World*, ed. Eric A. Havelock and Jackson P. Hershbell (New York: Hastings House, 1978), 23–36.

12.   Carson, *Eros*, 49.

13.   *Grammatici Graeci*, ed. Alfred Hilgard (Leipzig: Teubner, 1901), 1.3.183; quoted by Carson, *Eros*, 56.

14.   Alberto Pérez-Gómez, "The Myth of Daedalus," *AA Files* 10 (1985): 50. The connotations of this common noun are inferred particularly from the works of Homer and Hesiod.

15.   *Oxford English Dictionary*, s.v. "harmony," 1.

16.   Ruth Padel, *In and Out of the Mind: Greek Images of the Tragic Self* (Princeton, NJ: Princeton University Press, 1992), 12.

17.   Shigehisa Kuriyama, *The Expressiveness of the Body and the Divergence of Greek and Chinese Medicine* (New York: Zone Books, 1999), 111.

18.   Galen, *On the Usefulness of the Parts of the Body;* quoted in Kuriyama, *Expressiveness of the Body*, 123, 128.

19.   Kuriyama, *Expressiveness of the Body*, 128–129.

20.   Ibid., 129.

21.   According to *Physiognomics*, a pseudo-Aristotelian treatise quoted in ibid., 134.

22.   Kuriyama, *Expressiveness of the Body*, 136.

23.   Ibid., 135.

24.   Hence the word "chorography," which designates a regional map in ancient and Renaissance geographic texts.

25.   Homer, *Iliad* 16.68, 23.68, trans. A. T. Murray, Loeb Classical Library, 2 vols. (Cambridge, MA: Harvard University Press; London: Heinemann, 1924–1925).

26.   Carson, *Eros*, 84.

27.   J. Eckermann, "Sonntag, den 20 März 1831," *Gespräche mit Goethe*, in Johann Wolfgang von Goethe, *Gedenkausgabe der Werke, Briefe, und Gespräche*, ed. Ernst Beutler (Zurich: Artemis, 1948–1950), 24:484; quoted in Froma Zeitlin, "The Poetics of Eros," in Halprin, Winkler, and Zeitlin, eds., *Before Sexuality*, 420.

28.   Zeitlin, "Poetics of Eros," 430.

29.   Ibid.

30.   Ibid., 454–455.

31.   Ibid., 458.

32.   A critical edition of the 1499 text with notes (in Italian) by Giovanni Pozzi and Lucia Ciapponi was published in 1968 and reprinted in 1980 (Padua: Antenore). In English only a large section of the first part was translated under the title *The Strife of Love in a Dream*, published in 1592 and 1890. A new English translation of the full text by Joscelyn Godwin has become available recently (New York: Thames and Hudson, 1999). While the book is handsome and the text is quite readable, the annotations are not adequate and many subtleties of the original language are missed, mostly for lack of appropriate philosophical contextualization.

33.   Tracey Winton, "A Skeleton Key to Poliphilo's Dream: The Architecture of the Imagination in the *Hypnerotomachia*" (Ph.D. diss., University of Cambridge, 2001). Winton's text is the most lucid and comprehensive interpretation of the *Hypnerotomachia,* carefully disclosing its intellectual context.

34.   For a more extensive discussion of the text, see my own "The *Hypnerotomachia Poliphili* by Francesco Colonna: The Erotic Nature of Architectural Meaning," in *Paper Palaces: The Rise of the Renaissance Architectural Treatise,* ed. Vaughan Hart and Peter Hicks (New Haven, CT: Yale University Press, 1998), 86–104. A full bibliography of recent studies on the *Hypnerotomachia* is also provided in that volume.

35.   Lucretius, *On the Nature of the Universe* 1.21–23, trans. R. E. Latham, rev. John Godwin (London: Penguin, 1994), "Prayer to Venus," p. 10.

36.   Sappho, frag. 188 L-P; quoted in Carson, *Eros,* 170.

37.   Plato, *Symposium* 177d and *Theages* 128b; quoted in Carson, *Eros,* 170.

38.   Plato, *Apology* 21d; quoted in Carson, *Eros,* 172.

39.   Plato, *Symposium* 211d; quoted in Vernant, "One . . . Two . . . Three: Eros," 472.

40.   Aristotle, *Physics* 2.1, 193a, trans. Robin Waterfield (Oxford: Oxford University Press, 1999).

41.   Aristotle, *On the Parts of Animals* 645a; quoted in Kuriyama, *Expressiveness of the Body,* 127.

42.   Vitruvius, *Ten Books on Architecture,* trans. Ingrid D. Rowland, ed. Rowland and Thomas Noble Howe (Cambridge: Cambridge University Press, 1999), book 1, chap. 1, pp. 21–24.

43.   Plato, *Timaeus* 49, in *Timaeus and Critias,* trans. Desmond Lee (Harmondsworth, England: Penguin, 1965). This edition is hereafter cited parenthetically in the text.

44.   Jean-Pierre Vernant, *Mythe et pensée chez les Grecs* (Paris: Maspero, 1965), 1:124.

45.   Bruno Snell is cited in Carson, *Eros*, 38; see Snell, *The Discovery of the Mind: The Greek Origins of European Thought,* trans. T. G. Rosenmeyer (Cambridge, MA: Harvard University Press, 1953).

46.   Padel, *In and Out of the Mind*, 190–192.

47.   Aristotle, *Poetics* 4.12, 1449a, trans. S. H. Butcher, *Aristotle's Theory of Poetry and Fine Art* (1895; reprint, New York: Dover, 1951).

48.   Jane Harrison, *Ancient Art and Ritual* (1913; reprint, London: Moonraker Press, 1978), 40.

49.   Władysław Tatarkiewicz, *History of Aesthetics*, ed. C. Barrett, trans. R. M. Montgomery (Warsaw: Polish Scientific Publishers, 1970), 1:16.

50.   See Pérez-Gómez, "The Myth of Daedalus."

51.   In modern Greek, κωρα, often transliterated "hora," is the word for place, used also as a proper noun to designate the most important city on some islands. (There is also a Hora in the Peloponnese, near Pylos.) *Chōra* denoted place in Homeric literature. The word for dance, on the other hand, is κορά, written with an omicron rather than an omega and accented on the last syllable. In ancient Greek there were probably differences in pronunciation that have been lost today. But because accents were never used in Greek until the third century BC, the phonetic connection between words was even more significant.

52.   See Hermann Kern, "Image of the World and Sacred Realm," *Daidalos* 3 (1983): 11.

53.   Vitruvius, *The Ten Books on Architecture,* trans. Morris Hickey Morgan (1914; reprint, New York: Dover, 1960), book 5, chap. 3, p. 137.

54.   Padel, *In and Out of the Mind*, 48.

55.   Ibid., 189–191.

56.   Vitruvius, *Ten Books on Architecture,* trans. Morgan, book 5, chap. 3, p. 139; chap. 4, p. 140.

57.   Eric Voegelin, *The Ecumenic Age* (Baton Rouge: Louisiana State University Press, 1974), 186; more generally, see chap. 3.

58.   Nicholas of Cusa seemed capable of conceiving infinity as the product of the human mind. He defined the Christian God in geometric terms (as a ubiquitous sphere). Nevertheless, even for him the created infinity of the cosmos is not infinity in the full sense of the word; it remains infinitely distant from the absolute infinity of God. Karsten Harries has argued for the modernity of Cusanus in *Infinity and Perspective* (Cambridge, MA: MIT Press, 2001).

59.   See Jonathan Sawday, *The Body Emblazoned: Dissection and the Human Body in the Renaissance* (London: Routledge, 1995).

60.   Vitruvius, *De architectura,* trans. with commentary and illustrations by Cesare di Lorenzo Cesariano (Como, 1521), 5:83.

61.   See Dalibor Vesely, *Architecture in the Age of Divided Representation: The Question of Creativity in the Shadow of Production* (Cambridge, MA: MIT Press, 2004), 367.

62.   Aristotle, *Poetics* 1450b, trans. W. H. Fyfe, in *Aristotle: The Poetics; "Longinus": On the Sublime; Demetrius: On Style,* Loeb Classical Library (Cambridge, MA: Harvard University Press, London: Heinemann, 1927).

63.   The Greek term *prepon,* "seen clearly, conspicuous," captures the classical view of *decorum* (propriety) in which ethical and aesthetic values were never in conflict. See Vesely, *Architecture,* 364–367 and n. 25 citing M. Pohlenz, *"To Prepon:* Ein Beitrag zur Geschichte des griechischen Geistes," *Nachrichten von der Gesellschaft der Wissenschaften zu Göttingen* 16 (1933): 53–92.

64.   John Dee, *The Mathematical Praeface to the Elements of Euclid* (London, 1570), 2.

65.   See, for example, Alexandre Koyré, *Metaphysics and Measurement: Essays in Scientific Revolution* (London: Chapman and Hall, 1968), chaps. 1–4.

66.   Cited in Vesely, *Architecture,* 372.

67.   Giordano Bruno, *Cause, Principle and Unity and Essays on Magic,* trans. and ed. Robert de Lucca and Richard J. Blackwell (Cambridge: Cambridge University Press, 1998), 87.

68.   Maurice Merleau-Ponty uses the concept of flesh to designate the "first" element of reality, overcoming the dualism inherited by Western epistemology from Descartes. See *The Visible and the Invisible,* ed. Claude Lefort, trans. Alphonso Lingis (Evanston, IL: Northwestern University Press, 1979).

69.   Alberto Pérez-Gómez, "Juan Bautista Villalpando's Divine Model in Architectural Theory," in *Chora,* vol. 3 (Montreal: McGill-Queen's University Press, 1999), 125–156.

70.   Aristotle, *Physics* 44, 212a.

71.   Maurice Merleau-Ponty, *Phenomenology of Perception,* trans. Colin Smith (London: Routledge and Kegan Paul, 1962), 235. See also Alberto Pérez-Gómez and Louise Pelletier, *Architectural Representation and the Perspective Hinge* (Cambridge, MA: MIT Press, 1997), 330–340.

72.   See Antonio de Nicolas, *Powers of Imagining: Ignatius Loyola, a Philosophical Hermeneutic of Imagining through the Collected Works, with a Translation of These Works* (Albany: State University of New York Press, 1986).

73.   Richard Sennett, *The Fall of Public Man* (Cambridge: Cambridge University Press, 1977).

74.   Ferdinando Galli da Bibiena, *L'architettura civile* (1711; reprint, New York: Blom, 1971).

75. Karsten Harries, *The Bavarian Rococo Church: Between Faith and Aestheticism* (New Haven, CT: Yale University Press, 1983).

76. Abbé Marc-Antoine Laugier, *Essai sur l'architecture* (Paris, 1755).

77. Perrault was the first to deny the importance of "optical correction" as the central technical problem for architects. See my and Pelletier's *Architectural Representation*, 97–104.

78. See *The Libertine Reader: Eroticism and Enlightenment in Eighteenth-Century France,* ed. Michel Feher (New York: Zone, 1997), especially Feher's introduction.

79. Louise Pelletier, *Architecture in Words* (forthcoming, Routledge, 2007), chaps. 9, 10. See also Jean-François de Bastide, *The Little House: An Architectural Seduction,* trans. Rodolphe el-Khoury (New York: Princeton Architectural Press, 1997).

80. Pelletier, *Architecture in Words,* chaps. 9, 10.

81. Ibid., chap. 8.

82. David Spurr, "The Study of Space in Literature: Some Paradigms," in *The Space of English,* ed. Spurr and Cornelia Tschichold (Tübingen: Gunter Narr Verlag, 2005), 15–34.

83. Adolf Loos, "Ornament und Verbrechen" (1908), in *Sämtliche Schriften* (Vienna: Verlag Herold, 1972).

84. August Schmarsow's position about the importance of space in architecture was presented initially in two lectures, at the University of Leipzig (1893) and the Royal Saxonian Academy of Science (1896). His most coherent theoretical synthesis is *Grundbegriffe der Kunstwissenchaft am Übergang vom Altertum zum Mittelalter* (Leipzig: Teubner, 1905).

85. See August Schmarsow, "Raumgestaltung als Wesen der architektonischen Schöpfung," *Zeitschrift für Ästhetik und allgemeine Kunstwissenschaft* 9 (1914): 66–95.

86. Pérez-Gómez and Pelletier, *Architectural Representation,* 298–338.

87. Maurice Merleau-Ponty, "Eye and Mind," trans. Carleton Dallery, in *The Primacy of Perception, and Other Essays on Phenomenological Psychology, the Philosophy of Art, History and Politics,* ed. James M. Edie (Evanston, IL: Northwestern University Press, 1964), 181.

88. Carson, *Eros,* 111.

89. Ibid., 115.

90. Vitruvius, *Ten Books on Architecture,* trans. Rowland, book 2, chap. 2, p. 24.

91. For an analysis of the analogy between *erōs* and writing, see Carson, *Eros,* 117–133.

92.   Vitruvius, *Ten Books on Architecture,* book 3, chap. 1, p. 47.

93.   Carson, *Eros,* 136.

3   Eros and the Poetic Image

1.   Aristotle, *Rhetoric* 1.11, 1370a; quoted in Anne Carson, *Eros the Bittersweet: An Essay* (Princeton, NJ: Princeton University Press, 1986), 63.

2.   Carson, *Eros,* 170–171.

3.   Aristotle, *Rhetoric* 3.2, 1405a; quoted in Carson, *Eros,* 63.

4.   Hans-Georg Gadamer, *The Relevance of the Beautiful and Other Essays,* trans. Nicolas Walker, ed. Robert Bernasconi (Cambridge: Cambridge University Press, 1986), 14.

5.   Plato, *Phaedrus* 249c–d, in *Selected Dialogues of Plato,* trans. Benjamin Jowett, rev. Hayden Pelliccia (New York: Modern Library, 2001); all quotations from Plato, unless otherwise specified, are from this edition, hereafter cited parenthetically in the text.

6.   Carson, *Eros,* 161–162.

7.   Aristotle, *Rhetoric* 1.10, 1369b; quoted in Carson, *Eros,* 66.

8.   Shigehisa Kuriyama, *The Expressiveness of the Body and the Divergence of Greek and Chinese Medicine* (New York: Zone Books, 1999), 126–127.

9.   Lucretius, *De rerum natura* 1.443–446; quoted in Dalibor Vesely, "The Architectonics of Embodiment," in *Body and Building: Essays on the Changing Relation of Body and Architecture,* ed. George Dodds and Robert Tavernor (Cambridge, MA: MIT Press, 2002), 30.

10.   Vesely, "Architectonics," 30.

11.   Gilles Deleuze, "Eighteenth Series of the Three Images of Philosophers," in *The Logic of Sense,* trans. Mark Lester with Charles Stivale, ed. Constantin V. Boundas (New York: Columbia University Press, 1990), 127.

12.   Deleuze, *The Logic of Sense;* quoted in Mihai I. Spariosu, *Dionysus Reborn: Play and the Aesthetic Dimension in Modern Philosophical and Scientific Discourse* (Ithaca, NY: Cornell University Press, 1989), 148.

13.   For detailed account of the history of architectural representation and its relationship to building practice, see Alberto Pérez-Gómez and Louise Pelletier, *Architectural Representation and the Perspective Hinge* (Cambridge, MA: MIT Press, 1997).

14.   Marsilio Ficino, *Commentary on Plato's Symposium on Love* 6:6, trans. Sears Jayne, 2nd ed. (Dallas: Spring Publications, 1985), 113–115.

15.   Giordano Bruno, *Theses de magia* 15, vol. 3: 466; cited in Ioan P. Couliano, *Eros and Magic in the Renaissance,* trans. Margaret Cook (Chicago: University of Chicago Press, 1987), 91.

16. Giordano Bruno, *De magia* (1588); quoted in Couliano, *Eros and Magic,* 92.

17. Plotinus, *The Enneads,* trans. Stephen MacKenna (Harmondsworth: Penguin Classics, 1991), 46. There *are* in fact connections between the concept of symmetry and justice, having to do with equality and commensurability. Plotinus seems to be speaking rhetorically to make a point. The opposite position will appear more clearly in our discussion of *philia* and is articulated by Elaine Scarry, *On Beauty and Being Just* (Princeton, NJ: Princeton University Press, 1999).

18. Plotinus, *Enneads,* 46, 47, 48.

19. Jayne, introduction to Ficino, *Commentary,* 7. This edition of Ficino's *Commentary* is hereafter cited parenthetically in the text.

20. R. T. Wallis, *Neoplatonism* (London: Duckworth, 1972), 53.

21. This kind of representation appears during the sixteenth century in architectural treatises and books on military architecture by Pietro Cataneo and Jacques Androuet du Cerceau, among others. The tradition of "military perspective" continues into the modern period. See Pérez-Gómez and Pelletier, *Architectural Representation,* 243–272.

22. Francesco di Giorgio Martini, *Trattati di architettura ingegneria e arte militare,* ed. Corrado Maltese 2 vols. (Milan: Il Polifilo, 1967), "Primo trattato," 1:38–39.

23. Ibid., 2:303.

24. Tracey Winton, "A Skeleton Key to Poliphilo's Dream: The Architecture of the Imagination in the *Hypnerotomachia*" (Ph.D. diss., University of Cambridge, 2001).

25. Pérez-Gómez and Pelletier, *Architectural Representation,* 97–105, 119–122.

26. Frances Yates, *Giordano Bruno and the Hermetic Tradition* (London: Routledge and Kegan Paul, 1971), 197.

27. Alberto Pérez-Gómez, *Architecture and the Crisis of Modern Science* (1983; reprint, Cambridge, MA: MIT Press, 1992), 203.

28. Giordano Bruno, *The Ash Wednesday Supper,* trans. Stanley L. Jaki (The Hague: Mouton, 1975), 109, 107.

29. Vincenzo Danti, *Libri delle perfette proporzioni per il disegno* (Florence, 1568).

30. This debate resulted in diverging positions about the nature of Christian love. Compare Miguel de Unamuno, *El sentimiento trágico de la vida* (Madrid: Espasa-Calpe, 1967), and José Ortega y Gasset, *Estudios sobre el amor* (Madrid: Espasa-Calpe, 1966), 113–123.

31. Couliano, *Eros and Magic,* 85, 89.

32. See Antonio T. de Nicolas's introduction to Ignatius Loyola's "Spiritual Exercises," in *Powers of Imagining: A Philosophical Hermenentic of Imagining*

through the Collected Works of Ignatius de Loyola, with a Translation of These Works (Albany: State University of New York Press, 1986).

33.   Alberto Pérez-Gómez, "Juan Bautista Villalpando's Divine Model in Architectural Theory," in *Chora*, vol. 3 (Montreal: McGill-Queen's University Press, 1999), 134–140.

34.   See René Taylor, "Architecture and Magic: Considerations on the Idea of the Escorial," in *Essays in the History of Architecture Presented to Rudolf Wittkower,* ed. Douglas Fraser, Howard Hibbard, and Milton J. Lewine (New York: Phaidon, 1967), 81.

35.   See David Lindberg, *Theories of Vision from Al-Kindi to Kepler* (Chicago: University of Chicago Press, 1976), 202.

36.   Ibid., 204.

37.   Kepler, *Paralipomena;* quoted in Lindberg, *Theories of Vision,* 204.

38.   Anamorphosis became an important strategy in the work of avant-garde artists such as Duchamp. See Pérez-Gómez and Pelletier, *Architectural Representation,* 371.

39.   Jacques-François Blondel, *Cours d'architecture ou traité de la décoration, distribution et construction des bâtiments,* 9 vols. (Paris, 1771–1777), 1:390.

40.   For more about the linguistic analogy, see part II of this volume.

41.   Giovanni Battista Piranesi, *Carceri d'invenzione* (Rome, 1745, 1761).

42.   Thus Piranesi's *Carceri* became a precedent for much important art, architecture, and literature in the nineteenth and twentieth centuries, ranging from Lewis Carroll's *Alice* books to Flann O'Brien's *Third Policeman,* from Giorgio De Chirico's paintings to Daniel Libeskind's Jewish Museum in Berlin and the labyrinthine corridor in Mark Danielewski's *House of Leaves.*

43.   Giovanni Battista Piranesi, *Della magnificenza ed architettura de' romani* (Rome, 1761); *Parere sull'architettura* (Rome, 1765); *Diverse maniere d'adornare i camini* (Rome, 1769).

44.   Of course, Vico's view is not far from Aristotle's formulation of the character of fiction in his *Poetics.* For a comprehensive study of the architectural consequences of Vico's philosophy, see Donald Kunze, *Thought and Place: The Architecture of Eternal Place in the Philosophy of Giambattista Vico* (New York: Peter Lang, 1987).

45.   Giambattista Vico, *The New Science,* abridged trans. of the 3rd ed. (1744) by Thomas Goddard Bergin and Max Harold Fisch (1970; reprint, Ithaca, NY: Cornell University Press, 1979), 381.

46.   Ibid., 74.

47.   Ibid., 75.

48.   See Donald Verene, *Vico's Science of Imagination* (Ithaca, NY: Cornell University Press, 1981), 50–51.

49.   Marjorie Nicolson, *Newton Demands the Muse: Newton's Opticks and the Eighteenth Century Poets* (1946; reprint, Princeton, NJ: Princeton University Press, 1966).

50.   See Alberto Pérez-Gómez, "Charles-Etienne Briseux: The Musical Body and the Limits of Instrumentality in Architecture," in Dodds and Tavernor, eds., *Body and Building,* 164–189.

51.   Louise Pelletier, "Nicolas Le Camus de Mézières's Architecture of Expression, and the Theatre of Desire at the End of the Ancien Régime; or, The Analogy of Fiction with Architectural Innovation" (Ph.D. diss., McGill University, 2000), 296–298. See also Jean-François de Bastide, *The Little House: An Architectural Seduction,* trans. Rodolphe el-Khoury (New York: Princeton Architectural Press, 1996).

52.   Pelletier, "Nicolas Le Camus," 298.

53.   See David Leatherbarrow and Mohsen Mostafavi, *Surface Architecture* (Cambridge, MA: MIT Press, 2002).

54.   The text by Husserl, "Spatiality of Nature: The Originary Ark, the Earth, Does Not Move," trans. Leonard Lawlor, can be found in *Husserl at the Limits of Phenomenology: Including Texts by Edmund Husserl, Maurice Merleau-Ponty,* ed. Lawlor with Bettina Bergo (Evanston, IL: Northwestern University Press, 2002). See also Maurice Merleau-Ponty, *Phenomenology of Perception,* trans. Colin Smith (London: Routledge and Kegan Paul, 1962).

55.   Maurice Merleau-Ponty, *The Visible and the Invisible,* ed. Claude Lefort, trans. Alphonso Lingis (Evanston, IL: Northwestern University Press, 1979).

56.   Breton, *Mad Love,* trans. Mary Ann Caws (Lincoln: University of Nebraska Press, 1987), 8, 10.

57.   Ibid., 25.

58.   Rainer Maria Rilke, "Letters on Love," in *Rilke on Love and Other Difficulties,* ed. and trans. John J. L. Mood (New York: W. W. Norton, 1975), 33–35.

59.   Octavio Paz, *The Bow and the Lyre (El arco y la lira): The Poem, the Poetic Revelation, Poetry and History,* trans. Ruth L. C. Simms (Austin: University of Texas Press, 1991), 3–15.

60.   Giordano Bruno Nolano, *De gl'heroici furori* (Paris, 1585), 135.

61.   Gaston Bachelard dedicated a remarkable series of books to the material imagination, exploring the archetypal poetic images associated with the elements, water, air, fire and earth: *La psychanalyse du feu* (Paris: Gallimard, 1938), *L'eau et les rêves* (Paris: J. Corti, 1942), *L'air et les songes* (Paris: J. Corti, 1943), *La terre et les rêveries de la volonté* (Paris: J. Corti, 1947), and *La terre et les rêveries du repos* (Paris: J. Corti, 1948).

62.   Juhani Pallasmaa, *The Architecture of Image: Existential Space in Cinema* (Helsinki: Rakennustieto Oy, 2001).

63.   John Hawkes, *The Blood Oranges* (New York: New Directions, 1972).

64.   Paz is quoting Chang-Tzu in *The Bow and the Lyre*, 88.

65.   Alberto Pérez-Gómez, *Polyphilo or The Dark Forest Revisited: An Erotic Epiphany of Architecture* (Cambridge, MA: MIT Press, 1992).

66.   Philippe Duboy, *Lequeu: An Architectural Enigma*, trans. Francis Scarfe, additional trans. by Brad Divitt (Cambridge, MA: MIT Press, 1987).

67.   Octavio Paz, *Marcel Duchamp, Appearance Stripped Bare*, trans. Rachel Phillips and Donald Gardner (1978; reprint, New York: Arcade, 1990), vii.

68.   Frederick Kiesler, *Inside the Endless House; Art, People, and Architecture: A Journal* (New York: Simon and Schuster, 1964), 567.

69.   Kiesler, quoted in Hatje Cantz, *Frederick Kiesler: Endless House* (Frankfurt: Museum für Moderne Kunst, 2003), 17.

70.   Ibid., 63.

71.   Daniel Libeskind, "An Open Letter to Architectural Educators," in his *Radix-Matrix: Architecture and Writings* [trans. Peter Green] (Munich: Prestel, 1997), 155.

72.   Daniel Libeskind, *End Space: An Exhibition at the Architectural Association* (London: Architectural Association, 1980), 12, 22.

73.   Daniel Libeskind, quoted in Mark Taylor, "Point of No Return," in Libeskind, *Radix-Matrix*, 134.

74.   Carson, *Eros*, 168.

75.   Jean Baudrillard, *Seduction*, trans. Brian Singer (New York: St. Martin's Press, 1990).

Interlude: *Erōs, Philia,* and *Agapē*

1.   See Hans-Georg Gadamer, *The Relevance of the Beautiful and Other Essays*, trans. Nicholas Walker, ed. Robert Bernasconi (Cambridge: Cambridge University Press, 1986); John Brentingler, "The Nature of Love," in *Eros, Agape, and Philia: Readings in the Philosophy of Love,* ed. Alan Soble (New York: Paragon House, 1989), 136; and L. A. Kosman, "Platonic Love," in ibid., 149.

2.   Plato, *Symposium* 193d; in *Selected Dialogues of Plato*, trans. Benjamin Jowett, rev. Hayden Pelliccia (New York: Modern Library, 2001). Unless otherwise specified, all references to Plato in the chapter are to this edition, cited parenthetically in the text.

3.   Jean-Pierre Vernant, "One . . . Two . . . Three: Eros," in *Before Sexuality: The Construction of Erotic Experience in the Ancient Greek World,* ed. David Halprin, John W. Winkler, and Froma Zeitlin (Princeton, NJ: Princeton University Press, 1990), 473.

4.   Elaine Scarry, *On Beauty and Being Just* (Princeton, NJ: Princeton University Press, 1999), 57.

5.   Ibid., 52–53.

6.   Ibid., 28.

7.   Ibid., 47.

8.   Martin Heidegger, "The Origin of the Work of Art," in *Basic Writings from "Being and Time" (1927) to "The Task of Thinking" (1964)*, ed. David Farrell Krell (New York: Harper and Row, 1977), 143–188.

9.   Gadamer, *The Relevance of the Beautiful*, 121.

10.   See Maurice Merleau-Ponty, *The Visible and the Invisible*, ed. Claude Lefort, trans. Alphonso Lingis (Evanston, IL: Northwestern University Press, 1979). See also M. C. Dillon, "Temporality: Merleau-Ponty and Derrida," in *Merleau-Ponty, Hermeneutics, and Postmodernism*, ed. Thomas W. Busch and Shaun Gallagher (Albany: State University of New York Press, 1992), 189–212, and *Ecart et différance: Merleau-Ponty and Derrida on Seeing and Writing*, ed. M. C. Dillon (Atlantic Highlands, NJ: Humanities Press, 1997). Of particular interest in the latter volume are M. C. Dillon, "Introduction: Ecart & Différence," 1–17; Thomas W. Busch, "Merleau-Ponty and Derrida on the Phenomenon," 20–29; G. B. Madison, "Merleau-Ponty and Derrida: *La différence*," 94–111; and Robert Vallier, "Blindness and Invisibility: The Ruins of Self-Portraiture (Derrida's Re-reading of Merleau-Ponty)," 191–207.

11.   Anne Carson, *Eros the Bittersweet: An Essay* (Princeton, NJ: Princeton University Press, 1986), 107–109.

12.   See Richard Kearney, *The Wake of Imagination: Toward a Postmodern Culture* (Minneapolis: University of Minnesota Press, 1988).

13.   Hans-Georg Gadamer, *Gadamer in Conversation: Reflections and Commentary*, ed. and trans. Richard E. Palmer (New Haven, CT: Yale University Press, 2001), 78–85.

14.   Carsten Dutt in conversation with Gadamer, ibid., 81–82.

15.   Rainer Maria Rilke, "[Ah, not to be cut off]," in *Ahead of All Parting: The Selected Poetry and Prose of Rainer Maria Rilke*, ed. and trans. Stephen Mitchell (New York: Modern Library, 1995), 191.

16.   Soble, introduction to *Eros, Agape, and Philia*, xxiii.

17.   Jean-Luc Marion, *Le phénomène érotique* (Paris: Bernard Grasset, 2003), 9–21.

18.   Plato, *Lysis* 221e–222a; quoted in Carson, *Eros*, 33.

19.   Scarry, *On Beauty*, 80.

20.   See José Ortega y Gasset, *Estudios sobre el amor* (Madrid: Espasa-Calpe, 1966), 67, and Rainer Maria Rilke, "Letters on Love," in *Rilke on Love and Other Difficulties*, trans. John J. L. Mood (New York: W. W. Norton, 1975), 25–37.

21.   Aristotle, *The Nicomachean Ethics* 1166a, trans. J. A. K. Thomson (1953; reprint, London: Penguin, 2004).

22.   Ibid., 1161b.

23.   Gregory Vlastos, "The Individual as an Object of Love in Plato," in Soble, ed., *Eros, Agape, and Philia,* 96.

24.   Aristotle, *Rhetoric* 2.4, 1380b–1381a; quoted by Vlastos, "The Individual," 96.

4   *Philia,* Ritual, and *Decorum*

1.   Hannah Arendt, *The Human Condition* (Chicago: University of Chicago Press, 1958), chap. 2, and Richard Sennett, *The Fall of Public Man* (Cambridge: Cambridge University Press, 1977), chaps. 3–6.

2.   Vitruvius, *Ten Books on Architecture,* trans. Ingrid D. Rowland, ed. Rowland and Thomas Noble Howe (Cambridge: Cambridge University Press, 1999), book 2, chap. 1, p. 34.

3.   Ibid., book 6, pref., p. 75.

4.   José Ortega y Gasset, *El espectador,* vols. 5–6 (Madrid: Espasa-Calpe, 1966), 193.

5.   Vincent Scully, *The Earth, the Temple, and the Gods: Greek Sacred Architecture,* rev. ed. (New York: Praeger, 1969), 184; see Pausanias 3.11.9.

6.   For an account of Anaximander's theory and its sources, see G. S. Kirk, J. E. Raven, and M. Schofield, *The Presocratic Philosophers: A Critical History with a Selection of Texts,* 2nd ed. (Cambridge: Cambridge University Press, 1983), 100–110.

7.   Ibid., 111.

8.   Aristotle, *Physics* 2.2, 194a, trans. Robin Waterfield (Oxford: Oxford University Press, 1999).

9.   Ibid.

10.   Arendt, *The Human Condition,* 117.

11.   Stephen Miller, *The Prytaneion: Its Function and Architectural Form* (Berkeley: University of California Press, 1978), 13–14.

12.   Ibid., 15.

13.   Jean-Pierre Vernant, *Mythe et pensée chez les Grecs* (Paris: Maspero, 1965), 1:124.

14.   Ruth Padel, *In and Out of the Mind: Greek Images of the Tragic Self* (Princeton, NJ: Princeton University Press, 1992), 7.

15.   Ibid., 3.

16.   Ibid., 100.

17.   Miller, *The Prytaneion*, 18.

18.   Ibid.

19.   Vitruvius, *Ten Books on Architecture*, book 5, chap. 3, p. 65.

20.   Dalibor Vesely, *Architecture in the Age of Divided Representation: The Question of Creativity in the Shadow of Production* (Cambridge, MA: MIT Press, 2004), 367–368.

21.   Aristotle, *Poetics* 6.6, 1449b, trans. S. H. Butcher, in *Aristotle's Theory of Poetry and Fine Art* (1895; reprint, New York: Dover, 1951).

22.   Ibid., 6.9–10, 1450a; 9.2, 1451a.

23.   On this topic, see Oddone Longo, "The Theatre of the *Polis*," in *Nothing to Do with Dionysos? Athenian Drama in Its Social Context*, ed. John J. Winkler and Froma I. Zeitlin (Princeton, NJ: Princeton University Press, 1990), 13. Longo is himself citing Frank Kolb, "Polis und Theater," in *Das griechische Drama*, ed. Gustaf Adolf Seeck (Darmstadt: Wissenschaftliche Buchgesellschaft, 1979), 468–505.

24.   T. B. L. Webster, *Greek Theatre Production* (1956; reprint, London: Methuen, 1972), 2; quoted in Longo, "The Theatre of the *Polis*," 13.

25.   John J. Winkler and Froma I. Zeitlin, eds., introduction to *Nothing to Do with Dionysos?* 5.

26.   This polemic is still crucial for current critical writing on the discipline. It reflects a much broader discussion in philosophy that has taken place in the past few decades between existential phenomenologists and poststructuralist thinkers. I hope that without engaging the complex and often technical arguments, my position will open up alternatives beyond a simplistic dialectical opposition.

27.   Vitruvius, *Ten Books on Architecture*, book 1, chap. 2, p. 25. For the stories behind the different kinds of columns, see book 4, chap. 1, p. 54.

28.   See Hans-Georg Gadamer, *The Enigma of Health: The Art of Healing in a Scientific Age*, trans. Jason Gaiger and Nicholas Walker (Stanford, CA: Stanford University Press, 1996), 1–30.

29.   Georges Gusdorf, *Les origines des sciences humaines* (Paris: Payot, 1967), 42.

30.   Hans-Georg Gadamer, *Truth and Method*, [trans. and ed. Garrett Barden and John Cumming] (London: Sheed and Ward, 1975), 141.

31.   See Alberto Pérez-Gómez, *Architecture and the Crisis of Modern Science* (1983; reprint, Cambridge, MA: MIT Press, 1992), chap. 1; and Alberto Pérez-Gómez, introduction to Claude Perrault, *Ordonnance for the Five Kinds of Columns after the Methods of the Ancients*, trans. Indra Kagis McEwen (Santa Monica, CA: Getty, 1993), 1–44.

32.   For a discussion of *indole*, see Marc Neveu, "The Architectural Lessons of Carlo Lodoli (1690–1761)" (Ph. D. diss., McGill University, 2005).

33.   Jean-Nicolas-Louis Durand, *Précis des leçons d'architecture données à l'Ecole Polytechnique,* 2 vols. (Paris, 1802), 1:3–8.

5   Architecture at the Limits of Language

1.   Plato, *Euthyphro* 11c–e, in *Selected Dialogues of Plato,* trans. Benjamin Jowett, rev. Hayden Pelliccia (New York: Modern Library, 2001). See Indra McEwen, *Socrates' Ancestor: An Essay on Architectural Beginnings* (Cambridge, MA: MIT Press, 1993). McEwen brilliantly explores the ties between architecture and philosophy suggested by this statement.

2.   The concept of architecture operating at the limits of language is developed by Eugenio Trías, *Lógica del límite* (Barcelona: Ediciones Destino, 1991).

3.   George Steiner, *After Babel: Aspects of Language and Translation* (London: Oxford University Press, 1975), 51. I owe much to George Steiner for the concepts about language I draw on in this book. The pages that follow paraphrase many ideas from the first two chapters of his work and test them in the universe of architectural discourse.

4.   The presence of a categorical framework at the moment of ordinary perception is particularly clear in cases in which it fails (such as aphasia), and in young children as it precedes the acquisition of verbal language. See Maurice Merleau-Ponty, *Phenomenology of Perception,* trans. Colin Smith (London: Routledge and Kegan Paul, 1962), 191. See also Maurice Merleau-Ponty, *Consciousness and the Acquisition of Language,* trans. Hugh J. Silverman (Evanston, IL: Northwestern University Press, 1973).

5.   Steiner, *After Babel,* 47.

6.   See Paul Ricoeur, *Oneself as Another,* trans. Kathleen Blamey (Chicago: University of Chicago Press, 1992), and Martin Heidegger, "The Age of the World Picture," in *The Question Concerning Technology and Other Essays,* trans. William Lovitt (Toronto: Harper and Row, 1977), 115–154.

7.   Unlike Susan Sontag, who argued in her beautifully written book *Against Interpretation, and Other Essays* (New York: Farrar, Straus and Giroux, 1966) that phenomenology and interpretation were in opposition, hermeneutic philosophy has demonstrated the continuity between the two moments of experience and judgment.

8.   See Kenneth Frampton, *Modern Architecture: A Critical History* (New York: Oxford University Press, 1980).

9.   See Giorgio Agamben, *Means without End: Notes on Politics,* trans. Vincenzo Binetti and Cesare Casarino (Minneapolis: University of Minnesota Press, 2000).

10.   See, for example, the books by David Leatherbarrow (some coauthored with Mohsen Mostafavi) on twentieth-century architecture, particularly *Uncommon Ground: Architecture, Technology, and Topography* (Cambridge, MA: MIT Press, 2000) and his and Mostafavi's *Surface Architecture* (Cambridge, MA: MIT Press, 2002). See also Dalibor Vesely's interpretation of the baroque church in Zwie-

falten, in *Architecture in the Age of Divided Representation: The Question of Creativity in the Shadow of Production* (Cambridge, MA: MIT Press, 2004), 216–226.

11.   My own view on hermeneutics has been shaped by the works on the nature of history by José Ortega y Gasset, by Heidegger's ontological hermeneutics, and especially by Hans-Georg Gadamer's *Truth and Method,* [trans. and ed. Garrett Barden and John Cumming] (London: Sheed and Ward, 1975), and *Philosophical Hermeneutics,* trans. and ed. David E. Linge (Berkeley: University of California Press, 1976), as well as by Paul Ricoeur's vast bibliography on the subject, particularly *History and Truth,* trans. Charles A. Kelbley (Evanston, IL: Northwestern University Press, 1965); *The Conflict of Interpretations: Essays in Hermeneutics,* ed. Don Ihde (Evanston, IL: Northwestern University Press, 1974); and *Time and Narrative,* trans. Kathleen McLaughlin and David Pellauer, 3 vols. (Chicago: University of Chicago Press, 1984–1988).

12.   Giambattista Vico, *The New Science,* abridged trans. of the 3rd ed. (1744) by Thomas Goddard Bergin and Max Harold Fisch (1970; reprint, Ithaca, NY: Cornell University Press, 1979), 63.

6   The Language of *Philia* in Architectural Theory

1.   Vitruvius, *The Ten Books on Architecture,* trans. Morris Hickey Morgan (1914; reprint, New York: Dover, 1960), book 1, chap. 1, pp. 5–13. Another twentieth-century translation, with a parallel Latin text, is also useful to clarify the semantic horizon of particular terms: *On Architecture,* trans. Frank Granger, 2 vols., Loeb Classical Library (1931–1934; reprint, Cambridge, MA: Harvard University Press, 1983). Compare also the most recent English translation by Ingrid D. Rowland (ed. Rowland and Thomas Noble Howe [Cambridge: Cambridge University Press, 1999]).

2.   Vitruvius, *Ten Books on Architecture,* trans. Morgan, book 1, chap. 1, pp. 11–12.

3.   For a lucid discussion of the connotations of the terms "theory," "technology," and "praxis" in their original and modern senses, see Hans-Georg Gadamer, *The Enigma of Health: The Art of Healing in a Scientific Age,* trans. Jayson Gaiger and Nicholas Walker (Stanford: Stanford University Press, 1996), 1–30.

4.   Vitruvius, *Ten Books on Architecture,* trans. Morgan, book 1, chap. 1, p. 5. For the Latin text, see the Granger edition, 1:6.

5.   Vitruvius, *On Architecture,* trans. Granger, book 1, chap. 1, 1:6, 7.

6.   Aristotle, *Rhetoric* 3.2,1405a; quoted in Anne Carson, *Eros the Bittersweet: An Essay* (Princeton, NJ: Princeton University Press, 1986), 63.

7.   Vitruvius, trans. Granger, book 1, chap. 2, pp. 25–30.

8.   Proclus, *A Commentary on the First Book of Euclid's Elements,* trans. Glenn R. Morrow (Princeton, NJ: Princeton University Press, 1970), 31–33; this

edition of the *Commentary* is hereafter cited parenthetically in the text. Elsewhere, Proclus writes: "As the forms of knowledge differ from each other, so also are their objects different in nature. The objects of intellect surpass all others in the simplicity of their modes of existence, while the objects of sense-perception fall short of the primary realities in every respect. Mathematical objects, and in general all the objects of the understanding, have an intermediate position" (4).

9.   For an interpretation of catoptrics, see Alberto Pérez-Gómez and Louise Pelletier, *Architectural Representation and the Perspective Hinge* (Cambridge, MA: MIT Press, 1997), 101.

10.   See Ruth Padel, *In and Out of the Mind: Greek Images of the Tragic Self* (Princeton, NJ: Princeton University Press, 1992), chap. 2.

11.   Ibid., 17.

12.   Pérez-Gómez and Pelletier, *Architectural Representation*, 97.

13.   Vitruvius, *Ten Books on Architecture,* trans. Morgan, book 5, chap. 3, p. 37.

14.   Ibid., book 1, chap. 2, p. 13. After being used to qualify the concept of "order" itself, the concept of correction or adjustment is used often in the text (with regards to the thickness of columns, the projection of entablatures, etc.).

15.   "Acts of the Constitution of Masonry" (ca. 1400), in John Harvey, *The Mediaeval Architect* (London: Weyland, 1972), 191–207.

16.   Dionysius the Areopagite, *The Divine Names and Mystical Theology,* trans. C. E. Rolt (1971; reprint, London: SPC, 1987), 87, 195.

17.   See Ivan Illich, *In the Vineyard of the Text: A Commentary to Hugh's Didascalicon* (Chicago: University of Chicago Press, 1993). Illich demonstrates the far-reaching consequences of alphabetic indexing, which literally transformed the book into a fully accessible repository of memory quite unlike its earlier incarnations.

18.   From Władysław Tatarkiewicz, *History of Aesthetics,* ed. C. Barrett, trans. R. M. Montgomery (Warsaw: Polish Scientific Publishers, 1970), 2:198–199.

19.   See Dalibor Vesely, *Architecture in the Age of Divided Representation: The Question of Creativity in the Shadow of Production* (Cambridge, MA: MIT Press, 2004), 110–173.

20.   See Colin Rowe, "The Mathematics of the Ideal Villa" (originally published in 1947), in his *The Mathematics of the Ideal Villa and Other Essays* (Cambridge, MA: MIT Press, 1976), 1–28.

21.   See for example, René Taylor, "Architecture and Magic: Considerations on the Idea of the Escorial," in *Essays in the History of Architecture Presented to Rudolf Wittkower,* ed. Douglas Fraser, Howard Hibbard, and Milton J. Lewine (New York: Phaidon, 1967), 81–109, and my own "Juan Bautista Villalpando's Divine Model in Architectural Theory," in *Chora,* vol. 3 (Montreal: McGill-Queen's University Press, 1999), 125–156.

22.   Philibert de L'Orme, *Traités d'architecture,* ed. Jean-Marie Pérouse de Montclos (Paris: Léonce Laget, 1988); originally published in Paris as *Nouvelles intentions pour bien bastir et à petits fraiz* (1561) and *Premier tome de l'architecture* (1567).

23.   Juan Bautista Villalpando, *In Ezechielem explanationes et apparatus urbis ac templi hierosolymitani* (Rome, 1596–1604). See Pérez-Gómez, "Juan Bautista Villalpando's Divine Model."

24.   For a seventeenth-century interpretation of Villalpando's "discovery," see Juan Caramuel de Lobkowitz, *Architectura civil recta y oblicua considerada y dibuxada en el Templo de Ierusale[m]* (Vigevano, 1678).

25.   See Hans Jonas, *The Gnostic Religion: The Message of the Alien God and the Beginnings of Christianity,* 2nd ed., rev. (Boston: Beacon Press, 1963), 31.

26.   See, for example, the treatises of Guarino Guarini and Juan Caramuel de Lobkowitz. I discuss their implications in both *Architecture and the Crisis of Modern Science* (1983; reprint, Cambridge, MA: MIT Press, 1992), and *Architectural Representation and the Perspective Hinge.*

27.   Michel Foucault, *The Order of Things: An Archaeology of the Human Sciences* (London: Tavistock, 1970), 46.

28.   See Lily Chi, "An Arbitrary Authority: Claude Perrault and the Idea of *Caractère* in Germain Boffrand and Jacques-François Blondel" (Ph.D. diss., McGill University, 1997). See also my own introduction to Claude Perrault, *Ordonnance for the Five Kinds of Columns after the Methods of the Ancients,* trans. Indra Kagis McEwen (Santa Monica, CA: Getty, 1993).

29.   Charles Perrault, *Parallèle des anciens et des modernes,* 4 vols. (Paris, 1692–1696), 1:132.

30.   Johann Bernhard Fischer von Erlach, *Entwürff einer historischen Architektur* (Vienna, 1721).

31.   François Blondel, *Cours d'architecture* (Paris, 1698), 768–774.

32.   Jacques-François Blondel, *Architecture françoise* (Paris, 1752), 318.

33.   Jacques-François Blondel, *Cours d'architecture ou traité de la décoration, distribution et construction des bâtiments,* 9 vols. (Paris, 1771–1777), 1:376.

34.   Ibid., 1:390.

35.   Ibid.

36.   See Alberto Pérez-Gómez, "Charles-Etienne Briseux: The Musical Body and the Limits of Instrumentality in Architecture," in *Body and Building: Essays on the Changing Relation of Body and Architecture,* ed. George Dodds and Robert Tavernor (Cambridge, MA: MIT Press, 2002), 164.

37.   For the analogy between Piranesi's *Carceri* and modern film, refer to the well-known essay by Sergei Eisenstein, "Piranèse ou la fluidité des formes" (Piranesi or the Fluidity of Form), in *La non-indifférente nature,* trans. Luda and Jean

Schnitzer, vol. 1 (Paris: Union Générale d'Editions, 1976), 271–338. See also Pérez-Gómez and Pelletier, *Architectural Representation,* 370–383.

38.   Etienne-Louis Boullée, *Architecture, essai sur l'art* (Paris: Hermann, 1968), 67–69.

39.   Pérez-Gómez, *Architecture and the Crisis of Modern Science,* chap. 9.

7   A Tale of Two Brothers: Jean-Louis and Charles-François Viel

1.   Jean-Marie Pérouse de Montelos, "Charles-François Viel, architecte de L'Hôpital Général et Jean-Louis Viel de Saint-Maux, architecte, peintre et avocat au Parlement de Paris," *Bulletin de la Société de l'histoire de l'art français* (1966): 257–269.

2.   See, for example, *Annales françaises des sciences, des arts, et des lettres* 5 (January 1820): 230–234.

3.   Even the modern reprint of the book *Lettres sur l'architecture des anciens et celle des modernes* (Geneva: Minkhoff, 1974) is attributed to a hypothetical Charles F. Viel de Saint Maux by Michel Faré in his preface.

4.   Charles-François Viel, *Principes de l'ordonnance et de la construction des bâtimens* (Paris, 1797), dedication.

5.   *La Minerve* (1777) and *Les Neufs Soeurs* (1779). See Ramla Ben Aissa, "Erudite Laughter: The Persiflage of Viel de Saint-Maux," in *Chora: Intervals in the Philosophy of Architecture,* vol. 5 (in preparation).

6.   Jean-Louis Viel de Saint-Maux, *Lettres sur l'architecture des anciens et celle des modernes, dans lesquelles se trouve développé le génie symbolique qui préside aux monuments de l'antiquité* (Paris, 1787), sixth letter.

7.   Jean-Louis Viel de Saint-Maux, *Lettre sur l'architecture à M. le comte de Wannestin* (Brussels, 1780) and *Seconde lettre sur l'architecture à Monseigneur le duc de Luxembourg* (Brussels, 1780).

8.   See Alberto Pérez-Gómez, *Architecture and the Crisis of Modern Science* (1983; reprint, Cambridge, MA: MIT Press, 1992), 79.

9.   Viel de Saint-Maux, *Lettres sur l'architecture,* sixth letter, 12.

10.   Ibid., first letter, 5.

11.   See, for example, his ironic critique of Alberti's *Art de bâtir* (in ibid., first letter, 22–23) and of Cordemoy and others (sixth letter, 16).

12.   Viel de Saint-Maux, *Lettres sur l'architecture,* vi.

13.   Dupuis (citoyen Français), *Abrégé de l'origine de tous les cultes* (Paris, 1820), chap. 1. Dupuis (1742–1809) originally published his influential book in 1797.

14.   Ibid., 4, 10, 447.

15.   Viel de Saint-Maux, *Lettres sur l'architecture,* first letter, 17.

16.   Claude-Nicolas Ledoux, *L'architecture considérée sous le rapport de l'art, des moeurs et de la législation* (Paris, 1804).

17.   Viel de Saint-Maux, *Lettres sur l'architecture,* first letter, 21, 6.

18.   Ibid., 20. In a footnote to his second letter, he emphasizes: "The Ancients never confused, like we do, their Sacred Architecture with the art of building private houses; the latter having no relationship with the architecture of Temples and Monuments" (18 n. 1).

19.   Ibid., first letter, 9.

20.   Court's work is cited on several occasions. See, for example, ibid., 23.

21.   Antoine Court de Gébelin, *Histoire naturelle de la parole, ou Précis de l'origine du langage et de la grammaire universelle. Extrait du monde primitif* (Paris, 1776), 1, 4.

22.   "L'arbitraire n'a nulle autorité et ne peut jamais faire loi, dans les mots, comme dans la 'Conduite des Peuples et de Familles'" (ibid., 11).

23.   Court believed that the first language was composed of monosyllables uttered by natives painting physical objects; these monosyllables became the source of all words. All languages are founded on a small number of one-syllable radicals: "physical" words expressing moral or intellectual ideas (ibid., 37–39).

24.   Antoine Court de Gébelin, *Monde primitif analysé et comparé avec le monde moderne, considéré dans son génie allégorique et dans les allégories auxquelles conduisit ce génie* (Paris, 1773), 6. He writes that man finds in nature "les Éléments de tout ce dont il s'occupe—la musique est fondée sur une octave qui ne dépend jamais du Musicien . . . la Géométrie, sur les rapports et les proportions immuables des corps." Poetry's "marche cadencée" is related to the extension of our voice and the motions of our body (22).

25.   Court de Gébelin, *Histoire naturelle,* 14.

26.   Ibid., 107.

27.   Court de Gébelin, *Monde primitif,* 3; *Histoire naturelle,* 382–383.

28.   Court de Gébelin, *Monde primitif,* 5.

29.   Ibid., 64–70.

30.   Ibid., 90–93.

31.   Viel, *Principes,* chaps. 16–19. This work is bound in three volumes in an edition that includes two volumes of other writings under the title *Architecture de C. Viel* (Paris, 1797). I consulted the copy in the Vaudoyer collection at the Canadian Centre for Architecture in Montreal.

32.   Ibid., 96. Viel notes: "Architects use lines like authors use words. Neither conveys thoughts until they are subordinated to rules. From the diversity of lines are born the lines that constitute the orders, just like in discourse we compose phrases with words."

33.   Court de Gébelin, *Histoire naturelle,* 141.

34.   Viel, *Principes,* chap. 20. This work is hereafter cited parenthetically in the text.

35.   Abbé Laugier, *Observations sur l'architecture* (Paris, 1765). See Pérez-Gómez, *Architecture and the Crisis of Modern Science,* 64.

36.   The way nature brings about form in a fetus, for instance, starting with the head to elicit the most important features of the face—the nose starting as a line (*filet*), and the eyes as two black dots—is a model, according to Viel, for the way an architect starts to sketch and compose the massing of a future building (26).

37.   These short works will be discussed briefly, since I have analyzed them more fully in *Architecture and the Crisis of Modern Science;* they include *De l'impuissance des mathématiques pour assurer la solidité des bâtimens* (Paris, 1805), *Dissertations sur les projects de coupoles* (Paris, 1809), and *De la solidité des bâtimens, puissé dans les proportions des ordres d'architecture* (Paris, 1806).

38.   Viel, *De l'impuissance des mathématiques,* 5. The edition cited is published in a collection with other small texts in the second volume of his *Architecture* (Paris, 1797).

39.   Viel, *De la solidité des bâtimens,* 49–50.

40.   Ibid., 50. The orders, after all, were "the basic principles of composition and construction," which, like stars in the sky, illuminated the way for the architect in search of harmony and solidity.

41.   Viel, *De l'impuissance des mathématiques,* 6. In a footnote he reports De Quincy's words: "Il est difficile que tout ne soit pas connexe dans toutes les parties d'un même art."

42.   Ibid., 11–25.

43.   Viel, *De la solidité des bâtimens,* 12; *Dissertations,* 19–20.

44.   Viel, *Dissertations,* 48.

45.   Charles-François Viel, *Des anciennes études d'architecture: De la nécessité de les remettre en vigueur et de leur utilité pour l'administration des bâtiments civils* (Paris, 1807), 1.

46.   Ibid., 5.

47.   Ibid., 6.

48.   Ibid., 25.

49.   Ibid., 3.

50.   Viel, *Des anciennes études d'architecture,* 2.

51.   Ibid., 3.

52.   Charles-François Viel, *Inconvéniens de la communication des plans d'édifices avant leur exécution* (Paris, 1813), 7–8.

53.   Ibid., 25. It must be emphasized that only during Viel's time did techniques of notation (in architecture, as in music) become effectively reductive. Given these developments, which would soon be taken for granted as the legitimate modus operandi of these disciplines, his insight is evident. For the important parallel transformations in music theory, see Lydia Goehr, *The Imaginary Museum of Musical Works: An Essay in the Philosophy of Music* (Oxford: Clarendon; New York: Oxford University Press, 1992).

54.   Jean Rondelet, *Traité théorique et pratique de l'art de bâtir* (Paris, 1802).

55.   Charles-François Viel, *Décadence de l'architecture à la fin du dix-huitième siècle* (Paris, 1800), 25.

56.   Charles-François Viel, *De la construction des édifices publiques sans l'emploi du fer* (Paris, 1803), 15.

57.   Viel, *Des anciennes études d'architecture*, 25.

58.   Viel argued long to prove that Gothic was not an original invention. The diversity of early and late medieval structures, he believed, proved that medieval builders were merely adapting and misusing the models that were accessible to them. He claimed that the only reason for the public's enthusiasm for Gothic churches was the sheer size of the buildings.

59.   Vaudoyer's marginal notes suggested that these architects could be Ledoux and Boullée, or even Wailly. See page 8 of the copy of Viel, *Décadence de l'architecture,* at the Canadian Centre for Architecture, Montreal (in vol. 1 of *Architecture*).

60.   Pérez-Gómez, *Architecture and the Crisis of Modern Science,* 322.

61.   Viel, *Dissertations,* 23.

62.   Viel, *Décadence de l'architecture,* 8–10.

63.   Viel, *De l'impuissance des mathématiques,* 71.

64.   In distinction to eighteenth-century authors on the history of architecture who concentrated on formal taxonomies, Viel discusses the importance of use in relation to form. Despite his preference for Doric (for example, in *Principes,* chap. 31, "On Modern Temples"), he points out that the cellas of ancient temples were used only to house the statue of a god, in contrast to modern Christian churches in which the congregation worships inside. Roman basilicas, though, were often transformed into churches.

65.   Viel, *Décadence de l'architecture,* 10.

66.   I use "weak faith in progress" in the sense of Gianni Vattimo. See *The End of Modernity: Nihilism and Hermeneutics in Postmodern Culture,* trans. Jon R. Snyder (Baltimore: John Hopkins University Press, 1988).

67.   Jean-Nicolas-Louis Durand, *Précis des leçons d'architecture,* 2 vols. (Paris, 1819), and *Recueil et parallèle des édifices de tout genre, anciens et modernes* (Paris, 1801). In his *Précis* Durand explains his methodology or "mechanism of composition" based on the grid, complementing the "Grand Durand," his large-format historical compilation of buildings from all periods drawn at the same scale.

68.   Viel, *Des anciennes études d'architecture*, 5, 13.

69.   Charles-François Viel makes this rejection unambiguous as part of his critique of the new ways of producing projects through descriptive geometry and analytical applications. See *Inconvéniens de la communication des plans*, 23.

8   Poetry and Meaning from within *a* (Western) Architectural Tradition

1.   See Alberto Pérez-Gómez, "Charles-Etienne Briseux: The Musical Body and the Limits of Instrumentality in Architecture," in *Body and Building: Essays on the Changing Relation of Body and Architecture*, ed. George Dodds and Robert Tavernor (Cambridge, MA: MIT Press, 2002), 164–189.

2.   Lodoli left no writings, but his theories are known to us through his students: most significantly, Andrea Memmo and Giovanni Battista Piranesi.

3.   Romantic philosophers and writers such as Novalis, Baudelaire, and Rilke would recover Vico's understanding of poetic language, often without knowing his earlier formulation. Vico's reflections, furthermore, seem to have been key for the masterful and challenging use of poetic language in the avant-garde works of James Joyce.

4.   Nietzsche, *Human, All Too Human*, trans. R. J. Hollingdale (Cambridge: Cambridge University Press, 1986), frag. 223, p. 105.

5.   Ibid., frag. 175, p. 91.

6.   Ibid., frag. 218, p. 101.

7.   For recent developments in the debate between poststructuralism and phenomenology, particularly over the late and unfinished works of Merleau-Ponty, see *Merleau-Ponty Vivant*, ed. M. C. Dillon (Albany: State University of New York Press, 1991), especially preface, chaps. 5, 8, and Dillon, "Temporality: Merleau-Ponty and Derrida," in *Merleau-Ponty, Hermeneutics and Postmodernism*, ed. Thomas W. Busch and Shaun Gallagher (Albany: State University of New York Press, 1992), 189–212.

8.   See Alberto Pérez-Gómez, *Architecture and the Crisis of Modern Science* (1983; reprint, Cambridge, MA: Cambridge University Press, 1992), 79.

9.   Maurice Merleau-Ponty, *La prose du monde*, 163; quoted in George Steiner, *After Babel: Aspects of Language and Translation* (London: Oxford University Press, 1975), 128.

10.   For example, see Paul Ricoeur, "The Function of Fiction in Shaping Reality," *Man and World* 12 (1979): 123–141; Richard Kearney, *The Wake of Imagination: Toward a Postmodern Culture* (Minneapolis: University of Minnesota Press, 1988), especially the introduction and conclusion.

11.   Steiner, *After Babel*, 128–129.

12.   In his *Ars poetica* Horace writes that the epic poet "hastens into the action and precipitates the hearer into the middle of things" (lines 148–149); cited in

Walter Ong, *Orality and Literacy: The Technologizing of the Word* (London: Methuen, 1982), 142 (see also pp. 16–27).

13.   Vitruvius, *The Ten Books on Architecture,* trans. Morris Hickey Morgan (1914; reprint, New York: Dover, 1960), book 1, chap. 2, 13–14. Vitruvius associated "ideas" to constructive operations in situ rather than to architectural drawings in the modern sense. See Alberto Pérez-Gómez and Louise Pelletier, *Architectural Representation and the Perspective Hinge* (Cambridge, MA: MIT Press, 1997), 88–104, for an extensive discussion of this question.

14.   Ong, *Orality and Literacy,* 83–93.

15.   Plato, *Phaedrus* 274–277, in *Selected Dialogues of Plato,* trans. Benjamin Jowett, rev. Hayden Pelliccia (New York: Modern Library, 2001).

16.   David Abram, *The Spell of the Sensuous: Perception and Language in a More-Than-Human World* (New York: Pantheon, 1996), 93–135.

17.   See Gianni Vattimo, *The End of Modernity: Nihilism and Hermeneutics in Postmodern Culture,* trans. Jon R. Snyder (Baltimore: Johns Hopkins University Press, 1988).

18.   Ong writes: "Over the centuries, until the Age of Romanticism (when the thrust of rhetoric was diverted, definitively if not totally, from oral performance to writing), explicit or even implicit commitment to the formal study and formal practice of rhetoric is an index of the amount of residual primary orality in a given culture" (*Orality and Literacy,* 109).

19.   Octavio Paz, "Signs in Rotation," in *The Bow and the Lyre (El arco y la lira): The Poem, the Poetic Revelation, Poetry, and History,* trans. Ruth L. C. Simms (Austin: University of Texas Press, 1991), 241.

20.   Pérez-Gómez and Pelletier, *Architectural Representation,* 281–321.

21.   Steiner, *After Babel,* 175.

22.   Ibid., 177.

23.   Rimbaud, quoted (untranslated) in Steiner, *After Babel,* 177.

24.   See Timothy Mitchell, *Colonising Egypt* (1988; reprint, Berkeley: University of California Press, 1991).

25.   Pérez-Gómez and Pelletier, *Architectural Representation,* 281–321.

26.   Mitchell, *Colonising Egypt,* 63–71.

27.   Ibid., 133–134.

9   The Ethical Image in Architecture

1.   See his projects for the city of Chaux, such as the *pacifère,* in Claude-Nicolas Ledoux, *L'architecture considérée sous le rapport de l'art, des moeurs et de la législation,* 2 vols. (Paris, 1806–1846).

2. Gilles Deleuze, *Logique du sens* (Paris: Les Editions de Minuit, 1969), 76.

3. From an aphorism by Malcolm de Chazal, *Sens-Plastique,* ed. and trans. Irving Weiss, 2nd ed. (New York: Sun, 1979), 93.

4. See Stuart Spicker, *The Philosophy of the Body: Rejections of Cartesian Dualism* (New York: Quadrangle, 1970), and Drew Leder, *The Absent Body* (Chicago: University of Chicago Press, 1990).

5. Jean Baudrillard, *Seduction,* trans. Brian Singer (New York: St. Martin's Press, 1990).

Index